The Idea of the Actor

The Idea

of the Actor

Drama and the
Ethics of Performance

WILLIAM B. WORTHEN

Princeton University Press

Publication of this book has been aided by a grant from
The Whitney Darrow Fund of Princeton University Press

This book has been composed in Linotron Garamond

Clothbound editions of Princeton University Press books
are printed on acid-free paper, and binding materials are
chosen for strength and durability

Printed in the United States of America by
Princeton University Press
Princeton, New Jersey

The illustrations on the title page show "Joy" and "Despair", from
Henry Siddons, *Practical Illustrations of Rhetorical Gesture and Action;
adapted to the English Drama from a Work on the Subject by M. Engel*
(London, 1822)

[iv]

For Lorrie

Acknowledgments

I am pleased to have the opportunity to thank several people for helping this book along its way. I am grateful to Alvin B. Kernan for his continued confidence, and for sound advice on a number of matters; grateful also to Michael Goldman for igniting, and often rekindling, my thinking about acting. In a small way I hope this book settles a longer-standing debt to Joseph W. Donohue, for at one time providing a needed respite in academe. Larry Carver, Neill Megaw, and Wayne Rebhorn each read portions of the manuscript and made careful and instructive criticism of it; thanks also to Denise Sechelski for her help in preparing the manuscript. For repeated and timely encouragement, my warm thanks to Katherine Oakley, Mark Patterson, and Joan Lidoff. To my parents, and especially to my wife Lorrie, a final word of gratitude, for much gracious and uncomplaining sacrifice.

An earlier version of this book was undertaken with the support of the English department and graduate school of Princeton University; the University Research Institute of the University of Texas at Austin provided a summer grant that enabled me to complete final revisions. Portions of the third chapter originally appeared in *Theatre Journal* and in *Modern Drama*.

Contents

The Idea of the Actor

Introduction

Let me raise two questions that will begin to clarify the close affinity between acting and drama: What is an actor? And what does he do? In one sense, to act is to deceive, to become a *hypocrite* (Greek for "actor"). And yet in another, to act is simply to do something, to express or create meaning through action (Greek *drama*: an "act" or "deed"). Acting seems to bring a certain kind of falsehood into focus. Onstage, the actor both is and is not there for us. He is present as an actor, strutting his stagey stuff; but he is also absent, negated by the dramatic illusion he creates. In performance, the actor is engaged in two performances, a "double effort" that reveals him as an actor while it conceals him within his dramatic role.[1] As audience, of course, we experience the drama through the actor's palpably double performance. The drama shapes and is shaped by its expressive instrument: the body, mind, and person of the actor.

The site of drama is the site of acting; acting and drama share the poetics of duplicity. A play in performance invites us to attend to the complex ambiguity of human action through the odd disjunction between stage doers and their deeds—between the actors' acts and the characters' acts, between what's really acted and what's only "acted." It might well be argued that a stage event becomes fully dramatic only when its performers can excite the histrionic sensibility of their audience. For, in the audience, we too enact a double performance, grasp both reality and artifice, actor and character. Our assessment of the drama is enabled by our response to its histrionic means. To capture it in a formula, the ethics of drama are the ethics of acting—what it means to "act," to be an "actor," to communicate through "acting" embodies a vision of dramatic action as well.

There is a dynamic kinship among drama, actors, and theater. In the three essays that follow—on the public theater of Elizabethan London, the "metropolitan" theater of the age of Garrick, and the international theater of modern Europe—I will suggest some of the ways that the actor's duplicity has been explored in theory and dramatized in practice. These theaters each witnessed an efflorescence of dramatic activity and a blossoming of interest in acting; each voices a vigorous controversy regarding the nature of acting, and each dramatizes that conflict in the action of the plays it produces onstage. In the English Renaissance, for example, the actor's doubleness inspires an intensely antitheatrical spirit that is thoroughly and appropriately realized in the moralistic literature surrounding the stage. Hamlet's question of the player—"Is it not monstrous"—is one that his audience commonly asks about acting. Is the actor a blasphemer, a Satanic deceiver undermining the order of creation, or is he a creating god, like Sidney's Neoplatonic poet, whose performance affirms the transcendent power of human creativity? This volatile paradox pervades writing about acting in the period, but the drama—I discuss *Hamlet, Volpone, Twelfth Night*, and *The Duchess of Malfi*—typically shuns this duality by figuring the actor's creativity antithetically, as both divine and demonic, as a magical extension of human potentiality and as a monstrous deformity of it.

In the mid-eighteenth century, the actor's performance in the sentimental theater complements his metaphorical role in social theory, and requires us to place acting not in the context of theatrical morals, but among studies of human nature and society. In Garrick's heyday, the attempt to relate the actor's feelings to his expression informs both a burgeoning acting literature and the incipient theory of the benevolent society, which demands a thorough identity between the inborn social passions and their outward expression in action and gesture. The universal "language of gesture" defines the social implications of acting onstage and off, and provides a theory of performance that sustains the dramatic action of three of the most generally familiar plays of the period, Home's *Douglas*, Cumberland's *The West Indian*, and Goldsmith's *She Stoops to Conquer*.

In many ways, acting violates the Romantic definitions of the self, of the sensitive, often inexpressible delicacy of the inward life. Acting, therefore, had to be conceptually redefined before it could assume the status of Romantic art. The explosive innovations sparked by Ibsen's recasting of the drama fuel a lively and overdue reconsideration of acting both in England and on the continent. The first response to this overhauling of the actor's art is a popular one, voiced in the theatrical criticism of the 1880s and '90s. Subsequently, Stanislavsky gathers these attitudes into a comprehensive mission for the modern actor, one that more recent theory has readjusted, but not entirely dismissed. As we shall see, the startling range of modern acting theory belies a consistent desire to define the actor's authenticity in performance, a desire that also unites plays as diverse as *Rosmersholm* and *Heartbreak House* with the plays of Pirandello, Beckett, and Pinter.

Although the actor's performance is invariably ambiguous, I propose to phrase that ambiguity in the varied terms provided by three important theaters. Of course, to relate acting and drama in this way is to be indebted both to the rich tradition of literary and theatrical scholarship, and to the insights of several theorists of the stage. Two recent books are perhaps representative of the polarities—theoretical and documentary—that guide the argument to follow.[2] In *The Actor's Freedom*, Michael Goldman provocatively amplifies the actor's duplicity as part of a prospective theory of drama. There is something inherently uncanny about any act of impersonation, however informal: think of how irritating and disturbing it is to have your mannerisms, walk, or speech imitated by someone. By harnessing this uncanniness, Goldman argues, the actor gains access to a special allure, one that enables him to command and subdue his audience, while also becoming vulnerable to it. His performance shapes a dazzling ontological ambivalence, for he "enjoys a kind of omnipotence, a privilege and protection not unlike that accorded sacred beings— whatever he is doing, whatever crimes he may appear to commit, he is not to be interfered with. Yet at the same time he seems abnormally exposed, abnormally dependent upon us" (p. 9). The actor both attacks and submits to his audience. He is our priest and our scapegoat, at once the bearer of a powerful and attractive energy, and the victim of our relentless attention. Through his unsettling yet magnetic performance, the actor becomes "terrific," at once sacred and blasphemous, fascinating and fearsome.

Goldman's deft elucidation of the actor's freedom leads him to a brilliant synchrony between acting and drama. The actor's doubleness, and the special license of the theater, lend the actor a unique independence, one akin to the freedom that children have when they use play to explore and organize their world. But instead of sharing toys, the actor and audience playfully share the dramatic roles that they create and witness. The leading roles of their plays "act out some version of a half-allowed, blasphemous, and sacred freedom characteristic of the era in which the play was written" (p. 55). This powerful vision of the dramatic consequences of the actor's doubleness provides a cogent theoretical framework for assessing the histrionic dynamics of drama. Indeed, Goldman's dialectic deserves a fuller fleshing-out than he is able to undertake within the theoretical constraints of *The Actor's Freedom*. As we shall see, the "sacred and blasphemous" dialectic is often realized within a particular ethic of performance. Writing for and about actors—whether in antihistrionic diatribe, in theories of acting, or in plays themselves—tends to phrase this dialectic as a *paradoxe sur le comédien*: the actor simultaneously affirms and transgresses a moral vision of the relationship between self, action, and world. In so doing, the actor's performance dramatizes the ethical dialectic that animates his audience's sense of theater.

The blasphemous dimension of the actor's freedom has been

meticulously documented in Jonas Barish's *The Antitheatrical Prejudice*. In a series of essays, Barish pursues the host of charges that have been leveled against the theater from Plato's time to the present, and persuasively voices the anxieties that the theater has persistently aroused. This is a distinguished and (as my frequent reference to it implies) indispensable guide to antitheatrical literature and its values, and in some respects it provides a wider context for my narrower examination of acting. Perhaps because the book is ballasted by Barish's seminal work on antitheatrical values in the sixteenth and seventeenth centuries, though, the "puritan" attitude comes to dominate *The Antitheatrical Prejudice*, and lends a seductive consistency to this history of fear and loathing. Because much of the hostility to the theater is so grotesquely exaggerated, we are led to assume that the obsessive, "puritan" critique of the stage is entirely irrational and suspect, that it completely evades any direct consideration of the true nature of theater. Moreover, Barish's magisterial survey of antitheatrical literature is surprisingly offset by a rather general, unstated, and unchanging sense of what values are legitimately "theatrical." Much as all attacks on the theater have a "puritan" cast to them, so the theater seems implicitly to be earnest and frivolous, worthwhile yet harmless, incisive but extravagant, moral and amoral— whatever value its obstreperous critics deny it. Part of this imbalance stems from a common tendency in theatrical studies, an unwillingness to consider the theoretical investigation of the stage by its practitioners as a serious contribution to our understanding of acting and drama. Admittedly, men and women of the theater sometimes grope when they turn from stage practice to more abstract issues; there's often a dismaying lack of rigor in the writing of a Heywood, or a John Hill, or even a Jerzy Grotowski. Nonetheless, we should not slight their informed efforts in what is clearly a complicated and obscure endeavor. Barish's examination of antitheatrical prejudice fittingly subordinates the chorus of protheatrical writers to the voices of their critics, but with the exception of Diderot, few acting theorists receive more than cursory attention. We have little sense of how the aims of acting have been defined, of the specific vision of acting that antitheatrical writers like Prynne, Collier, or Rousseau may be attacking. This bias is most damaging when Barish turns to twentieth-century attitudes toward acting and theater. Although he makes the valuable point that antitheatrical impulses lurk in the hearts of the theater's most vocal partisans, Barish scants the evident fascination that acting holds for theorists like Shaw, Stanislavsky, Brecht, and others, and mistakenly casts their determination to revivify the theater by throwing off its dead and burdensome acting conventions as a deeply and absolutely antitheatrical one.

By considering three theaters at some length, I hope to suggest further lines of inquiry in both theoretical and historical directions, to lend greater precision to our understanding of acting theory, and to place the literature of acting more firmly in its intellectual and dramatic context. Indeed, the prospective nature of these essays has, unhappily, forced me to sidestep several inviting issues. I barely touch on matters of acting style—theatrical chestnuts like the Elizabethan "men or marionettes" question, how high Betterton raised his arms, or the degrees of naturalism between the neoclassical actor's teapot stance and the Method actor's aggressive crouch—even though the actor's technique is surely implied in an overriding conception of his art. Since this is not a social history of acting, I mention the actor's social status only intermittently, to suggest how the actor's standing in society reveals the society's valuation of his profession. And, of course, in the interest of clarifying a relationship between acting and drama, I've been extremely selective both in the plays and in the theaters I have chosen to discuss. Several avenues for further exploration spring to mind: the elaborate conventionality of Noh and Kabuki, and the appeal of Far Eastern theater to modern playwrights in general; the remarkably controversial development of "The Method" in American acting of the 1940s, '50s, and

'6os; quasi-dramatic forms like *commedia dell'arte* and English music-hall, and quasi-histrionic events like puppet theater; whether the stage actor's duplicity is similarly catalyzed by film and television performance, and so on.

Finally, a word about my title, baldly appropriated from Francis Fergusson's classic *The Idea of a Theater*. Graceful, passionate, and idiosyncratic, *The Idea of a Theater* is a landmark study of drama; despite an overemphasis on ritual in drama, it is a book that is widely synthetic, yet vigorously original—and obviously inimitable. I do, however, presume with a purpose. Fergusson's readers will already have remarked on my use of the phrase "histrionic sensibility," Fergusson's term for the "basic, or primary, or primitive virtue of the human mind" that orders reality not through symbolic means, such as language or mathematics, but through the process of mimetic enactment.[3] In a sense, my work here is an excursus on that sensibility. Although my approach may suggest that we can understand that sensibility only in historically relative terms, my guiding impulse actually tends in another direction. In *The Idea of the Actor*, we will see how three theaters define acting in a way that dramatizes a particular kind of histrionic sensibility, a sensibility shared by actors and audiences. But certainly these models of performance are all attempts to grasp the same art, to frame the duplicity inherent in acting itself. A theater fixes on an aspect of the actor's doubleness that resonates most evocatively with its presiding sense of meaningful action, its sense of what is a significant act. The actor becomes a metaphor for the ambiguity of all our actions. His feigned performance enacts the problematic relation that we discover daily between the self and the deeds that should reflect or reveal it, but that sometimes seem to deny it, to transform the self into an uncomfortable fiction. By stressing the manifold histrionic determinacy of the drama, I mean to draw attention to the continuing variety of the histrionic appeal, to the actor's fertile challenge to the drama and to its audience.

[1] *Is it not monstrous:*
The Demonic Dialectic of Renaissance Acting

> Is it not monstrous that this player here,
> But in a fiction, in a dream of passion,
> Could force his soul so to his own conceit
> That from her working all his visage wanned,
> Tears in his eyes, distraction in his aspect,
> A broken voice, and his whole function suiting
> With forms to his conceit? And all for nothing!
> —*Hamlet*, 2.2.556-62[1]

A man playing a man called Hamlet watches another man playing a man, called simply "player," who plays a man in a play. Visibly moved by the player's performance, the man called Hamlet rebukes himself for failing to make his own actions in the court suit with such expressive forms to his conceit. Hamlet's self-criticism is fitting, for he has been playing a host of parts: Gertrude's melancholic son, Old Hamlet's dutiful heir, Horatio's thoughtful companion, Ophelia's distracted lover, the antic actor plaguing Rosencrantz and Guildenstern and Polonius, the hectic raging in Claudius' court. And at this point, Hamlet has yet to reach the full stretch of his riddling play. The masks of betrayed lover, playwright-director, scold, murderer, duelist, and fallen soldier still wait, in Fortinbras' words, to be put on.

A reflexive concern for the histrionic dynamics of drama is by no means unique to *Hamlet* or to Shakespeare. Actors like Hamlet's player frequently complicate the action of Elizabethan and Jacobean drama, both as professionals—in *The Taming of the Shrew*, or in Massinger's *The Roman Actor*, for instance—and as well-meaning amateurs like Peter Quince and Bottom, or Beaumont's Rafe. Nor is acting solely the player's province. In an important sense, role-playing is the exemplary activity of English Renaissance drama, and the blending of artful dissembling and subtle intrigue surely provides one of the drama's conceptual conventions. The major figures of the drama are obsessed with disguise and deceit, with their ability to entertain, manipulate, cozen, seduce, murder, or get and keep a kingdom through feigning and impersonation. Much as the unlocalized platform suits the epic sweep of Shakespearean history, so too do the histrionic designs of their many players fulfill the history plays' commanding image of the political stage. Think of Richard, still Duke of Gloucester, vowing to "Change shapes with Proteus" (*3H6*, 3.2.192) to pluck the English crown, or of Prince Hal plotting the course of his prodigal youth, only to redeem time with a splendidly dramatic peripeteia. This histrionic talent, and the metatheatrical sensibility it often implies, is even more thoroughly implicated in the ethos of revenge drama. In revenge tragedy, the revenger's disguise and the "mousetrap" play he puts on combine with other symbolic motifs—his madness, delay, and death, the vengeful ghost, the atmosphere of violent excess—to give a coherent expression to a peculiarly Elizabethan angst. The revenger's theatrical expertise dramatizes the difficulty of taking consequential action in a world dominated by illusion, by irrational and chaotic seeming. In short, revenge drama meditates on the meaning of moral action in a theatricalized world, where the authority of the natural order has been critically weakened.[2] The genial enactment of comic players like Olivia's Cesario or Morose's Epicoene reflects the revenger's histrionic response to the occasions that spur him in a more benign light; like avengers, these actor-actresses negotiate the snares of romantic intrigue through a keen sense of the uses of play.

The theatrical self-consciousness of Renaissance drama, especially of Shakespeare's plays, has been well and amply explored.[3] But what meaning did acting—as an art, a profession, a language—hold for Shakespeare and his contemporaries? Acting has always been a highly suspect activity, and even a brief survey of theatrical pamphlets—*Th'overthrow of Stage-Playes* (1599), *A Mirrour of Monsters* (1587)—reminds us that violent antipathy toward the theater and its actors flooded the presses and the pulpits during the most explosive period of English theatrical culture. Acting was both a morally and a socially sensitive endeavor. Although in 1572 actors retained by noblemen could escape arrest as rogues and vagabonds only by being classed among protected retainers like fencers and bearwards, by the turn of the century several actors had risen to hitherto unknown national prominence, and a few, like Alleyn and Burbage, had amassed considerable wealth.[4] But such glittering success was emphatically not the rule. As Middleton's Sir Bounteous Progress laments, players "were never more uncertain in their lives. Now up and now down, they know not when to play, where to play, nor what to play; not when to play for fearful fools, where to play for Puritan fools, nor what to play for critical fools."[5]

The actor straddled a remarkably controversial imaginative boundary. The theater became a dominant influence on urban life in Elizabethan London, and provided a crucial metaphor of its culture. Celebrated in plays and imitated in courtly pageantry, the theater and its practitioners were nonetheless widely vilified. Outcast by society, actors could practice their profession only on the unrestricted margins of city life. And yet acting offered, as Michael Goldman argues, "one of the lightning careers of a speculative and chaotic age."[6] Acting epitomized man's ability to mold himself into the perfect courtier, the crafty new man of the Tudor bureaucracy, the eminent poet, the wily admiral, figures who share the actor's freedom both to transcend and to subvert the hierarchic order of Elizabethan society. The actor's art coordinates two sharply divergent world views and sparks a bitter clash between the "puritan" distaste for theatrical artifice—feigning, multiplicity, sensuality—and a "neoplatonic" sensibility that values all acts of creation as potentially godlike. Each of these views has its spokesmen, and various roles in the drama—Faustus and Prospero, for example—may seem predominantly colored by one attitude or the other. But the problem is more complex than either pro- or antitheatrical partisans will allow. Performance in the theater concentrates this unabated strain between demonic and sacred impulses on the actor himself. The actor's playing releases an electrifying ethical tension: acting images a Satanic duplicity, a "blasphemous" subversion of the order of things, while at the same time acting imitates the creative principle that sustains that order. The drama appeals to its audience by dramatizing this sense of theater.

The task of elaborating the ethics of acting in the Renaissance is a difficult one, for a number of reasons. Each side of the theatrical controversy is remarkably unwilling to engage, or even to acknowledge, the opposing position. A writer like William Prynne can hardly be aware of the subtle and qualified defense of the theater that emerges in plays like *The Tempest* or *A Midsummer Night's Dream*; not surprisingly, the playwrights themselves are often more scrupulous in their criticism of the theater than their enemies are. And yet, despite the virulence of the Puritan assault on the stage, the theater voices no effective rebuttal, even though several writers treat the stage indirectly or by analogy to poetry as Sidney does. Many scholars have addressed the obscure problem of Elizabethan acting technique, but the "men or marionettes" dilemma sheds little light on the meaning that performance itself—whether formal or natural in style—held for an audience.[7] In the absence of an Elizabethan Stanislavsky, the meaning of acting must be gleaned from more remote materials, from conduct books, from remarks on acting in the popular antitheatrical press, from the few apologies for the stage and for literature in general, and more distantly from the literary use of actor and theater as metaphors. The drama is also an extremely articulate source. For all their lampooning of Puritan manners and morals, playwrights in the period are especially sensitive both to the artistic deficiencies of their theater, and to the provisional morality of theatrical feigning. Through role-playing characters, actors, and plays-within-the-plays, dramatists explore the actor's double valuation, and critically examine the purpose and meaning—the ethic—of the actor's performance.

Acting is a creative and imaginative effort, and becomes an important focal point in the Renaissance controversy regarding the moral value of the feigning arts. We can take initial bearings on histrionic feigning from a passage in Thomas Heywood's *Apology for Actors* (1612), where Heywood apostrophizes the "bewitching" power of stage representation:

> what English blood, seeing the person of any bold English man presented and doth not hugge his fame, and hunnye at his valor, pursuing him in his enterprise with his best wishes, and as beeing wrapt in contemplation, offers to him in his hart all prosperous performance, as if the Personator were the man Personated, so bewitching a thing is liuely and well spirited action, that it hath power to new mold the harts of the spectators and fashion them to the shape of any noble and notable attempt.[8]

Heywood's *Apology* is a notoriously confused work, and throughout it Heywood unwittingly reinforces his opponents' arguments. Here, for instance, he blithely claims that the spectators are unable to distinguish the actor from his role, a charge that Puritan writers like Prynne will raise incessantly to scourge the theater's hypocrisy. Nonetheless, Heywood's text conveniently locates the two central themes of the critical discussion of acting: the potential of dramatic literature and its performance to encourage moral behavior in the audience, and the nature of the audience's response to the actor's feigning. In this passage, Heywood turns to the history play to introduce his consideration of the instructive virtues of the various dramatic genres. Predictably enough, the violent mayhem of tragedy is said to "terrifie men from the like abhorred practices" of murderous revenge; comedy uses amorous intrigue to reward virtue and ridicule folly; satire exposes the "subtleties and snares" of urban vice; and pastoral presents a pleasing image of rustic harmony, "the harmelesse love of sheepheardes diversely moralized, distinguishing betwixt the craft of the citty and the innocency of the sheep-coat." The histories have a more immediate purpose, to instruct "such as cānot reade in the discouery of all our *English* Chronicles" through the medium of the stage (F3ʳ-F4ᵛ).

The history play, with its evident mingling of fact and fiction, becomes the test case in the evaluation of stage feigning. Heywood commends both the subject matter of the dramatized "domesticke hystories" and their salutary effect on an audience. Both of these points are sharply refuted by critics of the theater, "puritans" in sect or simply in disposition. To present history on the stage violates the Puritans' sense of what A. C. Patrides has called the "horizontal unity" of recorded history, the perception of history from the Creation to the Last Judgment as the singular expression of God's will for mankind. However popular among audiences, historical drama demands the translation of the providential structure of history into the fictional structure of well-spirited drama, a recasting of absolute truth in a feigned form that seriously vitiates the didactic pretensions of such plays. The necessary fictions of the historical drama undermine the instructive powers traditionally ascribed to history, and obviate the distinction between the "truthful" subjects of history plays and the more overtly feigned inventions of the other dramatic modes.[9] As Stephen Gosson argues in *Playes Confuted in Fiue Actions* (1582), the transformation of history into drama inevitably falsifies it. Like other plays, histories "are no Images of trueth, because sometime they hādle such thinges as neuer were, sometime they runne vpon truethes, but make them seeme longer, or shorter, or greater, or lesse then they were, according as the Poet blowes them vp with his quill."[10]

The discussion of dramatized history epitomizes the wider debate concerning the didactic purpose of feigned literature in general. In *An Apologie for Poetrie* (publ. 1595)—partly conceived as a response to Gosson's *The Schoole of Abuse* (1579)—Sidney attempts to conflate the philosopher (teacher of abstract moral truth) and the historian (teacher of observed, material truth) in the role of the poet. Sidney's poet transcends both philosopher and historian by moving men to virtue by means of a feigned and liberating image of perfected nature; as William Rossky notes, the poet's superiority to the historian lies precisely in this "power to distort."[11] Unlike the poet, who imagines a golden world, the historian is tied to the lessons of the temporal world, "not to what shoulde bee but to what is, to the particuler truth of things and not to the general reason of things."[12] Moreover, Sidney's Neoplatonic understanding of poetic invention rests squarely on the principle of the poet's godlike creativity. His poet, rather than elucidating the moral precepts of revealed nature, "dooth growe in effect another nature, in making things either better then Nature bringeth forth, or, quite a newe, formes such as neuer were in Nature, as the *Heroes, Demigods, Cyclops, Chimeras, Furies,* and such like: so as hee goeth hand in hand with Nature, not inclosed within the narrow warrant of her guifts, but freely ranging onely within the Zodiack of his owne wit" (p. 156). To Sidney, the poet's feigned second nature renews God's creation, extending and perfecting nature through the poet's imagination. Instead of rivaling the natural world, the arts so depend on nature that they become "Actors and Players, as it were, of what Nature will haue set foorth" (p. 155). As Puttenham remarks in *The Arte of English Poesie* (1589), since poets are "able to deuise and make all these things of them selues, without any subiect of veritie," they are "as creating gods."[13] The godlike poet fulfills the animating principle of Perdita's great creating Nature; his feigning peoples the natural second world of art.

The humanists' vision of the poet's divine creativity breaks the bounds of literary dispute, and implies a sense of human identity as malleable and self-created. The poet enlarges the scope of divine creation through imitation. He is a maker of forms both in art and in life, and as Castiglione's *Courtier* (English version 1561) attests, the courtier's—and the courtly poet's—identity is constituted by a ceaseless, apparently effortless, series of posturings.[14] Castiglione's histrionic courtier realizes himself much as Sidney did, through the commanding performance of a variety of roles. Renaissance humanists generally envision man as such an acting animal. In the most familiar case, the Adam of Pico's *Oration* (1495) has no defining role in nature, and is unconstrained by any limitation. God tells this "indeterminate" creature, "thou mayest fashion thyself in whatever shape thou shalt prefer. Thou shalt have the power to degenerate into the lower forms of life, which are brutish. Thou shalt have the power, out of thy soul's judgment, to be reborn into the higher forms, which are divine."[15] Similarly, when the man of Vives' short *Fable About Man* (written 1518) astounds the gods with the wealth of his role-playing, including an impressive impersonation of Jove himself, he is invited to join their feast. At this point in the narrative, he asserts his essential humanity with a revealing gesture: "He put on his mask, which he had meanwhile laid aside, for this stage costume was so greatly honored. Since it had so well met the needs of man, it was deemed worthy of the most sumptuous feast and of the table of the gods."[16]

Like Sidney's poetic arts—the "Actors and Players, as it were, of what Nature will haue set foorth"—histrionic performance is a means of expressing man's fundamental nature, and of revealing his unique likeness to God. The actor's creation neither denies nor falsifies nature. In Mosca's words, the actor "had the art born with him;/ Toils not to learn it, but doth practice it/ Out of most excellent nature" (*Volpone*, 3.1.30-32).[17] Though Jonson will finally chain Mosca to the role of galley slave, this formulation of the actor's relation to burgeoning nature is commonplace. Webster's character "An excellent Actor" (1615) also conceives the player as refining nature:

> He doth not strive to make nature monstrous, she is often seen in the same Scaene with him, but neither on Stilts nor Crutches; and for his voice, tis not lower then the prompter, nor lowder then the Foile and Target. By his action he fortifies morall precepts with example; for what we see him personate, we thinke truely done before us.

The portrait continues, extending this view of the actor to its familiar conclusion:

> All men have beene of his occupation: and indeed, what hee doth fainedly that doe others essentially: this day one plaies a Monarch, the next a private person. Heere one Acts a Tyrant, on the morrow an Exile: A Parasite this man to-night, to-morow a Precisian, and so of divers others.[18]

Mosca today, Malvolio tomorrow—the actor speaks to the self-reliance of the humanists' man, his ability to shape a role to suit the changing needs of his elaborate performance. The classical and medieval identification between earthly mutability and the illusion of the stage is partly deflected by the histrionic sensibility of the Neoplatonists and their successors in and out of the theater, who find an emblem of substantial human value in the actor's art.[19] As we shall see, the widespread distrust of the "ontological subversiveness" of the theater, its means, and its practitioners is profound and intransigent; but it seems to be balanced by an acceptance of feigning as a means to truth, and as an acceptable, or inevitable, mode of being.[20] If all the world is a stage, man as actor has one commandment, to use his sophisticated playing to hold the mirror up to nature through artful performance.

Nonetheless, as an expression of human potentiality, the actor's indeterminacy could be terrifying as well as exhilarating. Ultimately, of course, the disposition of the theater fell into the hands of the antitheatrical Puritans who tended to see the actor's metamorphoses as demonic, not divine. Moreover, although Puritan pamphleteers lack the tact of a Sidney or a Hamlet, their vigorous, if hysterical, case against the theater amplifies the Renaissance actor's essential subversiveness. Barish has remarked that "the mimetic copy of a thing, in Plato's view, resembles the dream of a thing in that it is an impure and debased version of it which threatens our wholeness and sanity" (p. 29); the Puritan perspective on the actor's imitation is decisively Platonic in attitude, if not in spirit. The reciprocity between created nature and the artist's creation that animates the Neoplatonic vision of feigning is foreign both to Plato and to his Puritan followers, who rigidly reject all forms of feigning as illusory, even obscene.

In his compendious *Histrio-Mastix* (1633), for example, William Prynne clearly attempts to encompass literary, theatrical, and histrionic feigning in a comprehensive indictment of all such seeming. Devoting the first two "Acts" of "the actor's tragedy" to the origins of theater in primitive idolatry, Prynne then focuses his most telling arguments in Acts 3-5 of Part One, where he proceeds copiously from the artificial "stile and subject matter" of plays (Act 3), to a discussion of the social life of actors (Act 4), to a treatment of histrionic performance itself (Act 5), the "hypocrisie . . . obscenitie and lasciviousnesse . . . the grosse effeminacy . . . the extreame vanitie and follie, which necessarily attends the acting of Playes."[21] In fact, Prynne reinforces the connection between the feigned events of the dramatic text and the feigned behavior of the actors who perform it. Since plays themselves are "false and fabulous" (P1ʳ), so acting is "grosse hypocrisie. All things are counterfeited, feined, dissembled; nothing really or sincerely acted" (X2ʳ). Like the literature it embodies, impersonation imperils the sense of the visible world as the finite and inviolable expression of its divine creator. Acting is counterfeit, and threatens to obscure the clear relation between motive and act. It distorts the essential and absolute opposition between sin and virtue, between damnation and salvation. This sense of the sinfulness of feigning leads Prynne into a typical contradiction. Though acting is false—"nothing really or sincerely acted"—Prynne also argues that the actor actually commits the various deeds (murder, lechery, treason) that he performs onstage in character. Prynne echoes Heywood's confused blending of "Personator" with "man Personated":

> There is no difference at all between a foole, a fantastique, a Bedlam, a Whore, a Pander, a Cheater, a Tyrant, a Drunkard, a Murtherer, a Divell on the Stage (for his part is oft-times acted) and those who are such in truth, but that the former are farre worse, farre more inexcusable than the latter, because they wilfully make themselves that in sport.   (Z3ᵛ)

Prynne contradicts himself largely to be able to insist that the actor's performance is not inconsequential, that his feigning degrades his own moral nature as well as the public's. As both John Rainolds and Ben Jonson attest, there is a kind of psychological justification for Prynne's claims here, along the lines that the actors are brought to a gradual acceptance of sin through the continual rehearsal of sinful deeds.[22] Prynne, though, ignores this argument, and his rhetorical somersaults imply how thoroughly the actor's feigning resists the Puritan intellect. Both false and true, the actor not only challenges established moral categories, he evades them altogether.

Prynne's antipathy to acting stems from the actor's falsification of his identity. In *Bartholomew Fair* (1614), Jonson's Rabbi Busy draws on Deuteronomy 22:5 to argue Prynne's case against the puppet Dionysus: "Yes, and my maine argument against you, is, that you are an *abomination*: for the Male, among you, putteth on the apparell of the *Female*, and the *Female* of the Male."[23]

The puppet's easy repudiation of the Puritan "by playne demonstration" tends to overshadow the disturbing perception of role-playing contained in the Puritan case. Prynne contends that the player's impersonation sets in the place of his God-given self one of his own making. Actors impiously attempt, "yea, affectedly, to vnman, vnchristian, vncreate themselves" (Z2ᵛ). In many respects, the invocation of Deuteronomy is simply a smoke screen; acting uniformly provokes the Puritans' outrage, regardless of whether transvestite playing is involved. But the Deuteronomic injunction provides Scriptural substance to the Puritans' most compelling concern, that when the actor undertakes his feigning he unmakes what God has created, demonically obliterating "that most glorious Image which God himself hath stamped on us" (5X3ᵛ). Much as the humanists argue, the actor envisions human nature as potential, rather than as a received entity or calling. To the Puritans, though, the actor's creations violate God's order instead of fulfilling or imitating it. The actor breaks God's command

> not to alter that forme which God hath given them by adding or detracting from his worke; not to remove the bounds that he hath set them; but to abide in that condition wherein he hath placed them . . . so I may likewise condemne these Playhouse Vizards, vestments, images and disguises, which during their usage in outward appearance offer a kinde of violence to Gods owne Image and mens humane shapes, metamorphosing them into those idolatrous, those brutish formes, in which God never made them. (5X4ʳ)

Impersonation is not merely ostentation or exhibition. Stage acting directly challenges God's established order in the person of the individual actor, and implies a demonic attempt both to efface the image of the Creator and to usurp his role in the cosmos.

Prynne's rhetoric is at best off-putting, yet the complex of imagery with which he and other critics—Northbrooke, Rainolds, Rankins, Gosson, Stubbes, and the like—attack acting bears further scrutiny, for it expresses as much as any of their arguments do the spirit of this antihistrionic anxiety. Beyond the disturbing identification of the "Personator" with the "man Personated," it is the "bewitching" sensuous spectacle of the theater that arouses the Puritans' loathing. To the Puritan sensibility, the theater's physicality, its invitation to the senses, is itself appallingly demonic. Much like precise Malvolio gazing uncomprehendingly at the "uncivil rule" that Sir Toby and his cohorts concoct in *Twelfth Night*, the Puritans regard the theater as a Falstaffian, fleshly threat to everything uncompromised, absolute—in a word, pure. The theater epitomizes the sensuous temptation of the seductive world, as Gosson suggests in *The Schoole of Abuse*:

> There set they abroche straunge consortes of melody, to tickle the eare; costly apparel, to flatter the sight; effeminate gesture, to rauish the sence; and wanton speache, to whet desire too inordinate lust. Therefore of both barrelles, I iudge Cookes and Painters the better hearing, for the one extendeth his arte no farther then to the tongue, palate, and nose, the other to the eye; and both are ended in outwarde sense, which is common too vs with bruite beasts. But these by the priuie entries of the eare, slip downe into the hart, & with gunshotte of affection gaule the minde, where reason and vertue should rule the roste.   (B6ʳ-B7ʳ)

The actor's performance rapes the spectator's sensibility, penetrating the privy entries of the sense and ravishing the right rule of reason. His affecting performance topples the psychological hierarchy much as his subversive social role as rogue and vagabond threatens the elaborate rankings of civil rule.

By turning the spectator's attention from the transcendent spirit to the flesh, the actor decisively involves him in the realm of earthly mutability, where change itself reveals the impress of Satan. Feigned poetry is, in this sense, perfectly suited to the actor's histrionic feigning, for the verse allows Satan's stagey ministers to insinuate themselves more easily into the spectator's consciousness:

> Because the sweete numbers of *Poetrie* flowing in verse, do wōderfully tickle the hearers eares, the deuill hath tyed this to most of our playes, that whatsoeuer he would haue sticke fast to our soules, might slippe downe in suger by this intisement, for that which delighteth neuer troubleth our swallow. Thus when any matter of loue is enterlarded though the thinge it selfe bee able to allure vs, yet it is so sette out with sweetnes of wordes, fitnes of Epithites, with Metaphors, Alegories, Hyperboles, Amphibologies, Similitudes, with Phrases so pickt, so pure, so proper; with action, so smothe so liuely, so wantō; that the poyson creeping on secretly without griefe chookes vs at last, and hurleth vs downe in a dead sleepe. As the Diuell hath brought in all that Poetrie can sing, so hath hee sought out euery streine that musicke is able to pipe, and drawē all kind of instruments into that compasse, simple and mixte. (*Playes Confuted in Fiue Actions*, D8ᵛ-E1ʳ)

The manifold sensuous address of the stage—through language, action, music—invades the spectator and contaminates him. Gosson here anticipates Prynne's charge that the actor tries to "vnman, vnchristian, vncreate" himself, and transfers it to the theatrical audience. The stage's appeal to the senses degrades the spectator from his true estate as a Christian: "To seeke this, is, to spend our studies in things that are meere naturall, to spende our time so is to be carnally minded, but to be carnally minded is death, howe then can wee looke to bee Partakers of the benefittes of Christ, which runne a contrary race to him?" (E1ʳ).

The actor provides an analogy to Satan's operation in the world through his enticing appeal to the appetites of his audience. The actor-as-devil is a recurrent image in antitheatrical writing, and surfaces in anecdotes about real devils frolicking among the actors during performances of *Doctor Faustus*.[24] Moreover, the actor's subversion of the rational order enforces on all participants in the theatrical spectacle a kind of madness. As Prynne observes,

> Yea, what else is the whole action of Playes, but well personated vanity, artificiall folly, or a lesse Bedlam frenzie? He who shall seriously survay the ridiculous, childish, inconsiderate, yea, mad and beastly actions, gestures, speeches, habits, prankes and fooleries of Actors on the Stage, (if he be not childish, foolish, or frentique himselfe) must needs deeme all Stage-players children, fooles, or Bedlams; since they act such parts, such pranks, yea, use such gestures, speeches, rayment, complements, and behaviour in Iest, which none but children, fooles, or mad-men, do act, or vse in earnest. (Z3ᵛ)

Acting severs motive from deed, it complicates the actor's meaning, and makes his relation to the world around him unstable; like the madman, the actor's performance is illogical, irrational, and unreal.

Most conspicuous to modern readers is what we might call the erotic dimension of the Puritans' attack on the actor, their continual characterization of actors as emblems of lust and effeminacy and lewdness. In a sense, "lust" here is a shorthand term for the Puritans, gathering under one heading the various sensuous appeals of the stage. And yet the pervasiveness of this charge certainly implies that to the Purtian mind eros and the hypocrite player were more than kin, if less than kind. As Katharine Eisaman Maus has recently pointed out, there is a marked similarity, both in form and in specific detail, between antihistrionic and antifeminist writing in the period, and women and actors are frequently abused for the same behavior: dissembling, provoking lust, undertaking Satan's duplicitous service.[25] Not surprisingly, the Deuteronomic rule prohibiting transvestism surfaces in both indictments. Why does this charge carry such weight against the evidently playful role-playing of the theater?

[24]

First, as we have seen, the Puritans read Deuteronomy 22:5 as a lesson forbidding not simply disguise, but also the transformation of the self that a new form of expression represents. As Gosson remarks in *Playes Confuted*, the actor engages his role with frightening fidelity, putting on "not the apparrell onely, but the gate, the gestures, the voyce, the passions" of the women, or men, that he portrays (E3ᵛ). The consequences of this impersonation resonate throughout the social hierarchy, since "for a boy to put one the attyre, the gesture, the passions" of a woman is as serious a violation as for "a meane person to take vpon him the title of a Prince with counterfeit porte, and traine"—Perkin Warbeck's crime (E5ʳ). Here, Gosson links the actor's effeminacy with the social and cosmic subversiveness that his impersonation implies. To Gosson, Prynne, and others, the actor's transformation suggests that chaos could come again, a chaos framed in the actor's blurring of the distinction between men and women. What the Puritans fear is the actor's localizing of an undifferentiated reality, particularly of a frightening sexual indeterminacy. As Prynne argues, transvestite acting—and by extension all acting—"perverts one principall use of garments, to difference men from women; by confounding, interchanging, transforming these two sexes for the present, as long as the Play or part doth last." The confusion of the sexes predictably "excites many adulterous filthy lusts, both in the Actors and Spectators," lusts of a markedly narcissistic kind. Transvestite playing drives both actors and audiences to "selfe-pollution, (a sinne for which Onan was destroyed:) and to that unnaturall Sodomiticall sinne of uncleanesse, to which the reprobate Gentiles were given over" (2D4ʳ-2D4ᵛ). Acting undermines the principle of hierarchy itself, the principle of degree. It makes kings of vagabonds, and women of men. It allows reason to be ruled by the passionate senses. Far from being an avatar of the divine impulse to create, the actor incarnates a sterile perversion of it.

In the violence of the Puritan response to the actor's duplicity, as much as in the heady beauty of the Neoplatonic vision of histrionic man, we can see the depth of response excited by the actor's feigning. To the humanists, the actor's art is a creative expression of the world's dazzling fruitfulness, and of man's preeminent place in it. To the Puritans, the actor represents man's fallen inconstancy, and his evanescence implies the threatening chaos immanent in the natural order when nature's degrees and differences are erased. If the Neoplatonic vision of the actor's divine creativity suggests the attractive freedom of acting, the Puritan response suggests something of the fear that such freedom could inspire. The actor's performance implies a world become "absurd" and irrational, and arouses the fear of a hostile and protean chaos in which feigning, dreaming, and madness trap the self in an impenetrable and godless darkness. The world as theater is, to the Puritans, a prison much like Malvolio's cell in *Twelfth Night*; entangled in such webs of seeming, even the virtuous man will be unable to see the light.

I will have more to say about the special vision of acting that animates *Twelfth Night*; here, though, let me conclude this survey of the ethics of performance with some remarks on *Hamlet*. *Hamlet* is so thoroughly infused by the question of acting that it nearly becomes the kind of theoretical investigation of performance that the Renaissance theater otherwise failed to produce. Among other things, *Hamlet* is a play about taking a role; as Maynard Mack has shown, acting provides the "radical metaphor" of a play suffused with the imagery of acting and theater.[26] The action of *Hamlet* turns at every point on some form of performance, often feigned—think of Claudius greeting the court, Laertes' advice to Ophelia, Hamlet and the players, the Mousetrap, the duel. Moreover, *Hamlet* measures histrionic performance against other kinds of behavior, and undertakes both a "neoplatonic" and a "puritan" critique of acting. *Hamlet* phrases the contrary ethics of acting as complementary, and alerts us to how dramatic action imagines a critique of the actor's duplicitous performance.

A play begins with an actor taking his part; it also begins with a character taking his part, choosing a role in the play at hand. In his first scene, Hamlet poses the question of histrionic feigning in a disturbing yet familiar way. Although Hamlet enters *cum aliis*, he is from the outset clearly set apart, his nighted color dark against the raiments of the courtiers, his dejected havior frustrating Gertrude's solicitude and highlighting Laertes' earnestness, his sharp puns jarring against Claudius' fulsome periods. Hamlet presents both the audience and the court an interpretive problem, but an apparently comprehensible one. His motives, though unstated, are nonetheless signified in the conventional demeanor of grief, or at least seem to be.

> Seems, madam? Nay, it is. I know not "seems."
> 'Tis not alone my inky cloak, good mother,
> Nor customary suits of solemn black,
> Nor windy suspiration of forced breath,
> No, nor the fruitful river in the eye,
> Nor the dejected havior of the visage,
> Together with all forms, moods, shapes of grief,
> That can denote me truly. These indeed seem,
> For they are actions that a man might play,
> But I have that within which passes show;
> These but the trappings and the suits of woe.
>
> (1.2.76-86)

Hamlet's bitter rejection of seeming is deeply unsettling, for the prince not only withdraws from a world where all acts may be feigned, he also denies that any deed, in Prynne's words, can be "really or sincerely acted." Hamlet's alienation here challenges the value both of sincere action and of dramatic performance. Since no act can be unequivocally expressive, all acts are to Hamlet perniciously "histrionic." As Robert Weimann has noted, Hamlet's pointed reference to, and denial of, his conventional signs of grief has the effect of questioning the reality of the entire dramatic illusion from within.[27]

But Shakespeare refuses to rest with Hamlet's simplistic repudiation of seeming. *Hamlet* forces both characters and actors to explore the actor's ethical dilemma. Can acting express "that within" through an imaginative, feigned creation of meaning, or is it an empty sham, a parody of meaningful behavior bordering on madness? Many scenes in the play explicitly coordinate acting and madness, and evaluate the actor's feigning by comparing it with other forms of seeming. Shakespeare measures the effects of Hamlet's acting by presenting it as at once a form of explorative creation (in the play-within-the-play, for instance), and as an activity that often seems near to madness. The long scene that culminates in Hamlet's decision to catch Claudius' conscience in a theatrical ruse, for example, examines the nature and effect of Hamlet's enactment, or "transformation: so call it,/ Sith nor th'exterior nor the inward man/ Resembles what it was" (2.2.5-7). Hamlet's behavior is opaque and ambiguous. His madness impresses Claudius primarily as a threat to political stability. To Polonius, his actions suggest only that "The very cause of Hamlet's lunacy" lies in his lust for Ophelia. To the audience, Hamlet's madness has a histrionic dimension; it may be the "antic disposition" that Hamlet had forewarned Horatio about. That is, Hamlet's performance early in the play coordinates the imagery of the Puritan vision of the actor. His mask becomes at once the sign of madness, of lust, and of deceit.

By the close of the play, Hamlet himself will conceive his experience in theatrical terms—"Being thus benetted round with villains,/ Or I could make a prologue to my brains,/ They had begun the play" (5.2.29-31). But he will also keep the "mad" interpretation alive as well, urging Laertes to blame "His madness . . . poor Hamlet's enemy" for the murder of Polonius (5.2.241). In 2.2, though, Hamlet more directly voices his attitude toward acting, and in so doing, phrases the characteristic paradoxes of Renaissance performance:

> it goes so heavily with my disposition that this goodly frame, the earth, seems to me a sterile promontory; this most excellent canopy, the air, look you, this brave o'erhanging firmament, this majestical roof fretted with golden fire: why, it appeareth nothing to me but a foul and pestilent congregation of vapors. What a piece of work is a man, how noble in reason, how infinite in faculties, in form and moving how express and admirable, in action how like an angel, in apprehension how like a god: the beauty of the world, the paragon of animals; and yet to me, what is this quintessence of dust? (2.2.305-16)

Conceive the world as sterile promontory and all values become chillingly stagey; Gosson could be Hamlet's tutor here. The angelic nature of Neoplatonic man is reduced to the malleable quintessence of dust, capable of being shaped into a variety of forms; but (as the Puritans would remark) each of these forms is an illusion, a vain and ostentatious facade concealing an essentially unchanged, degraded nature.

To reject playing in Hamlet's world is to reject action altogether, to return to the static isolation of the "Seems" speech. Shakespeare fittingly advances Hamlet's understanding of playing here by introducing the players, and by juxtaposing two images of Hamlet's task in the role of Pyrrhus that both Hamlet and the player perform. An able player who speaks "with good accent and good discretion," Hamlet first voices the vision of manic vengeance that Pyrrhus personifies, an image that is at once heroic and brutal. "Black as his purpose," Pyrrhus is transformed by revenge into the efficient man of blood that Hamlet will ironically become, "total gules, horridly tricked/ With blood of fathers, mothers, daughters, sons" (2.2.464-65). Pyrrhus is to Hamlet a "painted tyrant," a feigned and ideal image of the course of his revenge. But as a feigned image, the figure of Pyrrhus is deceptively multiple in its instruction; not only is savage Pyrrhus both attractive and repellent, but his murder of old Priam both forecasts Hamlet's revenge and compares it to Claudius' murder of Old Hamlet. Shakespeare suggests that the didactic effects of the actor's performance are actually quite limited, for although Hamlet responds to the player's speech, he seems to miss the complex reflection of roles that the image of Pyrrhus coordinates.[28]

Hamlet's soliloquy response to the player's enactment is more baffling, for Hamlet both registers the impact of the performance and imitates it, cleaving the general ear with a torrid parody of the rhetoric of revenge:

> Bloody, bawdy villain!
> Remorseless, treacherous, lecherous, kindless villain!
> O, vengeance!

Again, the actor provides Hamlet with a partly inappropriate model. Earlier, acting had seemed inexpressive to Hamlet, but now it seems artificial, excessive, "histrionic": "Why, what an ass am I!" In 1.2, acting had offered Hamlet the choice between the real and the feigned, the actual and the seeming. His recapitulation of the player's performance here, though, implies that he has rejected such a distinction—is his soliloquy deeply felt, or is it a bombastic parody of the player?—and turns to acting as what Lawrence Danson has aptly termed a "mode of discovery."[29] Feigning provides Hamlet with a sense of acting that is itself part of the answer he searches for, as his decision to use the play to trap Claudius affirms.

Much as it is difficult to detach Hamlet from the role of revenger in this soliloquy, so too is it difficult to detach him from his "antic disposition." In some scenes, chiefly those involving Polonius and Claudius (the "fishmonger," "Buzz, buzz," and "Very like a whale" scenes, for instance), Hamlet's feigning is evidently artificial, a guise put on to thwart the scheming couple's falsehood and indirection. But in others, particularly in the "nunnery" and closet scenes, Hamlet's passionate outbursts seem more genuinely out of control. In the closet scene, Hamlet obviously prepares us to witness and evaluate a scene in which he will play the role of chastening scourge. Hamlet works himself into the part—"Now could I drink hot blood"—and uses his role to articulate his feelings clearly—"My tongue and soul in this be hypocrites" (3.2.402-405). Student of theater that he is, Hamlet attempts to play didactically, but the effects of his performance are again uncertain. At first, Hamlet's acting seems to have the intended results, forcing Gertrude's inward eye "into my very soul,/ And there I see such black and grainèd spots/ As will not leave their tinct" (3.4.90-92). But Shakespeare subtly modulates Gertrude's response to Hamlet's performance, in order to modulate our consideration of his acting. Early in the scene, she affirms both his instruction and his methods, remarking on Hamlet's stagey excess, "Ay me, what act,/ That roars so loud and thunders in the index?" (3.4.52-53). Gertrude's first response to Hamlet reinforces our view of him as player. When the scene progresses, though, our vision of Hamlet the antic actor is radically altered. As T. S. Eliot recognized, Hamlet's outbursts are increasingly out of proportion to their "objective correlative," and his "disgust envelops and exceeds" poor Gertrude.[30] Hamlet's rhetorical overkill weakens our confidence in his histrionic detachment; Gertrude's inability to see the Ghost further undermines our certainty that Hamlet is in full control of his antic mask. As Hamlet attempts to calm and reassure his mother that he is only acting— "I essentially am not in madness,/ But mad in craft"—we observe him more and more objectively, taking Gertrude's part as audience rather than Hamlet's as actor. Hamlet opens the scene as hypocrite, but our last vision of him is through Gertrude's eyes, as she describes him to Claudius: "Mad as the sea and wind when both contend/ Which is the mightier" (4.1.7-8). Shakespeare cunningly alters our response to Hamlet's feigning so that we can no longer differentiate absolutely between the histrionic "Personator" and the antic "man Personated." The actor and the madman become indistinguishable. Hamlet's acting frustrates both the Neoplatonists' secure vision of the omnipotent artist, whose creation never exceeds his ability to control it, and the Puritans' demonic feigner, whose acting cannot effect real change in the world. Hamlet's performance is creative yet destructive, both actual and enacted, both real and feigned.

Hamlet's problem is the player's problem, to suit the action to the word and the word to the action. Meaning itself is a critical difficulty in *Hamlet*, and suggests a final measure of the play's address to the actor. Language in *Hamlet* is fully consistent with the deceptions of histrionic seeming that complicate the play. *Hamlet* embraces a wide range of verbal styles—Hamlet's punning, Claudius' oily oxymorons, Polonius' platitudes, Ophelia's ravings, the gravediggers' jests—and like the actor's playing, all these speech modes make the attribution of sense uncertain. Ophelia's mad speeches are particularly important in this regard. As one of two female roles in the play, Ophelia might well coordinate a certain antipathy toward acting. A Puritan lured into the theater might not be surprised by Hamlet's crudeness in the "nunnery" scene, where he confronts both Ophelia's duplicity and also an effeminate boy actor tricked out as a girl, or by his "country" banter with her in the "Mousetrap" scene, where Hamlet displays a lewdness appropriate to the special license of the theater audience. But Ophelia more importantly coordinates the imagery of acting, madness, and lust that in some respects reflects Hamlet's own predicament. As David Leverenz has recently remarked, since she "is only valued for the roles that further other people's plots," she resembles an unwitting actor in much the way that Hamlet resembles a canny one.[31] In her mad scenes, Ophelia's expression recalls Hamlet's in his outburst against seeming, for her evident expression is divorced from the "within" of sense. As Claudius notes, she is "Divided from herself and her fair judgment,/ Without the which we are pictures or mere beasts" (4.5.86-87). Like the actor, Ophelia incarnates both sides of the histrionic coin. Her madness is unnatural and irrational, severing her motives from her significant behavior. But her actions are also darkly meaningful, for she voices the complexity of her feeling toward Hamlet, Polonius, and Laertes more fully than sane Ophelia ever could.

The Polonius children refine aspects of Hamlet's performance: Ophelia intensifies the image of the actor as madman; Laertes presents the madness of a too-thorough engagement with a conventionally "histrionic" role:

> How came he dead? I'll not be juggled with.
> To hell allegiance, vows to the blackest devil,
> Conscience and grace to the profoundest pit!
> I dare damnation. To this point I stand,
> That both the worlds I give to negligence,
> Let come what comes, only I'll be revenged
> Most throughly for my father.   (4.5.131-37)

On his return to Denmark, Laertes parodies what we see of Hamlet's progress through the play, recalling Hamlet's daring of damnation on the battlements, his prompting by heaven and hell, and his final sense that the "readiness is all," that he too can let come what comes. Yet Laertes lacks Hamlet's sense of the limitations of the revenger's posture, and falls "a-cursing like a very drab," unpacking his heart to Claudius. Fully committed, Laertes ignores Polonius' advice to give his thoughts no tongue and speaks his mind to Claudius, only to become the king's willing instrument. Claudius takes the measure of his man, skillfully questioning the reality of Laertes' pose in order to entrench him in it more fully: "Laertes, was your father dear to you?/ Or are you like the painting of a sorrow,/ A face without a heart?" (4.7.107-

109). Claudius easily ensnares Laertes in his plot, a plot that requires them to "put on" those to "varnish" Laertes' reputation, to search for "what convenience both of time and means/ May fit us to our shape," and to safeguard against "bad performance" (4.7.131-51).

In the abandon of Laertes' acting, rather than in Hamlet's careful experimentation, Shakespeare depicts the dangers of artless play. As Hamlet's final remarks to the "mutes or audience" of his play suggest, histrionic feigning is increasingly indistinguishable from sincere acting in *Hamlet*. When Hamlet imitates Laertes' ranting in Ophelia's grave, for instance, *his* emphasis and phrase of sorrow mocks Laertes' excess, but it also voices his own grief. Osric's formality can be parodied by Hamlet and Horatio, but it fully expresses his fawning waterfly nature. Our experience through the play, from the Pyrrhus scene onward, tends to qualify any simple reduction of the reality of the actor's deceit. Although playing is necessary in *Hamlet*, playing is neither as easy to control as the humanists imagine, nor as easy to identify and discriminate from other activities as the Puritans claim. *Hamlet* presents an image of the actor's potentiality that combines the Neoplatonic and Puritan perspectives in a coherent vision of the actor's dangerous seeming. The protean actor concentrates in his own performance the radical ambivalences of Renaissance feigning. Acting may discover truth, but only through cunning indirections; the most adept actor in the play chafes against this necessary artifice, and lesser actors are oblivious to, and done in by, the consequences of their feigning. Acting is man's natural inheritance in *Hamlet*, an inheritance that involves him in the endless contradictions, paradoxes, and contingencies of the actor's stage.

Hamlet presents the actor in this double perspective. Few plays in the period exploit the Renaissance actor's duplicity so evidently, but many are fully sustained by a sense of the contradictory values of his performance. By exploring three plays from the crowning decade of Shakespeare's theater—*Volpone, Twelfth Night, The Duchess of Malfi*—we can see the various ways in which the actor's monstrous creativity comes to shape a sense of the drama.

Volpone

The disturbing duality of Renaissance acting frequently guides the characterization of aggressively histrionic roles, parts that image the actor's task in the character he plays. The most striking criticism of *Volpone* regards the desire to perform, rather than greed or lust, as the play's driving motive. Acting is an unusually prominent activity in the play. The rich performances of Volpone and Mosca, the plotting of Voltore, Corvino, and Corbaccio, the posturing of Sir Politic and his wife, Peregrine's little scenario, the various plays-within-the-play, the open allusion to *commedia dell'arte*, and the dense texture of theatrical language and imagery all contribute to our sense that the play's primary focus is on the artifice of acting itself.[32] Although the structure of the play, proceeding to the exposure and punishment of its actors, casts acting in an ironic light, the final sentencing of the actors does not quite solve the problems that impersonation raises in the play. *Volpone* is unique partly in its evident fascination with the pleasure of acting, a pleasure that eludes the restrictions that the Scrutineo attempts to impose. Particularly in the role of Volpone himself, Jonson considers, and partly censures, the kind of pleasure that acting provides both the player and his audience.

The familiar problem of the play's unity supplies a convenient approach to the subtle dynamics of Volpone's part. Addressing Jonson's drama in his "Essay of Dramatick Poesie" (1668), Dryden approved the "labyrinth of design" that controls the intricate plotting of *The Alchemist* and *Epicoene*, but balked at *Volpone*, hesitating at the apparently improvised action of the fifth act:

I was going to have named the *Fox*, but that the unity of
design seems not exactly observ'd in it; for there appear two
actions in the Play; the first naturally ending with the fourth
Act; the second forc'd from it in the fifth: which yet is the less
to be condemn'd in him, because the disguise of *Volpone*, though
it suited not with his character as a crafty or covetous person,
agreed well enough with that of a voluptuary.[33]

Dryden argues that the character of Volpone bridges the partial
resolution of the Act 4 trial scene and the fresh complications
that bring the play to a close. Beyond that, Dryden also defines
the essential quality of Volpone's acting, recognizing that Volpone's performance in Act 5 is undermotivated if he is conceived
as merely lewd and grasping. The vitality of the play's finale lies
in Volpone's continuing development as a vividly histrionic "voluptuary."

Volpone's voluptuousness, his luxuriant sensuality, is his defining trait. Sensual indulgence prompts both Volpone's extravagant hymn to gold and his sudden pursuit of Celia, and increasingly Volpone's self-gratification is realized through the
particular pleasure that acting affords. Jonson characterizes acting
by comparing histrionic pleasure to erotic pleasure throughout
the play. Volpone first plays Scoto of Mantua, for instance, in
order to inspect Celia, and when he later seduces her he offers to
spice their lovemaking with artful impersonation:

> Whilst we, in changèd shapes, act Ovid's tales,
> Thou like Europa now, and I like Jove,
> Then I like Mars, and thou like Erycine;
> So of the rest, till we have quite run through,
> And wearied all the fables of the gods. (3.7.221-25)

Should Ovid stale, there are modern roles to pique their interest.
Later in the play, savoring both the gulling of the *avocatori* and

the detailed perfection of the courtroom performance, Mosca pointedly questions the nature of Volpone's delight:

MOSCA.   You are not taken with it enough, methinks?
VOLPONE.   O, more than if I had enjoyed the wench.
          The pleasure of all womankind's not like it.
                                        (5.2.9-11)

Jonson specifically fulfills the Puritan vision of acting in the sybaritic thrill that Volpone finds in it. Volpone discovers a sensuous appeal reminiscent of, and often identical to, the lustful allure of the flesh.

But there is another, more pervasive way in which acting becomes a dangerously indulgent activity in *Volpone*. Part of Volpone's voluptuousness is expressed through his typical extravagance, his tendency to intensify desire, to magnify language, and to complicate already elaborate plots. Volpone's acting is similarly magnificent, a part of his complex thrust toward self-realization through exaggeration and self-amplification. To use the Puritans' vocabulary, Volpone's acting is "lascivious" because it is obsessively, and somewhat pointlessly, virtuoso; he is a "professional virtuoso exulting in virtuosity," as C. H. Herford remarks.[34] His mountebank performance in Act 2 is impressively vivacious and precise, but as Scoto Volpone creates a situation that strains the limits of his acting: he comes in broad daylight, wearing a disguise that suggests theatrical artifice, to the house of a man who has just seen him on his deathbed. Even Corvino recognizes the *commedia dell'arte* elements of the scene. This proud extravagance of means typifies Volpone's acting throughout the play. In Act 1, Jonson emphasizes Volpone's concern for detail by showing him taking on his deathbed role, preparing his part: "Now, my feigned cough, my phthisic, and my gout,/ My apoplexy, palsy, and catarrhs" (1.2.124-25). Volpone then puts his talents to a stringent histrionic test:

VOLPONE. Mosca.

MOSCA.   My patron?

VOLPONE.   Bring him near, where is he?
             I long to feel his hand.

MOSCA.   The plate is here, sir.

VOLTORE. How fare you, sir?

VOLPONE.   I thank you, Signior Voltore.
             Where is the plate? mine eyes are bad.

                         (1.3.14-17)

Volpone draws Voltore closer, forcing the vulture's attention to his weak and palsied hands, his failing eyesight. In so doing, Volpone's illness becomes more affecting, but at the real risk of the actor's unmasking. As with the magnitude of his greed and lust, Volpone tests the limits of histrionic art by drawing his audience's attention precisely to the thorough verisimilitude of his deceptive feigning.

Volpone undertakes a similar performance before the court in Act 4. This time, the relationship between sensuousness and virtuosity is set in a more austere moral context, for Volpone's seeming momentarily threatens to deflect all other values. The terms of Volpone's performance are established in the opening lines of Act 4, Sir Politic's "I told you, sir, it was a plot; you see/ What observation is" (4.1.1-2). The authority of ocular proof is steadily subverted here, for in quick succession we hear Sir Pol advising Peregrine on the Polonian virtues of deceit ("beware/ You never speak a truth"), and see Lady Would-be accuse Peregrine of being "a lewd harlot, a base fricatrice,/ A female devil in a male outside" (4.2.55-56). In the courtroom, Bonario's inability to dramatize himself permits Voltore to turn his good reputation against him:

> 2ND AVOCATORE. The young man's fame was ever fair and
>   honest.

VOLTORE.   So much more full of danger is his vice,
               That can beguile so under shade of vir-
               tue.   (4.5.60-62)

In this setting, Celia's despairing swoon seems, naturally enough,
to be "Prettily feigned" (4.5.133).

Volpone's performance completes this rupture between the
seeming and the actual. Much as in Act 1, Volpone provokes the
scrutiny of his audience, for Voltore's defense tempts the court
to see through the fox's invalid mask:

>   Here, here,
> The testimony comes that will convince,
> And put to utter dumbness their bold tongues.
> See here, grave fathers, here's the ravisher,
> The rider on men's wives, the great impostor,
> The grand voluptuary! Do you not think
> These limbs should affect venery? Or these eyes
> Covet a concubine? Pray you, mark these hands.
> Are they not fit to stroke a lady's breasts?
> Perhaps he doth dissemble!   (4.6.20-29)

Again the details of Volpone's enactment are pointedly described,
forcing our attention both to the actor's performance and to
Volpone's. Furthermore, we see "what observation is" in a world
where sincere action and the judgments attendant upon it are
vitiated by histrionic performance. In the context that Voltore
and Volpone establish, Bonario's legitimate request to have the
old magnifico "proved" seems monstrous. Unable to act in their
own defense, Bonario and Celia become the dissembling "prod-
igies," and Voltore is commended for their "discovery."

The rhythm of this performance is also an index to the unique
energy that Volpone's acting taps. The fifth act opens with a
tableau of severely diminished vitality, a weak and chastened
actor catching his breath:

> Well, I am here, and all this brunt is past.
> I ne'er was in dislike with my disguise
> Till this fled moment. Here, 'twas good, in private,
> But in your public—*Cavè*, whilst I breathe.   (5.1.1-4)

Volpone's tone here is a new one in the play, markedly different from the splendid vigor of his hymn to gold in Act 1, or of Mosca's hymn to himself in Act 3. Moreover, Volpone's fatigue is disappointing, because we expect the exhilarating release that usually follows his performances. Following the gulling of Corbaccio in Act 1, for example, Volpone is elated:

> VOLPONE.   O, I shall burst!
>   Let out my sides, let out my sides.
> MOSCA.   Contain
>   Your flux of laughter, sir.   (1.4.132-34)

The irrepressible energy that controls Volpone's performance is released through the involuntary flux of laughter. The fifth act, in contrast, shows an enervated fox, who needs to recover the deep and spontaneous, laughter-like energy that acting has aroused in the past. So, he drinks:

> 'Tis almost gone already; I shall conquer.
> Any device, now, of rare, ingenious knavery
> That would possess me with a violent laughter,
> Would make me up again. So, so, so, so. *Drinks again.*
> This heat is life; 'tis blood by this time!

The shift in circumstances from private to public performance, from indulgent to enforced acting, has exhausted Volpone. To recover himself, to be made up again, he must be possessed by an inspiriting and violent laughter, a Dionysian vigor that acting both requires and promotes. The old voluptuary feels himself returning the longer he luxuriates, so he drinks again, then plots and acts.

Acting, then, is part of the complex of desires and satisfactions that defines Volpone as a voluptuary. Volpone's acting is sensuous, erotic, irrational, egocentric, obsessive, obscene. The fulfillment that Volpone pursues through acting is intimately related to the principal danger that the actor's power poses in the play, the ease with which his attractive self-reliance becomes a dangerously corrupt indulgence. The balance is gradually tipped in *Volpone*, as Jonson narrowly limits the freedom that Volpone can achieve through acting. In the course of the play, Volpone's roles symbolically enact the progress of his moral degeneration—from magnifico to mountebank to lecher to buffoon to prisoner—and the satisfactions of acting decline as well, as Volpone's parts become more restricted and confining.[35] The spirited gulling of Act 1 and the impromptu performance as Scoto in Act 2 give way to a succession of roles that trap Volpone in performance rather than releasing him through it. The arrival of Lady Would-be in Act 3 confines Volpone in the uncomfortable role of invalid confidant. Later, his attempted seduction of Celia has more serious results, for the presence of an audience, Bonario, finally forces Volpone to choose between active and passive roles, between the seduction bed and the deathbed. The consequences of this choice are immediate. In Act 4, Volpone gives a debilitating performance, harnessing all of his talent to feign an utterly passive immobility, "the punishment of a Dantesque *contrapasso*" that forces the spiritually moribund fox to enact his own death.[36] In Act 5, Volpone "dies" and is disinherited. His acting has "uncreated" him; he has become so superfluous that he can regain identity and social definition only by unmasking himself, by turning himself in. Once Volpone does decide to "uncase" himself, the Scrutineo swiftly devises a fit punishment. Volpone's crime has been his relentless effort to make action in Venice insubstantial, unreal, and the Scrutineo appropriately confiscates the material "substance" of his magnifico role. The court sentences Volpone to uncreate himself, condemning him to endure—in irons that will restrain further metamorphosis—the role that he has so artfully created:[37]

> And since the most was gotten by imposture,
> By feigning lame, gout, palsy, and such diseases,
> Thou art to lie in prison, cramped with irons,
> Till thou be'st sick and lame indeed.   (5.12.121-24)

In conceiving the title role of *Volpone*, and in elaborating much of the action of the play, Jonson concentrates the characteristic dynamics of Renaissance acting. Like the Puritan critics, Jonson defines part of the energy of acting as deriving from fundamentally antisocial and unnatural desires, from vanity and the impulse toward self-magnification and self-indulgence, and he uses the structure of the play to censure that impulse. But Jonson recognizes and articulates the powerful attraction that acting offers, voicing it most clearly in Mosca's opening soliloquy in Act 3, and demonstrating it throughout the play in Volpone's exuberantly extravagant enactment. Our own response to Volpone's feigning is, I think, more varied and ambivalent than the Scrutineo's, and is a more telling index to Jonson's subtle equipoise of contrasting moral attitudes. In the audience, our own "flux of laughter" enforces our identification with Volpone's histrionic capacity throughout the play. This identification is reinforced for the last time in Mosca's repudiation of Voltore, Corvino and Corbaccio in Act 5, where Volpone, concealed behind a curtain, is our representative on the stage, and voices our own mirth. Although acting is undoubtedly criticized in the play, it nevertheless provides the only means of realizing the self in action that the play offers; Bonario and Celia are helpless in Venice because they lack even enough histrionic sensibility to represent themselves effectively in court, to show virtue her own feature through well-spirited acting. Although acting in Volpone's Venice is the endemic symptom of the city's moral degeneration, virtue remains impotent insofar as it can so easily be undermined by the histrionic talents it rejects. In the play's final vision, the punishment of the actors provides only a brief stay to the voluptuous allure of the actor's art.

Twelfth Night

A much gentler play than *Volpone*, *Twelfth Night* also offers a surprisingly "puritanical" vision of the actor's performance, and persistently evaluates acting in terms of madness, sexual confusion, and demonic deception.[38] From the outset, *Twelfth Night* fuses the actor's erotic, histrionic, and demonic duplicity in the process of Viola's captivating acting. Viola is one of Shakespeare's most resourceful and most defenseless heroines; indeed, Shakespeare stresses her vulnerability by consigning her to the actor's contingent domain. Cast on the shores of Illyria without home, father, or brother, Viola has no choice but to engage herself in histrionic play:

> Conceal me what I am, and be my aid
> For such disguise as haply shall become
> The form of my intent.   (1.2.53-55)

Twelfth Night immediately depicts the sexual indeterminacy of the Renaissance performer in the form that most quickly suits Viola's histrionic intent. Neither boy nor girl, Viola puts on the garments of the male in order to play Orsino's eunuch, and much of the action of the play elaborates the consequences of Viola's rather desperate decision to act.

The early scenes of *Twelfth Night* repeatedly confirm Viola's androgyny as the critical feature of her role-playing. Although she is far from the polluted creature that Puritan critics might have seen, Viola does blend male and female qualities—"all is semblative a woman's part," as Orsino remarks (1.4.34). Accordingly, the play highlights Cesario's puzzling sexual ambiguity both in his first scene with Orsino, and in his first scene with Olivia as well. Olivia, trying to discover "What is he at the gate," is at first frustrated by Toby ("Let him be the devil and he will, I care not"), and still further perplexed by Malvolio:

> OLIVIA.   What kind o' man is he?
> MALVOLIO. Why, of mankind.
> OLIVIA.   What manner of man?
> MALVOLIO. Of very ill manner. He'll speak with you, will
>   you or no.
> OLIVIA.   Of what personage and years is he?

$$(1.5.149\text{-}54)$$

Malvolio finally answers Olivia, but answers darkly nonetheless; Cesario is "in standing water, between boy and man."

"What manner of man?"—Olivia's question gains force on Cesario's entrance, for his evident posturing only intensifies the problem of his manner. Cesario's sex, his personage, and his years—all qualifications for becoming a fit lover for Olivia—are all uncertain, but Viola makes Cesario's deportment more unsettling by stressing his detachment, the extent to which his interview with Olivia is a feigned performance. "I would be loath to cast away my speech; for, besides that it is excellently well penned, I have taken great pains to con it," Cesario remarks, stalling the play until he can determine his audience by refusing to answer any question that is "out of my part." Olivia, herself masked, is at first aware of Cesario's histrionic insincerity ("Are you a comedian?" she asks, 1.5.180), and urges him to condense his poetical flattery, for as poetry, "It is the more like to be feigned" (1.5.194).

And yet, for all the vivacity of Viola's seeming, Olivia's response to her acting is finally naive, much like her response to Feste's fooling earlier in the scene. Despite Cesario's confessed feigning—"I am not that I play" (1.5.182)—Olivia takes his performance to express his essential nature, and reads in his speech, face, limbs, actions, and spirit a "fivefold blazon" of gentle nature and breeding (1.5.290-91). The exchange between Olivia and Viola here encapsulates the characteristic dynamics of Shakespearean acting. In one sense, Viola's performance expresses her inherent nature in action: Olivia rightly perceives Viola's virtues through Cesario's mask, virtues that Viola presumably shares with Olivia's eventual husband, Sebastian. But Viola's enactment entails some disturbing consequences: Olivia wrongly attributes Viola's virtues to the role and not to the actor.

Moreover, in this remarkable scene the theme of sexual difference is dramatized through the enactment of sexual identity. Not only do we witness, as J. L. Styan notes, "a love scene between two boys playing girls" (one of whom plays a boy), but we are aware of many similarities between the two roles. Both boy actors play young women conspicuously shorn of fathers and brothers, both women are sensitive to the effect of self-display, both are in love, and even their names are nearly anagrams of one another.[39] Furthermore, Viola's role-playing fuses histrionic and erotic seeming in a way that recalls the Puritan charges against transvestite acting, in substance if not in tone. Recognizing that Olivia has been "charmed" by her performance, Viola comments on the moral complexity of her deceptive acting:

> I am the man. If it be so, as 'tis,
> Poor lady, she were better love a dream.
> Disguise, I see thou art a wickedness
> Wherein the pregnant enemy does much.
> How easy is it for the proper false
> In women's waxen hearts to set their forms!
> Alas, our frailty is the cause, not we,
> For such as we are made of, such we be.
> How will this fadge? My master loves her dearly;
> And I (poor monster) fond as much on him;
> And she (mistaken) seems to dote on me.
> What will become of this? As I am man,

> My state is desperate for my master's love.
> As I am woman (now alas the day!),
> What thriftless sighs shall poor Olivia breathe?
>
> (2.2.25-39)

Although Viola leaves it to time's whirligig to unravel her problems, she presents a set of terms that coordinates the ethical attitude of the central action of the play. The results of her acting, much as they are in writers like Prynne and Gosson, are defined through images of sexual confusion, dreams, and madness. Dreams, in *Twelfth Night*, are neither innocent nor easily ignored. As Malvolio and Olivia both discover, dreams in the play verge on hallucination. Even Sebastian is brought to this pass in the course of the play—"Or I am mad, or else this is a dream" (4.1.62)— as an effect of Viola's performance. And yet the dream of madness offers more to Olivia than Viola's false seeming does, for the dream at least gratifies her fantasy, while Cesario lacks the "little thing" to provide more fleshly fulfillment (3.4.305). Contemplating the erotic effects of her acting, Viola explicitly recalls that disguise is traditionally the instrument of the "pregnant enemy" Satan. Moreover, Viola's role ("poor monster") is analogous to the image of "pregnant" Satan; both fuse creative power and moral sterility through the monstrous deformity of the natural difference between the sexes.

This ethical network animates much of the action of the play, particularly the action of the Malvolio plot. Puritan or not, Malvolio has a keen sense of the value of self-expression, although he makes little distinction between sincere and feigned behavior. "Sick of self-love," Malvolio shares Viola's exquisite sense of performance, but lacks her sensitivity to the paradoxical self-denial that role-playing can entail.

> I frown the while, and perchance wind up my watch, or play with my—some rich jewel. Toby approaches; curtsies there to me—. . . . I extend my hand to him thus, quenching my

familiar smile with an austere regard of control—. . . . Saying, "Cousin Toby, my fortunes having cast me on your niece, give me this prerogative of speech." (2.5.57-69)

Malvolio visualizes his purposeful gesture and intonation; Maria's letter merely provides the script that will enable him to act his fantasy. His reaction is swift and thorough. Like Hamlet, Malvolio wipes away all trivial fond records of personality in order to adopt his new role with persuasive thoroughness:

> This is open. I will be proud, I will read politic authors, I will baffle Sir Toby, I will wash off gross acquaintance, I will be point-devise, the very man. . . . I will be strange, stout, in yellow stockings, and cross-gartered, even with the swiftness of putting on. (2.5.156-68)

While Viola feels forced into her role by circumstances, and plays the messenger Cesario with sophisticated irony, Malvolio leaps into his role headlong. Viola's disguise, the ambiguous "fivefold blazon" of her virtues, integrates her into Illyrian society, but Malvolio's performance actualizes a private, regressive fantasy ("The Lady of the Strachy married the yeoman of the wardrobe"— 2.5.37-38) that ultimately isolates him in the prison of his own seeming. Acting as the expression of "self-love" provides Malvolio with neither protection nor blazon, and his vulnerability is tellingly remarked by Sir Toby: "Why, thou hast put him in such a dream that, when the image of it leaves him, he must run mad" (2.5.189-90).

In the long scene at the play's center (3.4), Shakespeare again coordinates madness and acting, and creates a verbal context for the action that highlights Satan's subtle role in the improvised feigning of Illyria. The scene opens with Olivia's call for Malvolio. His entrance prepared by Maria's suggestion ("He's coming, madam, but in very strange manner. He is sure possessed, madam."), smiling Malvolio arrives, apparently distracted. Again, Sir Toby derides Malvolio's simplistic sense of the dangers of duplicity: "What, man, 'tis not for gravity to play at cherry-pit with Satan." Once Malvolio departs, Olivia briefly meets Cesario, and voices her infatuation with the messenger in typically excessive terms— "A fiend like thee might bear my soul to hell"—that lend verbal density to the figure of the Vice shadowed forth in Viola the actor. Olivia's departure gives Sir Toby the chance to offer Sir Andrew's contrived challenge to Cesario, and once again the play develops a clear contrast between the evident reality of the situation ("I am no fighter," pleads Viola), and Toby's ability to direct the scene through clever manipulation of its characters. Like the duel in *Hamlet*, this duel both is and is not a duel, for it is predicated on Toby's skill in puffing up the two antagonists. Appropriately enough, he makes each actor appear to the other as "a very devil."[40]

A mock duel between mock devils over a mock issue—Antonio rushes into this empty combat to the side of "Sebastian." Without the protection of disguise, Antonio is immediately recognized and arrested, his appearance in his own person underlining the irony of his confrontation with Toby's actors. Like Olivia and Malvolio, Antonio is perplexed, driven to the edge of his reason by this encounter with histrionic play. Though his devotion to Sebastian is genuine, its consequences are completely undercut in a scene where the pregnant enemy actively dissembles all appearances:

> But, O, how vild an idol proves this god!
> Thou hast, Sebastian, done good feature shame.
> In nature there's no blemish but the mind;
> None can be called deformed but the unkind.
> Virtue is beauty; but the beauteous evil
> Are empty trunks, o'erflourished by the devil.
>
> (3.4.368-73)

To the sailor Antonio, as to Viola's sea captain ("thou hast a mind that suits/ With this thy fair and outward character"—

1.2.50-51), the equation between the apparent and the actual is a fundamental natural principle. In the most profound sense, those are deformed who do not express their "kindness" directly in action. The "beauteous evil," the feigning, "unkind" distortion of nature, is not a positive force, but a negative one, trunks empty of meaning. As Antonio suggests, Satan o'erflourishes much of the action of *Twelfth Night*—Viola's disguise, Malvolio's possessed performance, Olivia's love, the duel—concealing the inward deformities that undermine virtuous action. Antonio forcefully reiterates a common image of the nullity of histrionic evil, recalling the actors of William Rankins's *A Mirrour of Monsters* (1587), empty "wels without water" who are sent "from their great captaine Sathan" to work their mischief.[41]

Malvolio's prison provides a complementary image of the nullity of acting in *Twelfth Night*. Illyria's saturnalian freedom exacts a heavy toll, for the potential for festive release is repaid with the dangers of confining self-indulgence. If Malvolio's prison is the prison of self-love, it is also the prison of indulgent feigning, for its only realities are theatrical. As Feste's closing song of the Vice and the devil suggests, the scene (4.2) images an exemplary chastisement, and has a conventional basis in the morality tradition.[42] The prison scene has a histrionic complexity similar to that of the duel scene; mad Malvolio, not actually possessed, is given confession by Sir Thopas, not really a priest. Too, Malvolio's problem is something like Olivia's or Antonio's, in that he is unable to perceive the histrionic ambiguity of his situation. Unable to accept the relative, "readiness is all" attitude Feste offers—

"That that is is"; so, I, being Master Parson, am Master Parson; for what is "that" but that, and "is" but is? (4.2.15-17)

—Malvolio remains identified with his role, incapable of seeing the light offered by Sir Thopas, or the irony of his remark to Feste, "I am as well in my wits, fool, as thou art."[43] Malvolio insists on a strict division between self and role that his own behavior, and the rest of the play, has made difficult to achieve.

[49]

Unwilling to commend his wits to heaven, or to leave his "vain bibble-babble," Malvolio wants redress, and refuses to leave an unsuccessful and questionable role behind.

The end of *Twelfth Night* extends and resolves the interplay between actual and apparent action, contrasting an actual marriage (Olivia-Sebastian) with an apparent one (Olivia-Cesario), revealing the servant to be his "master's mistress," showing Malvolio to be perhaps more madly used than mad in fact, and finally juxtaposing Sebastian and Viola in the natural perspective that restores sexual order to Illyria. The final scene of *Twelfth Night* always seems to provide an ambivalent resolution to the problems raised in the play, a play that is willing to risk the marriage of two women in order to enable the proper marriage between women and men. The scene has its moments of violence, which threaten to rend the delicate tissue of its festive finale. Olivia's attentions to Cesario make her liaison with Orsino's servant obvious to all, a liaison that Orsino vows vengefully to rupture by sacrificing "the lamb that I do love" (5.1.129). In this final extremity, Viola, though she does not doff her disguise, attempts to act *in propria persona*. She flies

> After him I love
> More than I love these eyes, more than my life,
> More, by all mores, than e'er I shall love wife.
> If I do feign, you witnesses above
> Punish my life for tainting of my love! (5.1.133-37)

Denying feigning, Viola is nonetheless aware that feigning has tainted her love for Orsino. But like Volpone's, Viola's role-playing eventually traps her in artifice, since she is still unable to disprove her apparent betrayal of the duke.

Olivia's command—"Be that thou know'st thou art"—suggests the difficulty of breaking free from the web of feigning in *Twelfth Night*. Indeed, Viola's predicament is further complicated when Olivia calls the priest to testify to their marriage:

A contract of eternal bond of love,
Confirmed by mutual joinder of your hands,
Attested by the holy close of lips,
Strength'ned by interchangement of your rings;
And all the ceremony of this compact
Sealed in my function, by my testimony;
Since when, my watch hath told me, toward my grave
I have traveled but two hours.   (5.1.155-62)

The priest stresses the ceremonial nature of their contract, the
bond between them witnessed by heaven. His emphasis on the
ceremonial aspect of the wedding is critical here; the marriage
will not only reorganize Illyrian society, but it also provides the
sustaining ceremonial structure that enables the desperate seeming of the play to be contained. As Lynda E. Boose has argued,
Shakespeare frequently invokes the structure of the marriage ceremony as an implied model for the process of family development
in his plays. She suggests that "the ceremonial activities associated
with marriage move from thesis through antithesis to synthesis;
the anarchic release of fertility is positioned between two phases
of relative stasis." Shakespeare builds his dramatic action upon
this ceremonial paradigm by evidently transferring his female
characters (and, Boose argues, the threatening femininity they
represent) from the domain of the father to the domain of the
husband. In *Twelfth Night*, the marriage ceremony's expression
of controlled sexual release is complicated by the remarkable
histrionic and erotic freedom of the play's women. Both Olivia
and Viola are left without father or brother for most of the play,
without those figures whose ceremonial role is at once to control
the daughter's sexual availability and to certify the purity of the
daughter given away in marriage. Sebastian, in fact, confirms
that Viola's father died on "that day when Viola from her birth/
Had numbered thirteen years," absenting himself at just the age
when Viola, like Juliet, enters sexual maturity. Shakespeare ex-

plicitly recalls the phases of the marriage ceremony by reminding us of Viola's relation to her father as a prelude to her "transition from one male domain to the other."[44] Shakespeare's reference to the marriage ceremony in this scene may well be intended to circumscribe Viola's sexuality, but she must undergo a more explicit ritual before her histrionic freedom can be similarly restrained.

"One face, one voice, one habit, and two persons"—if Sebastian and Viola present a natural perspective, so too do Viola and Cesario, the actor and her role. Orsino's remark initiates a marked change in the tone and attitude of the scene, introducing the long and somewhat tentative dialogue between Viola and her brother. Sebastian stands in for the father in the implied marriage ceremony of the scene ("Sebastian was my father;/ Such a Sebastian was my brother too" 5.1.232-33), but Viola's ceremonial greeting and leave-taking is made uncertain by the masculine role she has been playing. She postpones embracing Sebastian until she can rid herself entirely of her "masculine usurped attire":

> Do not embrace me till each circumstance
> Of place, time, fortune do cohere and jump
> That I am Viola; which to confirm,
> I'll bring you to a captain in this town,
> Where lie my maiden weeds; . . .   (5.1.249-54)

Nor can she turn from Sebastian to embrace Orsino; again, the sexual indeterminacy of Viola's role-playing disrupts the ceremonial structure of the scene. Orsino, too, perhaps relinquishing with difficulty the consuming illusion of his love for Olivia, also insists on seeing Viola in her "woman's weeds," and refrains from assuming the husband's role until the assumption of reality can be made with thorough certainty:

> Cesario, come—
> For so you shall be while you are a man,

But when in other habits you are seen,
Orsino's mistress and his fancy's queen.   (5.1.386-89)

In *Twelfth Night*, the stable relationships of the marital covenant, the "contract of eternal bond of love" that fixes sexual fidelity, can be established only when Viola's histrionic freedom has been finally curtailed.

If Sebastian's arrival begins to limit *Twelfth Night*'s feigning, Malvolio's release reminds us of the price that feigning exacts. The transparent device with which Malvolio has been duped becomes clearly exposed to Olivia. Without doubt, Malvolio's letter "savors not much of distraction." But although Olivia willingly makes Malvolio "plaintiff and the judge" of his cause, his adjudication is forestalled by Fabian's plea that Malvolio's story "May rather pluck on laughter than revenge" (5.1.366). Shakespeare's judgment of acting is more severe than Malvolio's, for the play finally offers no redress to those caught in their feigning. Time's whirligig apportions the play's endings without strict regard for justice. The play dramatically shifts our attention away from the victims of feigning—Malvolio, Toby, Antonio— without explicitly requiting them. The final festivity simply leaves them behind.

Feste's song reminds us of the manifold similarity between "man's estate" and the actor's. The difficulty of returning to one's proper role—which Viola, Olivia, Orsino, Sebastian, and Malvolio all experience—suggests why Shakespeare may have chosen to alter the model of *As You Like It* and give his epilogue to Feste instead of to Viola. *Twelfth Night* is a play whose histrionic and erotic imbalance is implicitly righted, but never actually demonstrated. Malvolio remains unjustly abused, Orsino withholds the proper naming of his wife, and Feste sings a melancholy song that, far from recalling golden Illyria, returns our attention to the eroding contingencies of our own rainswept world. Not that acting has served an entirely duplicitous service in the play; much as it does in *Hamlet*, acting both distorts and reflects the reality it imitates. As Cesario, Viola both represents and misrepresents herself—"Cesario" is, after all, an articulate blazon of Viola's virtues. Tricked into feigning, Malvolio is nonetheless both a presumptuous courtier and a kind of puritanical madman. For all the devils lurking in its language, Toby's little duel scene does reveal Cesario and Andrew for the womanish men they truly are. Indeed, conceived as a means to the revelation of an obscure truth, acting is related to the theme of epiphanic grace suggested by the play's title, and, as Barbara K. Lewalski has argued, demonstrated throughout in the counterpoint between suffering Viola ("the lamb that I do love") and transcendent Sebastian.[45] But although acting plays an important part in the gracious restoration of Illyria to health, the play's final gesture—Feste's doffing his mask—seems to me to set the histrionic release of the play within strict bounds. Feste's act is fitting, for much of the play censures the consequences of acting by criticizing the artifice of its own performance. Acting, even in Viola's capable hands, is consistently regarded as deceptive, as a demonic threat to the sexual and moral order. One way that *Twelfth Night* transcends the limits of Puritan antitheatricalism is by defining the place of this deceptive freedom in the workaday world. For although Shakespeare finally returns us to the world of wind and rain, he also censures Malvolio's "precisian" vision of a world lacking in cakes and ale, a world that cannot permit, within the proper limits of the theater, the threatening exuberance of the actor's play.

The Duchess of Malfi

More so than Jonson or Shakespeare, Webster deliberately creates his drama as theatrical spectacle. Both *The White Devil* and *The Duchess of Malfi* are loaded with stagey effects—waxen effigies, severed limbs, bizarre diseases, pimping, incest, madmen, tor-

ture, murdering dumb shows, and the like. Not only do Webster's characters typically engage in disguise and role-playing,
they often provide a mordant commentary on the "tedious theater" that they perform. Even Webster's copybook *sententiae* en-
hance this calculated artifice; rather than reinforcing a traditional
moral vision, Webster's allusions strike us as "fragments of an
older morality, to which Webster's characters refer but cannot
adhere."[46] In this regard, Webster's allusiveness vividly directs
our attention to the characters' language as a text and consequently
to their actions as performance, as acting. As J. R. Mulryne
suggests, acting is "the very idiom" of Webster's plays, plays in
which every attitude becomes "a pose 'acted up,' even the most
sincere of them appearing to be adopted like an actor's role."[47]

Not surprisingly, Webster's actors embody the paradoxical
valuation of Renaissance performance, and in *The Duchess of Malfi*
Webster focuses his concern for the dynamics of acting in a
number of ways. The dense imagery of the play suggests both
the theatricality of its world, and the specific dangers implied by
insubstantial feigning—the image of epidemic plague especially
comes to characterize the actor's mutability. And more than *The
White Devil*, *The Duchess of Malfi* questions the nature of sincere
acting, the effects that deeds "really or sincerely acted" can have
in a world suffused by such rampant seeming.

Acting pervades the action of *The Duchess of Malfi*. Much as
Webster orients the action of *The White Devil* in Lodovico's opening "Banish't," so he phrases *The Duchess of Malfi*'s vision of acting
in Antonio's demeanor on his return from France. As Delio remarks,

> You are welcome to your country, dear Antonio—
> You have been long in France, and you return
> A very formal Frenchman in your habit.   (1.1.1-3)[48]

Antonio's new French habits suggest his capacity for change and
alert us to the histrionic equivocation that such artful self-display

can entail. As Antonio describes the other courtiers, we realize that such doubleness is widespread in Malfi. Bosola deceptively "rails at those things which he wants," the Cardinal's superficial "flashes" of virtue belie his "inward character," and Duke Ferdinand's "mirth, is merely outside" (1.1.25, 156-57, 170). Nor need we rely on Antonio's description alone, for Webster's characters juggle their masks with alarming swiftness. In this scene, for example, Ferdinand urges his sycophants to merriment, and then turns a suddenly haughty glare on them:

> FERDINAND. I am of Pliny's opinion, I think he was begot by the wind; he runs as if he were ballasted with quicksilver.
>
> SILVIO. True, my lord, he reels from the tilt often.
>
> RODERIGO,
> GRISOLAN. Ha,ha,ha!
>
> FERDINAND. Why do you laugh? Methinks you that are courtiers should be my touch-wood, take fire, when I give fire; that is, laugh when I laugh, were the subject never so witty—
>
> (1.1.118-25)

Such fickleness subverts our sense of the characters' coherent identity; indeed, the notion of a perduring self is false to a play that repeatedly defines character as a function of situation.

Webster depicts his characters' actor-like freedom in the ease with which they alter their personae. Antonio, for instance, inhabits a number of offices; he rises from servant to reluctant suitor to husband, and then is cast out as exile, dismembered corpse, and hapless revenger. Ferdinand degenerates from man to machiavel to beast. The Duchess, too, is changed from widow to wife and mother, from prince to unwilling player, from duchess to prisoner to "box of worm-seed" to disembodied voice. These characters experience a continual redefinition of social and individual identity, and Bosola—"a good actor . . . curs'd/ For playing a villain's part" (4.2.289-90)—epitomizes their histrionic fluidity. Like Elizabethan actors themselves, Bosola is an indeterminate outcast, an exiled rogue searching for a secure niche in the play's hierarchic social world. In the opening scene, Bosola, like Antonio, is notably changed in station and manner. Having served as the Cardinal's galley slave, Bosola seeks both his due "reward" and his proper place in the courtly precedence, "where this man's head lies at that man's foot, and so lower, and lower" (1.1.68-69), from which he has been excluded. "Familiar," "quaint invisible devil, in flesh," "intelligencer," Ferdinand promises Bosola that by playing these roles he may "arrive/ At a higher place by't" (1.1.259-64). And Bosola plays brilliantly, not only "court-gall" but provisor of the Duchess's horse, soldier, gravemaker, bellman, and avenger. But as an actor, Bosola performs the one activity that, as both Puritans and humanists agree, explicitly negates the ideal of degree itself. Almost predictably, Bosola's playing undermines his place in the social world, rather than confirming it. When he finally discards the role of intelligencer in Act 5, he is still an outsider, unable to escape the theater he has created. Instead of integrating him into the social order, his actions remain actor-like, like mistakes "as I have often seen/ In a play" (5.5.95-96). The theater provides the only model for acting in *The Duchess of Malfi*, but the model it provides is a treacherously histrionic one.

Bosola's feigning, like the Duchess's dissembling of her marriage to Antonio, blurs the priorities of social degree. Webster naturally uses the image of the theater to evaluate his characters' feigning, but he amplifies his valuation of the actor's assault on degree through a more inventive metaphor, the image of plague. Plague, as René Girard has argued, traditionally images an anxious fear of chaotic undifferentiation. Pervasive, yet arbitrary, plague erases all distinctions of age, sex, station, or morality; it nullifies categories of good and evil and transforms all of its unlucky victims equally into its own image—the corpse.[49] Girard suggests that from Homer to Artaud plague has figured forth the obliteration of difference or degree, particularly the loss of individual and social identity. Like the epidemic contamination of plague, once acting infects the orderly society, all forms of organization are threatened with disintegration. The actor's seeming, as the Puritans' incessant charge of "effeminacy" implies, particularly threatens the secure delineation of sexual difference. Even the frequent closing of the theaters in Elizabethan London due to plague may have, in this sense, both a medical and a metaphorical rationale, proscribing the disease of undifferentiation in both its viral and histrionic forms.

Plague subsumes a variety of images in *The Duchess of Malfi*, those of disease, poison, bodily decay. Antonio voices this controlling metaphor in his first speech:

> . . . a prince's court
> Is like a common fountain, whence should flow
> Pure silver drops in general: but if 't chance
> Some curs'd example poison 't near the head,
> *Death, and diseases through the whole land spread.*
>
> (I.I.11-15)

Like *Hamlet, The Duchess of Malfi* is suffused by the imagery of disease.[50] Antonio's hidden poison spreads quickly through the court, and returns at the end of the scene to touch him through the Duchess's transforming affection. The Duchess's love is, as Cariola remarks, a secret to be guarded like poison: "For I'll conceal this secret from the world/ As warily as those that trade in poison/ Keep poison from their children" (I.I.352-54). And her affection is poisonously mortal in its effects, for like plague, the Duchess's proposal erases the essential differences of social degree:

> I do here put off all vain ceremony,
> And only do appear to you a young widow

[58]

That claims you for her husband, and like a widow,
I use but half a blush in't.   (1.1.456-59)

Webster relates fleshly decay to the actor's dissembling more overtly as the play progresses. In Act 2, Bosola teaches Castruchio how to play the unaccustomed role of "eminent courtier," and also remarks on the "witchcraft" of face-painting and ostentatious dress:

But in our own flesh, though we bear diseases
Which have their true names only ta'en from beasts,
As the most ulcerous wolf, and swinish measle;
Though we are eaten up of lice and worms,
And though continually we bear about us
A rotten and dead body, we delight
To hide it in rich tissue.   (2.1.52-58)

Man responds histrionically to the diseases that riot in his flesh, dissembling them with costume and make-up. Even the reputation of wisdom is, in this context, a deceptively "foul tetter that runs all over a man's body" (2.1.78-79). Bosola's leprous "tetter" anticipates Ferdinand's assessment of his inconstant sister: "methinks her fault and beauty,/ Blended together, show like leprosy,/ The whiter, the fouler" (3.3.62-64). The play repeatedly focuses our attention on such hidden or unacknowledged decay, and when Bosola mortifies the Duchess in Act 4, he appropriately directs her thoughts to the frailty of her flesh: "Thou art a box of worm-seed, at best, but a salvatory of green mummy:—what's this flesh? a little crudded milk, fantastical puff-paste" (4.2.124-26). The play's actions are feigned, its actors rotting, and its values corrupt; suitably enough, when the Cardinal has tricked Julia into kissing his poisoned Bible, he announces to the court that "she died o' th' plague" (5.2.321-22). The play's principal actor, Bosola, becomes the literal agent of death in the play, bringing his leveling and murderous plague to the Duchess,

[59]

Antonio, Ferdinand, the Cardinal, until he is consumed by it himself. Like the Duchess in her theatrical prison, the characters in *The Duchess of Malfi* are variously, and mortally, "plagu'd in art" (4.1.111).

The prominence of the plague motif, and its verbal figuration of the actor's poisonous seeming, raises a key point regarding Webster's integration of verbal and visual effects, and his reciprocal valuation of verbal and histrionic feigning. Webster's imagery is dense, diverse, sententious, and not infrequently just weird—"I would sooner swim to the Bermudas on/ Two politicians' rotten bladders, tied/ Together with an intelligencer's heartstring" (3.2.266-68). Webster has an unusual facility to make his verbal imagery concrete in the physical action of the play. In scene 1, for instance, Bosola characterizes the duplicity of the Aragonian brothers through the image of overripe fruit:

> He, and his brother, are like plum-trees, that grow crooked over standing pools; they are rich, and o'erladen with fruit, but none but crows, pies, and caterpillars feed on them: could I be one of their flattering panders, I would hang on their ears like a horse-leech till I were full, and then drop off:—I pray leave me. (1.1.49-54)

Horse-leech that he is, Bosola subsequently accepts Ferdinand's cover as the Duchess's provisor of the horse: "say then, my corruption/ Grew out of horse-dung: I am your creature" (1.1.286-87). These lines gather a range of association—dung, corruption, deceit, fruitfulness—that Webster brings into focus in Act 2, when Bosola tests the Duchess with his corrupted "apricocks." Ripened in horse dung, the delicate apricocks "swell" the Duchess, who falls immediately into labor and delivers the fruit of her hidden liaison with Antonio.

" 'Tis a pretty art," as Bosola remarks, "This grafting" of verbal and visual images. Webster's "grafting" exemplifies a crucial attitude informing Renaissance art. As Stephen Orgel remarks,

"We tend to slight the Renaissance pressure toward *explanation*, stressing instead the age's devotion to symbolic modes of expression. But again, the verbal was inseparable from the visual. Then as now, a symbol had meaning only after it was explained."[51] Webster's complex union of verbal and visual expression in the "apricocks" scene is explanatory rather than emblematic. The imagery of the play creates an amplifying context for Bosola's test, focusing the brothers' moral corruption and Bosola's deceit in the gift of the fruit, which is answered by the Duchess's own concealed bearing. As Webster remarks in his preface to *The Devil's Law Case*, the "grace" of this dramatic technique lies "where the decency of the Language, and Ingenious structure of the Scaene, arrive . . . to make up a perfect Harmony."[52]

Webster reverses this paradigm in his invocation of the theater in the play. Critics of *The Duchess of Malfi* have often remarked on the play's increasing reference to its own theatricality, particularly in the last two acts.[53] The image of the theater is critical to the play's entire movement, though, and when the verbal image of the theater arises late in the play, it confirms a fully developed pattern of physical action. The world-as-theater image fulfills what we have already seen, that all the characters are actor-directors using theatrical devices to further their private plots. The first scene, for example, presents a sequence of such actions. Webster introduces Antonio and Delio to the audience; they then stand aside as observers, as an onstage audience to the short scene between Bosola and the Cardinal. We witness the entrance of both Ferdinand and the Duchess; again Antonio and Delio stand aside to analyze them, describing their behavior and motives. And the scene closes with two self-evident performances. Ferdinand and the Cardinal persuade the Duchess not to remarry in a speech that comes so "roundly off" that it seems "studied" (1.1.329-30), and the Duchess playfully enacts her seduction of Antonio before a concealed audience, Cariola.

Webster builds the second act of the play on a similar series of performances. Bosola begins by satirizing Castruchio's manners and the Old Lady's face-painting, and strikes a melancholic pose that seems forced even to Antonio: "Because you would not seem to appear to the world puffed up with your preferment, you continue this out-of-fashion melancholy—leave it, leave it" (2.1.84-86). Bosola then unmasks the Duchess with the apricocks ruse, and Antonio replies with a counter-play, sealing the court, ostensibly to catch the Duchess's poisoner, while the Duchess delivers her child. In the third scene, Bosola draws the conventional comparison between the actor's seeming and the falsity of women— "Though lust do mask in ne'er so strange disguise,/ She's oft found witty, but is never wise" (2.3.76-77)—a remark that introduces the feigning of the following scene between the Cardinal and Julia, a woman who plays false to her husband by telling him she came "to visit an old anchorite/ Here, for devotion" (2.4.4-5). Acting discovers the Duchess's pregnancy and conceals it, allows her to dissemble her marriage, and provides the vehicle for Julia's unfaithful liaison. Finally, the Duchess's deception provokes Ferdinand's madness, his desire for revenge, and his decision to "study to seem/ The thing I am not" (2.5.62-63).

But the theater is a slippery instrument. In the bedroom scene (3.2), for instance, Antonio and Cariola steal out of the chamber in order to trick the Duchess into talking to herself. Watching her they become audience to a more fearsome scene, one that dramatizes—since Ferdinand assumes Antonio's role in the bedchamber—Ferdinand's desire to possess the Duchess or destroy her. This impulse underlies several other scenes in the play—the pilgrimage scene, the prison scenes—and lends the events of the play a theatrical tenor, an effect Webster intensifies by twice advancing the plot of the play through dumb show.

Nonetheless, Webster's actors are not all equally adept. The Duchess and Antonio especially seem to feel a sense of uncompromised, unchanging selfhood that often hinders their successful role-playing. Seducing Antonio in the first scene, the Duchess complains that she is forced into an uncomfortably masculine role:

> The misery of us that are born great—
> We are forc'd to woo, because none dare woo us:
> And as a tyrant doubles with his words,
> And fearfully equivocates, so we
> Are forc'd to express our violent passions
> In riddles, and in dreams, and leave the path
> Of simple virtue, which was never made
> To seem the thing it is not.   (1.1.441-48)

The Duchess regrets her equivocation, and voices a common vision of virtue: since virtue is absolute and inalterable, it has no need of the compromising falsehoods of role-playing and representation. Throughout the play, characters defend the opinion that virtue requires no dissembling. Even Ferdinand asks whether virtue is "but a bare name,/ And no essential thing?" (3.2.74-75). We may feel, with the Duchess, that only "unjust actions/ Should wear these masks and curtains" (3.2.158-59), but the play relentlessly undermines any conviction that the virtuous can safely eschew the devices of well-spirited acting.

Antonio is a case in point. Antonio's newly "formal" manners and his sudden leap in station suggest that he grasps the dynamics of performance. He plays his part in the Duchess's court persuasively, so much so that "some said he was an hermaphrodite, for he could not abide a woman" (3.2.220-21). But his histrionic facility pales beside Bosola's clever feigning. In 2.1, for instance, he rightly conceives Bosola's unfashionable melancholy as a pose, but is nonetheless easily taken in by Bosola's request to "let me be simply honest." Claiming to understand Bosola's "inside," Antonio blindly ignores Bosola's role as the Cardinal's one-time servant and present intelligencer. Bosola understands Antonio rather better, for he sees that Antonio lacks the actor's sensibility. As he remarks to the Duchess,

>   His discourse rather delighted to judge itself, than show
>   itself.
>   His breast was fill'd with all perfection,
>   And yet it seem'd a private whisp'ring-room,
>   It made so little noise of 't.   (3.2.255-58)

Deceit, even display, is foreign to Antonio, and he chafes at his disguises much as Bosola does; like Bosola, he determines to act the avenger in Act 5 in his own "shape" (5.1.69). In one of the play's final ironies, Antonio's only "benefit in death" is belatedly "To appear myself," mistakenly slain by a now unwilling Bosola (5.4.49-50).

The actor's mutability informs the painfully changeable world of *The Duchess of Malfi*, and clarifies the problem of selfhood in the climactic prison scene. In this scene (4.1-2) Webster constantly changes our understanding of the action we witness, repeatedly weakening our simple categories of real and feigned. Ferdinand's reconciliation with his sister, for instance, instantly becomes punishment, when the lights come up and the hand he offers in friendship becomes the severed hand of Antonio. Later in the scene, after the Duchess's horror—and our own—has had time to take effect, Ferdinand informs us that the bodies and the hand were "but fram'd in wax," transforming a theatrically grotesque torture into tortuously grotesque theater. Not only does Webster shift our view of the action, but the characters themselves undergo stunning change. Ferdinand's madmen sing with a "dogged howl,/ Sounding as from the threat'ning throat/ Of beasts, and fatal fowl" that prefigures Ferdinand's sudden transformation from prince to the lupine beast who hunts "the badger, by owl-light." The madmen's song of woman's inconstancy reminds us not only of the Duchess's transgression, but also suggests her coming change, from life to death. And, typically, Bosola also plays a number of parts here, changing from tomb-maker to bellman so rapidly that even the Duchess remarks on it: "Even now thou said'st/ Thou wast a tomb-maker."

The Duchess's torment is to endure such transformation, to feel that her enduring self ("I am Duchess of Malfi still") is being eroded by her theatrical world ("I account this world a tedious theatre,/ For I do play a part in't 'gainst my will"). As Arthur C. Kirsch suggests, the Duchess appears "to assume a theatrical role," the role of the "reverend monument" that she seems to Cariola to resemble (p. 110). If she is Duchess of Malfi still, she nonetheless uses the devices of the theater to express herself. Her assertion of a self both expressed and confined by the theater anticipates Bosola's similar discovery later in the play. Indeed, all the play's actors increasingly strain against the insubstantiality of their performance, and long to unmask and declare themselves. Once Bosola has been cast out by Ferdinand, he, like the Duchess (and like Antonio in Act 5), vows to be Bosola still, throwing off "my painted honour" (4.2.336). Sunk again in station, Bosola casts off the actor's mask and attempts to act sincerely, to perform a deed commensurate with his suffering in the play: "somewhat I will speedily enact/ Worth my dejection" (4.2.373-74).

Bosola's unmasking provides an important continuity between the last two acts of the play, for when he becomes the focus of the play's action, he assumes the Duchess's affecting sincerity. Several critics view Bosola's performance in Act 5 as less "theatrical" than his earlier deeds, but such claims are foreign to the vision of the play, and to Webster's highly skeptical sense of the ethics of enactment.[54] Kirsch is surely closer to the play's impulse when he notes that the finale of the play most resembles "a play gone haywire, rife with mistaken cues, confused directions, and actors who can no longer control their parts" (p. 110). Antonio and Bosola both assume the role of avenger in their own shapes, but such sincerity has little effect on the outcome of the play. Most of the actors' intentions in Act 5—Bosola's plan to save Antonio, Antonio's revenge, the Cardinal's plan to murder both Bosola and Antonio, Julia's seductions—run awry, regardless of Bosola's or Antonio's final rejection of seeming. Feigning or not, Bosola is ultimately added to the list of the play's theatrical victims. Bosola, "an actor in the main of all/ Much 'gainst mine own good nature," is "i'th'end/ Neglected" both in his part and out of it (5.5.85-87). His acting cannot elevate him in the society of the play, nor can his unmasking spare him the consequences of his convoluted feigning. To act and to "act" are finally indistinguishable.

The Duchess of Malfi is radically skeptical of the actor's nature, and comes close to phrasing a purely Puritan vision of the actor's insubstantiality. Bosola's world is a Puritan nightmare, a world of chaotic change, in which the histrionic plague infects all certainty, all consistency. Although Delio attempts finally to right the play's wrongs by setting the Duchess's son "In's mother's right," we have little sense that Delio's actions will mitigate the theatrical vicissitudes of Malfi. The "Integrity of life" that Delio claims in his final couplet is reserved for those "beyond death." Here, in the sublunary world, the actor's metamorphoses preclude such an absolute sense of wholeness. Webster's actors also fail to evince any of the powerful attraction of acting that we see in both Jonson's and Shakespeare's actors. His actors are either villains or dupes, masterful machiavels or dull morons caught in someone else's plot. Finally, his actors are remarkably passive, entirely lacking the exuberance of Hamlet's or Viola's or Mosca's or Volpone's playing. Even Bosola—who exults after his successful play in the "apricocks" scene—comes to dislike his acting, even while he plays the parts of tomb-maker and bellman. Webster's actors recall the humanists' vision of man's limitless potential for change, but Webster empties that vision of all positive possibilities. His theater is "tedious" in this sense, that it images the actor's various changes not as a sign of divine omnipotence, but as a sign of degrading moral weakness. The "Actors and Players, as it were, of what Nature will haue set foorth" are not, for Webster, the lords of creation. They are, more like the Duchess herself, incurably "plagu'd in art."

The Renaissance actor mirrors both his audience's attraction to creative feigning and its anxious regard for the deception of histrionic imitation. The drama represents the actor's double valuation with remarkable consistency. For the most part, role-playing in the plays requires a conscious commitment to acting, and always involves bridging the gap between the real and the fictitious. Peter Quince's players fear the duplicity of feigning, and opt for the safety of a literal interpretation of their art: "I, one Snout by name, present a wall." More sophisticated players are more comfortable in their acting and, like Richard III declaring that he is to "prove a villain," conceive of themselves more overtly as performers. To engage in thoughtless play, as perhaps Falstaff does, is to risk the painful "uncreation" of the self and entrapment in a confining part. The images of Volpone bound, of Malvolio imprisoned, of Viola unable to speak her love to Orsino, of the Duchess's theatrical torture, or of Laertes fatally engaged in the revenger role, all depict a common vision of the actor. We see the performer finally unable, as the Puritans might argue, to enforce the distinction between the "Personator" and the "man Personated," between himself and his mask.

The characters in the plays continually dramatize a concern for the ethics of acting. Shakespeare, for example, frequently rephrases Hamlet's recognition of the galling disparity between seeming and "that within." Viola's acting—"I am not that I play"—tricks her out in usurped masculine attire, but betrays her into wooing her rival for Orsino, instead of wooing Orsino for herself. Acting, as Hamlet learns, can help to express our inner imperatives in action, but false seeming can also misrepresent or falsify them, make them seem "acted up" like the player's Pyrrhus role. To discover the fluid boundary between the authentic and the artificial aspects of the roles we play can be devastating. Lear must be unseated from both his throne and his reason before he can see that his regal authority is not coextensive with his personal identity—"They told me I was everything; 'tis a lie, I am not ague-proof." Richard II is left finally with two contradictory roles—king and beggar—which cannot be hammered out into "one person."

Shakespeare's vision of actors and acting is, to a large extent, part of his wider consideration of dramatic art and of the theater in which it is realized. As Alvin B. Kernan remarks, Shakespeare's drama reveals a keen sense of both the limitations and the potential of art: "In the end the theater seems to have been paradoxical for him: at one and the same time, only a transitory illusion and an image of transcendent reality, a trick and a vision, mere entertainment and a means of directing life to meaningful ends."[55] Shakespeare's actors dramatize the complicated ambivalence that their author and their audience felt toward the roguish professional actors, and toward the art of acting generally. Most are, like Nathaniel in *Love's Labour's Lost*, "a little o'erparted." Even consummate actors like Hal or Hamlet, Rosalind or Viola, often slip up: Hamlet, playing the "hypocrite" in Gertrude's chamber, kills the wrong man; Hal seizes the crown too soon, steps too early into his royal part. No actor is entirely competent, able to create a part that is thoroughly, or enduringly, convincing. But although acting is a demanding art, it seems to come naturally to a range of characters, good and bad, heroes and villains. If, as I suggested at the outset of this chapter, the acting motif is nearly a convention of Renaissance dramaturgy, it also seems to be part of our native inheritance, at least as the drama envisions it, to feign.

The role of the actor in the drama emblematizes the playwrights' total response to a guiding conception of the actor's art. The actor is at once Macbeth's ephemeral player, strutting and fretting his brief hour, and Prospero's incandescent Ariel, bodying forth the poet's feigned creation in well-spirited action. In the language and action of the plays, the actor is figured as man in his Protean aspect, radically undetermined, risking damnation through histrionic creation. Yet the leap from self-expression to self-multiplication, from doing to acting, exacts both a moral and a psychological toll. The likeness of acting and madness in *Hamlet* and *Twelfth Night* (and in *The Spanish Tragedy, King Lear, The Changeling*, and so on) suggests that the dramatists, like their Puritan critics, were alert to the irrational impulse behind all art, the impulse that turns the artist's attention from the material world to the potentially solipsistic grip of his fertile mind. Many actors seem almost specifically to embody a Puritan critique of acting. Perhaps because he is a precisian, Malvolio is a careless actor—his performance is banal, indulgent. Volpone's acting is lustful and gratuitous and, like Bosola's, plants the seed of a crippling moral illness that spreads to consume the commonwealth. Yet acting has many of the creative, even instructive, virtues that its defenders claim for it. Hamlet learns how to act by imitating the player, as does Hal. Viola experiments with her masculine role, and learns the difficulties of being faithful to herself long before she engages to be faithful to Orsino. To the extent that the Duchess of Malfi models her death scene on the pattern of stoic tragedy—her "reverend monument" may suggest as much—acting may even provide a kind of consolation. Both divine and demonic, creative and destructive, actual and illusory, these roles give a shape to the contrary ethical values that Renaissance culture attributes to the actor. The actor's performance seems, finally, to dramatize a profound concern. The actor's creative, deceptive feigning enacts the vital relation between God's transcendent, immutable order and our own fallen and contingent powers to create. Faced with the professional actor, the Renaissance theater audience, like the playwrights and the actors themselves, must have asked with all of Hamlet's fascination, "Is it not monstrous?"

[2] *Realize the feelings of his Character:* Gesture, Feeling, and Community in the Sentimental Theater

> Garrick will put his head between two folding-doors, and in the course of five or six seconds his expression will change successively from wild delight to temperate pleasure, from this to tranquillity, from tranquillity to surprise, from surprise to blank astonishment, from that to sorrow, from sorrow to the air of one overwhelmed, from that to fright, from fright to horror, from horror to despair, and thence he will go up again to the point from which he started. Can his soul have experienced all these feelings, and played this kind of scale in concert with his face? I don't believe it; nor do you.
>
> —Denis Diderot, *Le Paradoxe sur le comédien* (1778)

> —but I pronounce that the greatest strokes of Genius, have been unknown to the Actor himself, 'till Circumstances, and the warmth of the Scene has sprung the Mine as it were, as much to his own Surprize, as that of the Audience—Thus I make a great difference between a great Genius, and a good Actor. The first will always realize the feelings of his Character, and be transported beyond himself, while the other, with great powers, and good sense, will give great pleasure to an Audience, but never—pectus inanitor angit/ Irritat Malís & falcis, terroribus implet/ Ut Magus.
>
> —David Garrick, letter to Helfrich Peter Sturz, 3 Jan. 1769[1]

The personal stamp of David Garrick's acting fascinated the eighteenth-century audience, and Garrick's image dominated the public imagination both in and out of the theater. Garrick was continually cast before the eyes of his admiring public, as an actor, as a popular portrait subject, as the object of stage and literary parody, and as an important figure in fiction, biography, memoir, and correspondence. Predictably, Garrick played an exemplary role in acting and elocution manuals, and his stage performance provided an eloquent paradigm in more general studies of taste and beauty. Of course, Garrick himself was no mean publicist, and devoted his exceptional talents—as actor, manager, bibliophile, philanthropist, and socialite—to establishing the artistic and social credibility of professional actors. But it was the entrancing appeal of the Garrick *persona* that captivated the imaginative center of London life in the middle decades of the eighteenth century, the magnetic figure of the actor as model and metaphor.[2]

Part of Garrick's popularity arose from the unusual resonance his acting held for his audience. In the theater, he typically balanced a deft use of pictorial acting conventions with the appearance of immediate inspiration, and embodied contemporary concern for the place of the actor's feelings in performance. Garrick's acting was deeply implicated in its theatrical ecology. In striking a suggestive equipoise between formal convention and individual expression, Garrick epitomized a critical problem familiar to neoclassical audiences. His acting depicted a dialectic between passion and its formal expression that entirely suffused the sentimental theater, animating its acting, its drama, and its audience.

The ethical scope of Garrick's acting dilates significantly when we recall the special performance context of the eighteenth-century house. The actor at mid-century performed a repertory of new plays and old favorites in a small, well-lighted theater, to a public of habitual theatergoers. It was an actor's theater, attended by an experienced and discriminating public. The influence of tradition in this theater can hardly be overstated, and its effects on acting were profound. As Bernard Beckerman suggests, "in a highly traditional and articulate theater . . . audiences tend to be more cognizant of the performing features or surface," and the eighteenth-century audience paid close attention to the formal structure of the actor's performance.[3] The practice of "pointing"—detaching a famous speech from the action of the play and delivering it directly to the audience, repeating it if necessary—is just one instance of the extent of the audience's interest in this performing "surface." As a device emphasizing technique rather than meaning, pointing naturally provided the opportunity to compare the talents of various actors in the same part. More important, pointing tended to fix the dramatic role in the performance tradition. Woe to the actor who, under the misguided influence of an original conception of his character, scanted the public's keen anticipation of Hamlet's or Jaffier's or Sir John Brute's familiar points. And pointing was only one part of an integrated system of histrionic conventions—including gesture, facial expression, vocal tone—that controlled the meaningful passions of the dramatic role. While these conventions stressed the formal surface of the actor's performance, they also gave occasion for immediate emotional expression as well. The point forced the actor to present a specific passion to his audience, and many theorists of acting argued that the actor's expression could move the audience only if his own feeling sustained the character's passion. Finally, the formal point also prompted the spectators' active response to the play. The sentimental audience reacted decisively to the actor's conventional representation of feeling; the actor's pointed aria was directly answered by the audience's passionate reply, by tears or laughter, applause or abuse. The formal point voiced and structured a moment of intense emotion, coordinating the passions of actor, character, and spectator.

Garrick and Diderot raise a question that is essential to drama and theater, and one particularly appropriate to the dynamics of neoclassical acting. Beginning with Aaron Hill's articles in *The Prompter* in the 1730s, acting theory and stage criticism increasingly conceive of the actor from a sentimental perspective, probing the obscure relation between the player's sensibility and the necessary conventions of theatrical expression. Unfortunately, the expressive process proved exceedingly difficult to describe, and many eighteenth-century and modern critics have been eddied in the baffling currents of "Punch's feelings."[4] Hopelessly oversystematic in their dissection of the actor's sensibility, acting theorists in the period eagerly exploit the associationist model of the psyche, with its well-marked—and highly artificial—gradations of thought and feeling. In their investigation of the actor's formal representation, they are again seduced, this time by the pseudoscientific allure of a "universal" convention of physical expression, the "language of gesture."[5] As a representational medium, the language of gesture never really attains the coherent integration of symbols typical of a fully articulated system of signs. Yet the acting theorists' compelling invocation of a semiotics of gesture alerts us to the unacknowledged convictions that guide their misleading pursuit of the actor's feelings. By examining the content of the actor's gestures, how those gestures express a particular state of mind, and the nature of the audience's response, the theorists of the stage construct a consistent theory of theatrical communication. By harmonizing feeling and form, acting theory transcends the restricted problem of the actor's emotional engagement, and offers a distinctly neoclassical vision of the ethics of acting. In the widest sense, neoclassical acting theory defines the actor by defining how his acting creates and communicates meaning.

The sentimental theater's unashamedly affective mission—that "Those who would make us feel, must feel themselves"—frames the problem of the actor's feelings.[6] The indiscriminate character of much stage theory and criticism in the period reflects a radical transformation taking place in the theater itself, a redefinition of the theater's social function, and a changing perception of the affective dynamics of theatrical performance. In 1698, Jeremy Collier could launch a persuasive attack on the stage by anatomizing its failure to uphold its properly didactic social mission. "The business of *Plays*," he contends,

> is to recomend Virtue, and to discountenance Vice; To shew the Uncertainty of Humane Greatness, the suddain Turns of

Fate, and the Unhappy Conclusions of Violence and Injustice: 'Tis to expose the Singularities of Pride and Fancy, to make Folly and Falsehood contemptible, and to bring every Thing that is Ill Under Infamy, and Neglect.

To Collier, the theater's function is both instructive and repressive. Since dramatic performance aims to reform the audience's moral nature by appealing to its reason, Collier conceives of theatrical communication as occurring solely along a rational axis. He deeply suspects the stage's tendency to stimulate the audience's emotions, and censures the theater for arousing "those Passions which can neither be discharged without Trouble, nor satisfyed without a Crime: 'Tis not safe for a Man to trust his Virtue too far, for fear it should give him the slip."[7]

By Garrick's prime, though, the stage's address to its audience is perceived very differently. The theater's social justification is still a broadly didactic one, but the stage is understood to operate immediately on the spectator's emotional sensibility rather than on his rational moral sense:

> the elevated passions and incidents with which we are treated by [tragedy] may warm, melt, and astonish our feelings; while [comedy], playing with fancy in its natural, or some other familiar sphere, exhilarates our spirits, puts judgment in good humour, and pleasantly prepares us to receive some occasional necessary lashes of correction, applied to our vices or follies.[8]

Like Collier, Francis Gentleman distinguishes here between the instructive ends of tragedy and comedy, but whereas Collier's theater would throttle the passions, Gentleman's theater expresses them. The mid-century theater teaches by urging the spectator to exert a sensible taste, rather than intellectual judgment. The theater stimulates what J. G. Cooper calls a "good *Taste*" that "thrills throw our whole Frame, and seizes upon the Applause of the Heart, before the intellectual Power, Reason, can descend

from the Throne of the Mind to ratify it's Approbation."⁹ Collier's
stage chastens the impulsive Hobbesian spectator with static icons
of virtue rewarded and vice punished. The sentimental theater
serves a more benevolent public, and is fittingly redesigned

> To purge the passions, and reform the mind,
> To give to nature all the force of art,
> And while it charms the ear to mend the heart.¹⁰

In this theater, the actor aggressively arouses the passions of men
and women of feeling.

Mid-century acting theory responds to this changing sense of
theater by examining how the actor can most surely control the
heart-strings of his public. It places an affective actor on the
sentimental stage. In his series of articles in *The Prompter*, in
letters to actors, and especially in his verse treatise "The Art of
Acting" (1746) and in *An Essay on the Art of Acting* (1753), Aaron
Hill attempts a sweeping overview of the actor's affective means.
He definitively describes the affective performance situation, and
locates the actor's psychological process and expressive technique
at the center of a theory of stage communication:

> The time *shall come*—(nor far the destin'd day!)
> When soul-touch'd *actors* shall do more, than *play*:
> When passion, flaming, from th'asserted stage,
> Shall, to taught greatness, fire a feeling age:
> Tides of strong sentiment sublimely roll,
> Deep'ning the dry disgraces of the soul:
> *Pity, fear, sorrow*, wash'd from folly's foam
> Knock at man's breast, and find his heart at home.¹¹

On Hill's stage, the actor's representation, like the poet's, is
neither personal nor idiosyncratic. He arouses the audience's feelings and communicates theatrical meaning through a just representation of general human nature. The actor masters the ten
dramatic passions—joy, grief, fear, anger, pity, scorn, hatred,

jealousy, wonder, and love—that are uniquely suited to the presentational mode of the theater. These alone "can be distinguished by their outward marks, in action."[12]

The actor conveys these passions through a suitably conventional, and again highly generalized form of expression, the language of gesture. The notion that gestures, like words, have a specific and limited sign value has an extensive history in rhetorical practice—as well as in dance, the philosophy of language, and the education of the deaf and dumb—and Hill's application of this tradition to the stage is hardly startling.[13] Where Hill innovates acting theory is through his remarkable synthesis of the entire performance transaction. In his *Essay*, he draws a paradigm of the actor's emotional process from contemporary faculty psychology, in order to coordinate the actor's feeling with its gestural expression:

> 1st, The imagination must conceive a *strong idea* of the passion.
> 2dly, But that idea cannot *strongly* be conceived, without impressing its own form upon the muscles of the *face*.
> 3dly, Nor *can* the look be muscularly stamp'd, without communicating, instantly, the same impression, to the muscles of the *body*.
> 4thly, The muscles of the body, (brac'd, or slack, as the idea was an active or a passive one) must, in their natural, and not to be avoided consequence, by impelling or retarding the flow of the animal spirits, transmit their own conceiv'd sensation, to the sound of the *voice*, and to the disposition of the *gesture*. (p. 356)

The actor's stage gesture is not, strictly speaking, conventional at all. His formal expression follows ineluctably from his active conception of one of the inherently dramatic passions. Since it unites the actor's "idea" of passion with its means of expression, Hill's model of the actor's process is precisely attuned to the affective theater. And because passion and its pictorial expression are so closely allied, the young actor requires only the dressing-room mirror for his histrionic preceptor, "for *there*, only, will he meet with a sincere and undeceivable test of his having strongly enough, or too slackly, adapted his fancy to the purpose before him" (pp. 359-60). As Hill suggested to Garrick, the mirror is "a stiff *constraint*, upon both *mien*, and *memory*" and will not help the actor to discover a passion.[14] But since conception gives rise to expression in the actor's train of feeling, the mirror reveals the sincerity of his commitment of passion by reflecting to him his representation of it. By "annexing, at once, the *look* to the *idea*" (p. 362), the mirror encourages the actor to respond to the affective value of his own expression, to reinforce the coordination between the feeling and its consequent gesture.

Aaron Hill's synthesis of feeling and expression defines the neoclassical actor's ways and means. He lays the foundation for John Hill's more speculative study of the actor's passion, *The Actor* (1750; extensively revised, 1755). A translation and enlargement of Pierre Rémond de Sainte-Albine's *Le Comédien* (1747), *The Actor* pursues the ramifications of Aaron Hill's model by exploring the relationship between the gestural sign and its referent passion. In John Hill's view, the actor's commitment of feeling alone permits his dramatic signals to exert their full impact on the spectator. Unless the actor perceptibly engages his personal feelings in performance, he seems to stand apart from his role, and his signs of passion lose their ability to move the audience's feelings. The unfeeling actor is truly a hypocrite, and is treated as such by the discriminating spectator: "a feigned sensibility where the actor feels nothing . . . never fails to be treated, by those who are capable of discerning the fraud, with the greatest contempt."[15] But when the role is sustained by actual feeling, "we no longer perceive in him the cold player, who by his studied tones and forc'd gestures, is labouring to interest our hearts in imaginary adventures; he is to us the person he represents" (1750; p. 107). By grounding his gestural signs in actual feeling, the actor commands "the different steps thro' which his author means to lead the passions and the imaginations of his audience" (1750; p. 6). And as Fielding reminds us in *Tom Jones*, the actor's principal task is to lead his audience through these subtle gradations of feeling, much as Garrick orchestrates the passions of a feelingly stunned Partridge: "And during the whole speech of the ghost, he sat with his eyes fixed partly on the ghost and partly on Hamlet, and with his mouth open; the same passions which succeeded each other in Hamlet succeeding likewise in him."[16]

Furthermore, John Hill suggestively places the language of gesture within the larger arsenal of human signs, by comparing gestural language with verbal language. Expressive "signs which we use to express these several intentions of the soul"—facial expression, gesture, vocal tone—are not "merely arbitrary" signs in the way that words are. Instead, "they are dictated by nature's self, and are common to all mankind. The language of signs we all speak without having been taught it . . . and all that the player needs, or indeed is able to do, is only to avoid improprieties in it, and to be careful to use it only in such parts as nature shews it to be necessary and useful in" (1750; pp. 167-68). The actor's gesture has universal currency, not because it is shared by a common culture, but because it is the natural, unique manifestation of a universal psychological state. Since John Hill emphasizes the actor's feeling more exclusively than Aaron Hill does, there is no need for his actor to test his expression in the mirror. Studying his part, the actor should give priority to his own feeling, rather than to the propriety of his gestures. If the actor can "give himself up without restraint to the emotions he feels on this occasion. . . . The action and the expression will arise from the occasion, unstudied, unpremeditated, and as it were natural to him; and being natural as well as great, it will affect every body." To represent sincere feeling through conventional gesture, "this is the character of true sensibility" (1755; p. 97).

The acting theorists' concern for the language of gesture is neither eccentric nor overspecialized. The values and methods that guide their investigation of the actor also inform a wider reconsideration of the relationship between feeling and action in all social activity. The language of gesture is particularly instrumental to what might be called the sentimental theory of society, the theory of social benevolence.[17] As a means of externalizing the inborn social passions, the natural language of gesture frequently attracts the attention of benevolist social philosophers, and provides a critical link between performance on the stage and in society. In his *Elements of Criticism* (1762), for instance, Lord Kames carefully relates the function of the "external signs of emotions and passions" to both theatrical and social stages.[18] Like the acting theorists, Kames's orientation is at once empirical and sentimental. He attempts to derive a scientific theory of art from the associative process of perception, but the justification of his study is an explicitly affective one. By developing a theory of taste based on psychological principles, Kames hopes "no less to invigorate the social affections, than to moderate those that are selfish" (p. xiii). The stage provides Kames with a host of examples of art's ability to produce a feeling response, but he unites the structure of perception to the sympathetic basis of social communication most conclusively in his discussion of the language of gesture.

In chapter 15 of the *Elements*, Kames reiterates John Hill's distinction between the arbitrary and the natural signs of passion. With the exception of "a few simple sounds expressive of certain internal emotions," sighs and grunts and the like, words are arbitrary signs, bearing no essential relation to their referent passions. Gestures, arising directly from the passions, are natural signs since "every vivid passion hath an external expression peculiar to itself." The language of gesture provides the necessary means for realizing the native social inclinations of the man of feeling:

> The natural signs of emotion . . . being nearly the same in all
> men, form a universal language, which no distance of place,
> no difference of tribe, no diversity of tongue, can darken or
> render doubtful: even education, though of mighty influence,
> hath not the power to vary nor sophisticate, far less to destroy,
> their signification.   (p. 195)

Gesture is a part of all social involvement, because it expresses
an individual's motive passions in visible and unequivocal action.
This inborn and universal language naturalizes social formalities
(including the gestural conventions of the stage), and implies
that the conventions of social behavior are themselves the natural
outcome of inherent social instincts:

> if these signs were, like words, arbitrary and variable, the
> thoughts and volitions of strangers would be entirely hid from
> us; which would prove a great, or rather invincible, obstruction
> to the formation of societies: but, as matters are ordered, the
> external appearances of joy, grief, anger, fear, shame, and of
> the other passions, forming an universal language, open a direct
> avenue to the heart. As the arbitrary signs vary in every coun-
> try, there could be no communication of thoughts among
> different nations, were it not for the natural signs in which all
> agree: and as the discovering passions instantly at their birth
> is essential to our well-being, and often necessary for self-
> preservation, the author of our nature, attentive to our wants,
> hath provided a passage to the heart which never can be ob-
> structed while eyesight remains.   (pp. 195-96)

The language of gesture pervades Kames's phrasing of benevolist social theory. Kames's society is sustained by the innate
passions and sympathies of its members. For these feelings to
have their proper effect, though, they must be performable, dramatic. Kames's social man is an actor who, like Aaron Hill's
stage player, performs those passions—joy, grief, anger, and so

on—that "can be distinguished by their outward marks, in action." As they do in the theater, the enacted signs of passion invariably affect the social audience. They cannot be "beheld with indifference; they are productive of various emotions, tending all of them to ends wise and good" (p. 197). Gesture actively involves actor and spectator with each other, and subtly implicates them in their encompassing social milieu. In any gathering, as in the theater, "these external signs . . . diffuse through a whole assembly the feeling of each individual" and "contribute above all other means to improve the social affections." The unified gesture, where the "countenance, the tones, the gestures, the actions, join with the words in communicating emotions" has a "force irresistible":

> thus all the pleasant emotions of the human heart, with all the social and virtuous affections, are, by means of these external signs, not only perceived but felt. . . . one joyful countenance spreads cheerfulness instantaneously through a multitude of spectators.   (pp. 199-200)

The theater is a lively microcosm of this benevolent society, and the physical expression of both actors and audience serves a similarly amiable purpose. Of course, the entire theatrical experience in the sentimental theater reinforced the spectator's sense of social participation. On the architectural scale, the division of the theater into box, pit, and gallery audiences objectified the class distinctions that structured society at large, and the theater intensified the dynamics of performance that guided social interaction in the world beyond the stage. In the illuminated theater, each social group was conscious of the conventional role it performed before the rest of the public. Like many spectators, Goldsmith's Chinese visitor found the aristocratic patrons of the theater particularly noteworthy in this regard: "I could not avoid considering them as acting parts in dumb shew, not a curtesy, or nod, that was not the result of art."[19] Stage seating and side boxes also encouraged the drama's patrons to indulge themselves in the pleasures of performance, and if the Fine Gentleman of Garrick's *Lethe* (1740) is any measure, they played their parts with considerable verve:

> I dress in the evening and go generally behind the scenes of both playhouses; not, you may imagine, to be diverted with the play but to intrigue and show myself. I stand upon the stage, talk loud and stare about, which confounds the actors and disturbs the audience. Upon which the galleries, who hate the appearance of one of us, begin to hiss and cry "Off, off!" while I undaunted stamp my foot so, loll with my shoulder thus, take snuff with my right hand and smile scornfully, thus.[20]

The audience responded to its own performance much as it did to the performance on the stage, as the Earl of Egmont reports: "The Prince and Princess of Wales, the Duke, the Princesses were all at the Play. When the Prince came into the box he made a bow to the Duke and Princesses; the Duke returned it, but the Princesses did not, upon which the house hissed them."[21] The actor's performance of a highly structured role through the conventions of gestural expression reflects the social enactment of his theatrical audience, self-consciously performing itself for the greater amusement of the house.

We should not be blind to the special excitement of the sentimental theater. At its best, the formalized performances of both actors and audience were neither dull nor derivative. On the contrary, in the affective theater, the audience's reaction to performance was swift and vigorous. As Charles Beecher Hogan reminds us, despite the highly-structured quality of the performance, the spectators' feelings were expressed with striking immediacy: "They burst freely into tears; the ledges of the boxes were frequently white with the handkerchiefs that were in constant employ. Following a death scene both men and women wept; the women screamed, and sometimes fainted."[22] Unlike the modern spectator's deferred applause, the eighteenth-century spectator's sudden, public reaction to the events on the stage confirmed both his engagement with the dramatic action and his active participation in the theatrical community. The brassy theatricality of the spectators' behavior revealed their sympathetic involvement with one another. Rather than defeating the dramatic spectacle, the performance on the near side of the stage seemed to broaden it, to form part of the evening's entertainment. By responding both to the actors' and to its own performance, the audience certified the project of the sentimental theater. The actor's representation stimulated the spectators' response to the play, and to the play of their fellow citizens, producing the kind of harmonious social pleasure that Shaftesbury, among others, thought "superior to any other."[23]

In many respects, the theatricality of social performance frames the meaning of acting in the sociable theater. The audience's conventional performance within the theater was, in one sense, simply an extension of its highly formalized performance in society at large. Codes of behavior were finely detailed in the eighteenth century, and much like the high and low comedian, the gentleman and the commoner could be easily distinguished by their habitual byplay and business. The function of social performance may well have been, in part at least, to discriminate class in just this way. Nor was this sense of the interpenetration of society and theater lost on the public. As Fielding points out in *Tom Jones*, "stage and scene are by common use grown as familiar to us, when we speak of life in general, as when we confine ourselves to dramatic performances: and when transactions behind the curtain are mentioned, St. James's is more likely to occur to our thoughts than Drury Lane" (Bk. 7, ch. 1). By presenting individual passion through conventional means, the actor's performance becomes a radically simplified version of the more various activity that occupies his audience. The player's enactment emblematizes the spectator's involved social performance.

As Richard Sennett has convincingly shown in *The Fall of Public Man*, public conduct in the eighteenth-century city demanded a kind of social role-playing, and the image of man-as-actor underlies many contemporary notions of social involvement.[24] To perform in public, as Lord Chesterfield remarks, a "man of the world must, like the chameleon, be able to take every different hue; which is by no means a criminal or abject, but a necessary complaisance; for it relates only to manners and not to morals."[25] On the social stage, man must, like the actor, maintain a disciplined awareness of the conventions of his performance. But if the actor's use of the natural language of gesture epitomizes the principles of social interaction, his ability to depict the signs of passion disingenuously—to become a kind of sincere hypocrite— profoundly threatens the necessary spontaneity of expression that makes gesture so crucial to the benevolent society. Chesterfield's understanding of social performance was far from universal; Johnson remarked of his *Letters*, "they teach the morals of a whore, and the manners of a dancing master" (*Life of Johnson*, p. 188). Although Johnson's ambivalence toward stage acting can be partly attributed to his competitive relationship with Garrick, his anxious regard for the actor's passion suggests a more pervasive skepticism toward acting as a metaphor for social performance.[26] Johnson, unfortunately, never codified this concern in a treatise on acting, but his attitude is fully voiced by two articulate contemporaries, Rousseau and Diderot.

Conceived as a rebuttal to d'Alembert's article on Geneva in the *Encyclopédie*, which urged that a theater be founded in that city, Rousseau's *Letter to M. d'Alembert on the Theater* (1758) contends that the theater can provide only a debasing and inhuman model of urban society. Rousseau's scorn for acting and actors stems from his understanding of impersonation, which he regards as a dangerous form of self-abnegation:

What is the talent of the actor? It is the art of counterfeiting himself, of putting on another character than his own, of appearing different than he is. . . . What, then, is the spirit that the actor receives from his estate? A mixture of abjectness, duplicity, ridiculous conceit, and disgraceful abasement which renders him fit for all sorts of roles except for the most noble of all, that of man, which he abandons.[27]

As this passage suggests, Rousseau revives many familiar arguments against actors, and anticipates a typically Romantic bias against the actor's violation of his own integrity through his performance of a dramatic role. But the *Letter* focuses less on the morality of acting than on the troubling interrelation between histrionic and social performance. Like Chesterfield, Rousseau understands social life to demand role-playing, but to Rousseau this kind of acting is far from a "necessary complaisance" relating "only to manners and not to morals." Rousseau takes the histrionic aspect of social performance to be symptomatic of an underlying social malaise, what Lionel Trilling has called "the attenuation of selfhood that results from impersonation."[28] In contrast to the straightforward simplicity of social contact in provincial Geneva, the complex conventionality of Parisian social performance seems to Rousseau to erode individual authenticity, to undermine the ability to recognize the self and put its imperatives directly into action. The actor's performance typifies the kind of behavior demanded by metropolitan life, for Paris is a city of epidemic artificiality. Instead of imaging the process of benevolent, natural social exchange, Rousseau's actor and the theater in which he performs become metaphors for an opposing vision of social performance, one expressing the decadence of a society in which all relationships are empty, unreal, theatrical.[29]

Although Rousseau recalls many traditional antitheatrical arguments, when discussing the theater's social function he specifically addresses the model of the affective stage. Rousseau goes to great lengths to show that neither the theater nor the theatricalized society is truly sociable. In so doing, Rousseau directly confronts the affective theater's claim to social utility, that it stimulates the active social passions of the public. "People think they come together in the theatre," he writes, "and it is there that they are isolated. It is there that they go to forget their friends, neighbors, and relations in order to concern themselves with fables, in order to cry for the misfortunes of the dead, or to laugh at the expense of the living" (pp. 16-17). Since the actor's performance is only play, Rousseau determines that the audience's emotional reaction, however deeply felt, must be similarly illusory. The theater's preoccupation with feigning renders it incapable of arousing a truly social passion in its audience; more typically, it lulls the public into a dangerous complacency, a false sense of social participation. After the performance, when the spectator has wept "for imaginary miseries," Rousseau asks, "what more can be asked of him?"

> Is he not satisfied with himself? Does he not applaud his fine soul? Has he not acquitted himself of all that he owes to virtue by the homage which he has just rendered it? What more could one want of him? That he practice it himself? He has no role to play; he is no actor. (p. 25)

Rousseau implies that the audience responds only to the fiction that the actor represents, rather than to the process through which he represents it, as the affective theorists argue. As a result, he easily dismisses the spectators' passionate involvement with the play and with each other. Since it offers only unreal and ephemeral entertainment, the theater can arouse only a "fleeting and vain emotion which lasts no longer than the illusion which produced it; a vestige of natural sentiment soon stifled by the passions; a sterile pity which feeds on a few tears and which has never produced the slightest act of humanity" (p. 24). By discounting the audience's response to the actor's performance as artificial and narcissistic, Rousseau invalidates the theater as a social institution. To Rousseau, the theater provides only the fantasy of community.

In this context, Rousseau directs his most violent antipathy toward the idea of self-representation as a necessary social "complaisance." Rousseau rejects the theater because he rejects any society that is mediated by conventions of performance. Rather than seeking to stimulate sentiment through the performance of a formal role, Rousseau's social man is entirely autonomous and self-defining. His sense of selfhood has "the simplicity of true genius":

> all its resources are within itself; indifferent to insult and hardly conscious of praise, if it is aware of itself, it does not assign itself a place and enjoys itself without appraising itself.
>
> (p. 60)

The genuine self is neither self-regarding nor self-dramatizing; it simply is. When Rousseau, somewhat surprisingly, offers an alternative to d'Alembert's theater, he offers a form of entertainment precisely attuned to the anti-representational bias that informs this sense of identity: the festival. "Plant a stake" in the town square, he urges, call the people together and let "the spectators become an entertainment to themselves; make them actors themselves; do it so that each sees and loves himself in the others so that all will be better united." For Rousseau, the festival is a kind of theater that evades the inevitable duplicity of acting. And yet, when the Genevans perform their festivals, an arresting transformation takes place:

> Nevertheless, one must have been there with the Genevans to understand with what ardor they devote themselves to them. They are unrecognizable; they are no longer that steady people which never deviates from its economic rules; they are no longer those slow reasoners who weigh everything, including joking,

in the scale of judgment. The people are lively, gay, and tender; their hearts are then in their eyes as they are always on their lips; they seek to communicate their joy and their pleasures. They invite, importune, and coerce the new arrivals and dispute over them. All the societies constitute but one, all become common to all. (pp. 126-27)

In its apparently formless and democratic entertainment, Rousseau's festival could not be more removed from an English theater like Drury Lane. But in the experience that it is designed to produce, the festival actually restates the social mission of the sentimental theater. Rousseau's festival realizes the implicit bonds that unite his sympathetic society by allowing the public to perform itself, to become actors dramatizing their own social harmony. Although their performance is less artful than that of some of Garrick's patrons, the festive Genevans recall the behavior of the London theatrical audience. They actively perform themselves to one another, and through their performances they come to a stronger feeling of social unity. Indeed, their festival play realizes the Genevans' inner nature much more directly than their daily life does. The citizens are free from their everyday sobriety, and seek to "communicate their joys and pleasures" through Dionysiac release. Much like the London theater audience, Rousseau's pastoral society celebrates itself through a formal performance situation, one that integrates social and theatrical enactment. Rousseau clearly rejects the emblematic role that the actor and theater play in stimulating social sympathy, but the social mission of his festival largely confirms the social orientation of the sentimental stage.

In the *Letter to M. d'Alembert*, Rousseau offers a paradoxical program of theatrical reform, urging that the festival theater should articulate sociability while avoiding the means of the theater, particularly acting. Diderot's classic *The Paradox of the Actor* (1778), considers the claims of English affective theory more pragmatically. Planned as a reply to Antonio Fabio Sticotti's *Garrick ou les acteurs Anglais* (1769)—itself a translation of the 1755 edition of John Hill's *The Actor*—Diderot's *Paradox* reexamines the role of the actor's feeling in theatrical communication. Despite his blunt dismissal of the arabesques of English theory, Diderot shares many of his opponents' attitudes regarding the purpose of acting. First, Diderot is similarly concerned with the function of gesture in the theater. Like the English theorists, he argues that words alone are not capable of realizing complex dramatic meaning; words are only "symbols, indicating a thought, a feeling, or an idea; symbols which need action, gesture, intonation, expression, and a whole context of circumstance, to give them their full significance" (p. 5). The idea of gestural communication intrigues Diderot, and he frequently—in the *Dialogue on Le Fils Naturel* (1757), and in *Rameau's Nephew* (1773), for instance—returns to it. In his *Letter on the Deaf and Dumb* (1751), he even describes an experiment he undertook to test the affective value of stage gesture. When attending a familiar play, Diderot sometimes blocked his ears; watching the soundless spectacle, he nonetheless "shed tears at the pathetic passages, though I had my fingers in my ears."[30] Not surprisingly, then, the purpose of acting in the *Paradox* is similarly affective: the actor's talent "depends not, as you think, upon feeling, but upon rendering so exactly the outward signs of feeling, that you fall into the trap" (p. 16).

By distinguishing between the actor's feeling and his gestures, Diderot clearly departs from the English model. Instead of seeing the actor's immediate feeling as a perceptible referent for his gestural signs—the referent that gives his gestures meaning for an audience—Diderot argues that the actor's feelings are irrelevant to the passion that the gestures convey. Although the actor communicates passion through gesture, Diderot contends that he must learn the absolute value of an emotion by refining his representation of it, but not by feeling it during performance. The disengaged actor transforms the flux of his role's passion into a fixed, repeatable, theatrical sign:

> the actor who plays from thought, from study of human nature, from constant imitation of some ideal type, from imagination, from memory, will be one and the same at all performances, will be always at his best mark; he has considered, combined, learnt and arranged the whole thing in his head; his diction is neither monotonous nor dissonant. His passion has a definite course—it has bursts, and it has reactions; it has a beginning, a middle, and an end. The accents are the same, the positions are the same, the movements are the same; if there is any difference between two performances, the latter is generally the better. He will be invariable; a looking-glass, as it were, ready to reflect realities, and to reflect them ever with the same precision, the same strength, and the same truth.   (p. 9)

The actor presents his ideal role to the audience through a conscious manipulation of the theatrical languages of speech and gesture. Diderot's actor may still feel his character's feeling (perhaps when he is preparing his part), but this emotional identification is irrelevant to how well his acting will move his audience's passions.

This notion of acting is sustained in part by Diderot's understanding of the dramatic role. As he suggests here, he conceives the role as an Aristotelian organism, a whole whose parts must be brought into a consistent balance:

> On the stage, with what we call sensibility, soul, passion, one may give one or two tirades well and miss the rest. To take in the whole extent of a great part, to arrange its light and shade, its forts and feebles; to maintain an equal merit in the quiet and in the violent passages; to have variety both in harmonious detail and in the broad effect; to establish a system of declamation which shall succeed in carrying off every freak

of the poet's—this is matter for a cool head, a profound judgment, an exquisite taste,—a matter for hard work, for long
experience, for an uncommon tenacity of memory.

(pp. 95-96)

Diderot should not be considered as a Stanislavskian precursor
here; he stresses the unity of presentation that the actor ought
to pursue, not the psychological coherence of a naturalistic character. The actor's passionate points are subordinate to an overall
consistency of character, of style, and of theatrical effect. The
engaged actor may perhaps "intoxicate us" and "transport us with
admiration," but he does so only intermittently. As Diderot
finally asks, "would you rather have a fine moment than a fine
part?" (pp. 100-101). That is, part of Diderot's claim for the
actor's disengagement resides in his understanding of the dramatic
role and its effect on an audience. Although it is still an ideal
type presented through moments of passion, the role demands to
be balanced, to be resolved into a rational order, a demand which
requires the actor's full and disinterested attention.

Moreover, Diderot's vision of the actor closely corresponds to
his vision of social action. As Richard Sennett points out, Diderot's actor emblematizes an ideal of public action in which the
role-like conventions of social behavior forestall rather than facilitate the engagement and exposure of private feeling. His actor
is the model for the great courtier: "who in society makes it his
object, and unluckily has the skill, to please every one, is nothing,
has nothing that belongs to him, nothing to distinguish him, to
delight some and weary others. He is always talking, and always
talking well; he is an adulator by profession, he is a great courtier,
he is a great actor" (p. 61). But there is a price attached to this
vision of hypocritical society, even though Diderot largely ap-
proves of actors and their profession. By dissenting from the
English version of affectivity, he also rejects the player's active
performance of feeling through formal gesture as a metaphor of

social harmony. His disengaged actor implicitly repudiates the benevolist model of social process, in which, as Cahusac suggests in his *Encyclopédie* article on "Geste," gesture is "the universal language from the cradle . . . in all men from their infancy; gesture is and always will be the language of all nations."[31] Diderot's actor does not make his gesture "natural" by grounding it in actual feeling. For Diderot understands acting in real life to be even more artfully histrionic than acting on the stage, if only because in society we must write our own parts while we play them. Much as he contrasts the mimic Rameau and the idle philosophe in *Rameau's Nephew*, in *The Paradox* he argues that in "the great play, the play of the world, the play to which I am constantly recurring, the stage is held by the fiery souls, and the pit is filled with men of genius. The actors are in other words madmen; the spectators, whose business it is to paint their madness, are sages" (p. 14). The actor's art is to observe and reflect the earnest staginess of life, since he cannot possibly act more sincerely, or more theatrically, than we do ourselves. And on this note, Diderot concludes:

> Do not people talk in society of a man being a great actor? They do not mean by that that he feels, but that he excels in simulating, though he feels nothing—a part much more difficult than that of the actor; for the man of the world has to find dialogue besides, and to fulfill two functions, the poet's and the actor's. The poet on the stage may be more clever than the actor of private life, but is it to be believed that an actor on the stage can be deeper, cleverer in feigning joy, sadness, sensibility, admiration, hate, tenderness, than an old courtier? (p. 108)

Obviously not, we agree, and assent to Diderot's ruthless vision of social duplicity. The actor imitates the deceptive process of society, but does not extend it. The actor reflects a society in which all values have become theatrical, rather than using his performance to unify his theatrical audience through the expression of social feeling. In this respect, Diderot's actor, concealed by his theatrical mask, fulfills Rousseau's negative vision of the theater; he images a society enfeebled by the hypocritical performances of its estranged, manipulative citizenry.

Garrick's actor also disappears from view but, like the man of feeling, he vanishes by becoming at one with the expressive requirements of his passionate role. Garrick proves exemplary in Diderot's *Paradox* largely because he has been removed from the stage. Much as audiences in the theater trained their attention on points, private gatherings like the one that Diderot describes often asked Garrick to perform histrionic parlor tricks, points like "the Dagger Scene in Macbeth, ye Curse in Lear, & the falling asleep in Sr John Brute," as Garrick wrote to Colman from Paris (*Letters*, no. 317). We should not scant the attraction that this kind of imitation held for Garrick and his public. According to a well-worn anecdote, Garrick's fascination with his own mimetic abilities once led him to enact Fielding for a Hogarth likeness, much as he posed for portraits of Shakespeare and impersonated Johnson and others for the entertainment of his friends.[32] Recognizing that in the drawing room mimetic verisimilitude must overshadow the broader expression that audiences demanded in the theater, Garrick chose turns with a significant degree of realistic business. He relied primarily on his considerable pictorial skills, rather than on his affective talents.

But in the theater, Garrick was continually concerned with the role of feeling in performance. To many observers, Garrick's acting seemed to hold the actor and the role in a meaningful balance, one that presented both the formal outlines of the part and the animating movement of the actor's individual sensibility. As many scholars have argued, this tension frequently informs Garrick portraiture. In the familiar Hogarth portrait of Garrick as Richard III in the tent scene, Hogarth boldly counterpoints Garrick's alert posture and vivid facial expression with his formal gesture, the extended right hand with its fingers spread in the conventional sign of fear and surprise.[33] By locating Garrick's personal expression in the figure's face, and contrasting it with his formal gesture, Hogarth follows the advice of Charles Le Brun's influential treatise on the passions, which taught painters that "the Face is the Part of the Body where the Passions more particularly discover themselves," the eye and eyebrow being especially expressive of "Agitation of the Soul."[34] Theatrical criticism, too, often distinguishes between the actor's ocular and gestural expression, as a way of describing the contribution that his individual sensibility makes to his representation of a familiar role. Francis Gentleman remarks on Garrick's "natural, picturesque attitude" as "terror-struck" Hamlet in the Ghost scene, and commends the "harmonious gradation" of "speech and feeling" that kindled in the audience "the most pleasing, we had almost said, astonishing sensibility." But Garrick's eyes "anticipate his tongue, and impress the meaning upon us with double force" (vol. 1, p. 55). The affective actor, as Thomas Wilkes suggests, must have not only all the "gifts of Nature; viz. a penetrating wit, a clear understanding, and a good memory; with an articulate voice, ready utterance, a feeling heart, expressive countenance, a genteel figure"; to move the public, he must also possess "a piercing eye, which, at one glance, can convey the inward motions of the soul to the observing beholder."[35]

Garrick clarifies his own sense of the relation between actor and role in the letter to Sturz describing Mme Clairon. As the letter notes, when the actor performs on the stage, his "Genius" should enable him to be "transported beyond himself" into a passionate synchrony with his character's feelings. Although Garrick may seem to be anticipating Stanislavsky here, his actor is not really engaged in the project of the modern stage. The modern actor taps his own subconscious identity in order to vivify himself as an artist. Using emotional recall, the actor realizes himself through the character he plays, and both actor and character achieve a perceptible "life in art." Garrick's actor uses feeling, but not in pursuit of personal authenticity. Instead, his feeling motivates an autonomous dramatic role, gives the role's passion a significant stage reference in the actor's real emotions. The actor's feeling sustains the independent, universal signs that stimulate the audience's emotional response. Rather than presenting himself to the audience through the prism of his role, Garrick's actor uses personal feeling to substantiate the role's passions; he realizes *only* "the feelings of his Character" to the audience.

The problem of the neoclassical actor's feelings is a knotty one, and before turning to three plays from the Garrick era—Home's *Douglas*, Cumberland's *The West Indian*, and Goldsmith's *She Stoops to Conquer*—let me recapitulate briefly. In their preoccupation with feeling and expression, eighteenth-century acting theorists confront a difficulty crucial both to social and to theatrical performance: how to express the amiable passions that harmonize society through the formal codes of social behavior. Acting theory in the period participates in a broader effort to examine the nature of society, and to reconceive the Hobbesian vision of society along benevolent, sentimental lines. The actor's performance becomes a model for social activity outside the theater, and acting theory, by voicing an account of meaning in performance, defines the meaning of acting both on and off the stage. By revealing how the language of gesture communicates in the theater, acting theory provides the actor with a definable ethos, and suggests how the actor's performance epitomizes the process of polite social interaction.

The affective actor's continual study is to adjust his feeling to the expressive requirements of his role. He must be able to sustain his natural gestures with actual feeling. Although his gestures are universally significant, he must make his expression suit his feeling and make his feeling inform his conventional expression, in order to claim the passions of his audience. When feeling and expression are perfectly coordinated, the actor is attuned to the performance requirements of his stage and society, and becomes an emblem of the expressive man who performs his benevolent passions through the natural forms of social intercourse. To affect his audience, the actor must become sincere in this sense, as Kames remarks: "None but those who actually feel a passion, can represent it to the life" (p. 204).

In the miniature society of the theater, the actor's performance is a dynamic representation of social interchange in the world at large. This context places the actor in a singularly difficult position. The eighteenth-century actor lives to please in a very special sense, one defined by the wider implications of social performance. In the theatricalized society, public acting relates social performers to one another. As Sennett suggests, "man in public has an identity as an actor . . . and this identity involves him and others in a social bond" (p. 108). Performance itself has an intrinsic value in this culture, one that frames the more restricted meaning of theatrical performance. By failing to align his individual sensibility with the demands of his role, the actor does more than perform poorly. He collapses as an emblem of social involvement in a theater that expresses and intensifies the reciprocal delights of social performance. Unlike the modern actor, whose "public solitude" allows him to expose private feeling in an apparently spontaneous manner (to a similarly private audience), the eighteenth-century actor must actively perform the feelings of his character, enact them to an audience itself caught up in a public performance. If the actor cannot seem to infuse his gesture with feeling, he fails to affect his audience, and weakens the sympathetic structure of all social relationships. He becomes Diderot's courtier, or Rousseau's Parisian hypocrite, and confirms Rousseau's pessimistic vision of the moral vacuity of the theater and of the theatrical society. He vitiates the affective force of the natural language of gesture, and implies that the conventions that bind the amiable social audience together are fragile and arbitrary. This is the dialectic that defines the actor's performance in the mid-eighteenth century, and, as we shall see, it is the dialectic that resonates in the drama as well.

Douglas

Home's *Douglas* is a remarkable play in many respects, not least as it epitomizes the vicissitudes of the theater. An immediate success both in Edinburgh and in London, and a sturdy theatrical property for a quarter-century, *Douglas*, like much of the tragic drama of the period, today survives in the study if it survives at all. Our theatrical tastes are now so far removed from plays of this kind that we are rather uncertain about their original dramatic interest, and somewhat desperately invoke the rise of a sentimental ethos in the theater and in the culture at large to explain them. But tragedies like *Douglas*, in their straightforward address to the spectator's sympathies, frankly exploit the histrionic conventions of the eighteenth-century theater. No one would argue that *Douglas* is an endlessly stimulating piece of drama. Nevertheless, through its response to the affective actor, *Douglas* could, and did, generate considerable theatrical interest; we can regain a sense of the play's lost vitality by reimagining it on the sentimental stage.

Even in its own day, *Douglas* was not universally admired. Garrick read a manuscript version of the play, and in a letter to Home's patron suggestively anatomized the play's shortcomings:

> The Story is radically defective & most improbable in those Circumstances which produce dramatic Action—for instance— Lady [Randolph] continuing Seven Years togeather in that melancholly miserable State, just as if it had happen'd ye Week before, without discovering ye real Cause; & on a Sudden opening ye Whole Affair to Anna without any stronger reason, than what might have happen'd at any other Time since the Day of her Misfortunes—this I think, wch is ye foundation of y^e

Whole, Weak & unaccountable . . . *Lady* [Randolph's] speaking to *Glenalvon* imediatly in behalf of [Douglas], forgetting her own indelible Sorrows, & Glenalvon's Suspicions & Jealousy upon it (without saying anything of *his* violent Love for ye Lady, who cannot be of a Love-inspiring Age) are premature and unnatural . . . the Story is rather told, than represented . . . the Characters do not talk or behave suitably to ye Passions imputed to them, & the Situation in Which they are plac'd. (*Letters*, no. 166)

Garrick's attentive review of the play's lack of stageworthiness is commanding. As a playwright and an actor, Garrick is sensitive to both the outer and the inner action of *Douglas*, and finds both plotting and characterization to be weak and unpersuasive. Lady Randolph's mourning is fantastically protracted, her passionate revelation of a secret marriage and lost son is undermotivated, and the characters generally act upon each other for reasons that strain belief. Unlike many modern readers, though, Garrick is apparently not bothered by the play's shameless assault on the audience's compassion. He simply finds the structure of this version of *Douglas* to be too insubstantial to support such extensive claims.[36]

Although Garrick thought *Douglas* "incapable of raising the Passions, or comanding Attention," its shopworn formulas evidently made a powerful impression on audiences in the theater. As David Hume recalls in dedicating his *Four Dissertations* (1757) to his countryman,

the unfeigned tears which flowed from every eye, in the numerous representations which were made of it [in] this theatre; the unparalleled command, which you appeared to have over every affection of the human breast: These are incontestible proofs, that you possess the true theatric genius of *Shakespear* and *Otway*, refined from the unhappy barbarism of the one, and licentiousness of the other.[37]

[98]

Hume's allusion to Shakespeare and Otway accurately places *Douglas* in its theatrical milieu, in a repertory that numbered *Romeo and Juliet*, Tate's *King Lear, The Orphan*, and *Venice Preserv'd* (not to mention *Jane Shore, The Distrest Mother*, and *The Fair Penitent*) among its most enduring and popular plays.[38] We can enlarge our sense of the attraction *Douglas* exerted in the theater by attempting to master the variety of ways in which it articulates the attitudes of that theater, particularly regarding the actor's feeling and expression. In brief, *Douglas* responds to the ethos of the neoclassical actor in three ways: through the characters' means of representing their passions, through a contrast between engaged and disengaged acting, and through the affective responses of the onstage audience to highly structured points of feeling.

As Joseph Donohue has suggested, Home's most striking innovation in *Douglas* is his successful presentation of an expressive setting, one that prompts and externalizes the passions of the characters (see pp. 57-69). This reciprocal relation between character and physical environment, reminiscent of similar trends in poetry and painting, is especially prominent in Lady Randolph's opening soliloquy:

> Ye woods and wilds, whose melancholy gloom
> Accords with my soul's sadness, and draws forth
> The voice of sorrow from my bursting heart,
> Farewell a while: I will not leave you long;
> For in your shades I deem some spirit dwells,
> Who from the chiding stream, or groaning oak
> Still hears and answers to Matilda's moan.
> O, Douglas! Douglas! (1, 295)[39]

The play opens in this outdoor setting in order to frame Lady Randolph's passion in an expressive natural scene. But in its vague outlines, this wood sharply contrasts with more notable theatrical forests, the Arden of *As You Like It*, or the heath of *King Lear*. Instead, as Donohue remarks, the speech is a precursor of the

Romantic *paysage intérieur*, sketching a generalized forest of "woods and wilds," "shades," and "chiding stream, or groaning oak," that extends an appropriately general passion, Lady Randolph's "soul sadness" for her lost son Douglas (pp. 59-60). The forest "draws forth/ The voice of sorrow," and places Lady Randolph's operatic expression of grief within a significant setting that organizes, intensifies, and depicts the state of her passion to the audience.

The setting of the scene works in close harmony with the actress's expressive gestures. The actress's conventional attitudes provide a kind of middle term, a bridge from the inner source of feeling to the surrounding world that receives it. The scene continually directs the audience's attention to the variety of expressive instruments at the actress's command. Lord Randolph, for instance, condemns the "black weeds" that

> Express the wonted colour of thy mind,
> For ever dark and dismal. Seven long years
> Are pass'd, since we were join'd by sacred ties:
> Clouds all the while have hung upon thy brow,
> Nor broke, nor parted by one gleam of joy.   (1, 297)

Her clouded brow and dismal attire signify Lady Randolph's despair to her husband and to the audience, her utter loss of "pride, anger, vanity, the strong desire/ Of admiration" (1, 298). Garrick correctly criticized the unreality of both emotion and action in this scene. The scene's interest seems to lie elsewhere, perhaps in the spectator's desire to apply a catalogue of the passions, like the one Lord Randolph mentions, to Lady Randolph's expression. Lady Randolph's emphasis on expression permits the spectator to participate in the play's process, to attempt with the other characters to read and interpret her signs of passion.

Like the actress who plays her, Lady Randolph is conceived primarily as an expressive vehicle, a dominant passion striving to express itself through theatrical means. And as they do for the

actor, so the terms of Diderot's paradox frame for the character
the nature of performance in the play. The willingness to sustain
actions with actual feeling clearly distinguishes the heroes from
the villans in *Douglas*, and particularly opposes evil Glenalvon to
the nobly born Douglas. Glenalvon is typical of the villains of
pathetic tragedy, the scheming heir to Rowe's Lothario and Otway's Polydore. Unlike Lady Randolph, the pathetic center of
the play, Glenalvon acts to conceal his motives rather than express
them. Lady Randolph, the feeling actor, reflects her world; Glenalvon, the disengaged hypocrite, disrupts his.

> Subtle and shrewd, he offers to mankind
> An artificial image of himself:
> And he with ease can vary to the taste
> Of different men its features. Self-denied,
> And master of his appetites he seems:
> But his fierce nature, like a fox chain'd up,
> Watches to seize unseen the wish'd-for prey.
> Never were vice and virtue poised so ill,
> As in Glenalvon's unrelenting mind.   (1, 308)

Despite the fact that he is "brave and politic in war,/ And stands
aloft in these unruly times," the ambiguous relation between his
public deeds and his private motives and passions casts Glenalvon
as a threatening and unstable element in the play. He is, like
Rousseau's actor, naturally at odds with the play's sympathetic
society.

   Furthermore, Glenalvon's dissembling villainy disrupts the
sympathetic structure of communication in the play. Attempting
to persuade Lady Randolph that he will protect her newly returned
Douglas during the forthcoming battle, Glenalvon seems to re-
pent:

> One instant stay, and hear an alter'd man.
> When beauty pleads for virtue, vice abash'd

Flies its own colours, and goes o'er to virtue.
I am your convert; time will shew how truly.   (3, 342)

Glenalvon easily hits "the very tone/ In which she loves to speak,"
but his deception here is more than simple flattery. Glenalvon
phrases his conversion as an emotional and moral response to Lady
Randolph's beauty; her virtuous actions seem to have brought
him to reconsider and reject his illicit appetites and ambitions.
The action of *Douglas* turns on moments of natural sympathy like
the one Glenalvon feigns here—on Lady Randolph's recognition
of her lost son, on the natural affection between a son and mother,
on the broken bond of sympathy between Lady Randolph and
her husband. In this context, Glenalvon's deceit is deeply ironic.
By perverting the effects of sympathetic response, Glenalvon mocks
the fundamental moral and dramatic values of the play.

Douglas appropriately pits Glenalvon against Douglas, the disengaged against the expressive actor. Before he is recognized by
Lady Randolph, everyone assumes that Douglas—or Norval, as
he is called—is the son of a wandering shepherd. Yet while
"Norval" is a "low-born man," his inherent virtues are easily
discerned in his noble actions and attitudes. As Lord Randolph
remarks when the young shepherd rescues him,

> Whoe'er thou art, thy spirit is ennobled
> By the great King of kings! thou art ordain'd
> And stamp'd a hero by the sovereign hand
> Of Nature! blush not, flower of modesty,
> As well as valour, to declare thy birth.   (2, 314)

While Glenalvon is capable of "ironical derisive counsel" (4, 361),
false or equivocal expression is entirely foreign to Douglas. As a
kind of noble savage, "Norval's" native expression, in its radical
form, is the deed, not the word: "But as I am,/ I have no tongue
to rail. The humble Norval/ Is of a race who strive not but with
deeds" (4, 364). Expressive Norval operates at a primitive level

of communication, but one that confirms the natural priority of gesture over arbitrary words. Indeed, as Cahusac remarks of theatrical gesture, "gesture . . . must always precede speech, one feels more than speech can say . . . the gesture that sensibility renders agile always moves at the very moment that the soul feels the passion."

The conflict between expressive Douglas and deceptive Glenalvon is one feature of the play's preoccupation with passionate seeming. For a costume drama of this kind, *Douglas* is notably lacking in visual effects. Although the play takes place on the eve of an invasion, the battle begins only in the play's last moments. The ambush of Lord Randolph is shunted off stage, as is the duel between Douglas and Glenalvon, Lady Randolph's suicide, and Lord Randolph's suicidal rush into battle. Simply plotted, the play subordinates external to internal action, leading and structuring the audience's response through points of emotional expression. The significant scenes of the play tend to coordinate a passionate aria with a reflecting, qualifying response— Lady Randolph's grief is modified by its effects on Lord Randolph, and then on Anna in Act 1; in Act 3, Old Norval's patient narrative is swallowed up by the surge of Lady Randolph's wave of feeling. Lady Randolph's reaction to Norval and her subsequent discovery of his true identity present a model of affective response in the play. When Norval appears to her in Act 2, Lady Randolph's tears are immediately forthcoming, "for various affections,/ And strangely mingled, in my bosom swell;/ Yet each of them may well command a tear" (2, 316). Norval makes a natural claim on Lady Randolph's sympathies, one that is providentially affirmed by Old Norval's story: " 'Twas my child I saw!—No wonder . . . that my bosom burn'd" (3, 334). Lady Randolph's response reveals her feeling to herself, to her stage audience, and to the theatrical spectator; moreover, the expression of feeling implicates her more fully in her dramatic world. Like Old Norval's kindly rescue of the infant Douglas, or Douglas's instant attraction to his mother, the spontaneous expression of a characteristic virtue involves Lady Randolph with her stage society, and in the action of the play. In *Douglas*, passionate expression partly serves to arouse the audience's pity or sympathy, but it serves an important dramatic purpose as well. The characters' affective response connects them to the social world of the play, much as Lady Randolph's opening point relates her to her physical world.

Passion, in *Douglas*, creates a social bond; selfish passion weakens social feeling. Lady Randolph's passions, for example, are not only grotesquely enlarged, they are often destructive in intensity. Home guides our interpretation of Lady Randolph's chief points by providing a reflector, Lord Randolph, who defines the antisocial dimensions of her passion. In the opening of the play, Lady Randolph seems "To feed a passion which consumes" her, a passion that turns her attention from the "duty" that she owes to the living to the selfish, vain ministrations of the "silent dead" (1, 296). Even the restricted claims that Lord Randolph makes on her affections are ignored or deflected by her grief.

> I never asked of thee that ardent love,
> Which in the breasts of fancy's children burns.
> Decent affection and complacent kindness
> Were all I wish'd for; but I wish'd in vain.
> Hence with less regret my eyes behold
> The storm of war that gathers o'er this land:
> If I should perish by the Danish sword,
> Matilda would not shed one tear the more.   (1, 299)

Although Lady Randolph's response to Douglas will momentarily reawaken her social sympathies, at the beginning of the play her remorse has extinguished them. The course of the play fulfills Lord Randolph's prophecy, as Douglas's death drives Lady Randolph into suicide, and her husband into battle. Fittingly, Lady Randolph's final rejection of the claims of society is again reified

[104]

on the stage through the interplay between character and setting, in Anna's description of her death.

> She ran, she flew like lightning up the hill,
> Nor halted till the precipice she gain'd
> Beneath whose low'ring top the river falls,
> Ingulph'd in rifted rocks: thither she came,
> As fearless as the eagle lights upon it,
> And headlong down—
> . . . O had you seen her last despairing look!
> Upon the brink she stood, and cast her eyes
> Down on the deep: then lifting up her head
> And her white hands to heaven, seeming to say,
> Why am I forced to this? she plunged herself
> Into the empty air.   (5, 384)

At the close, Lady Randolph inhabits a Gothic wasteland, one that extends and amplifies her final desolation, and seems to justify her suicide.

It is not surprising that a serious dramatic vehicle like *Douglas* would play so lugubriously on the spectator's heart-strings; to endure in the sentimental theater, perhaps it could do little else. But although *Douglas* no longer seems to rival the emotional intensity of Shakespeare's or even of Otway's plays, it clearly uses a range of strategies to arouse the tragic complex of fear and pity. Of course, Lady Randolph's uniform pathos, Glenalvon's melodramatic villainy, and Douglas's cloying virtue appeal directly to the audience's sympathies. But *Douglas* responds to its stage more variously, both in action and in characterization. *Douglas* clearly contrasts engaged and disengaged characters, and emphasizes the role that expressive action plays in externalizing a virtuous character like Douglas's. Like the actor's performance, the play's dramatic action proceeds through points of emotional expression and response. Characters perform themselves to one another as the actor performs them to the audience. Finally, in its use of expressive setting, *Douglas* extends the actor's universal gesture to the encompassing stage world. Gesture and setting work in tandem to create an expressive sign of passion. In many respects, the impact that a play like *Douglas* could have on an audience must remain conjectural. But by conceiving the play in the affective theater we can understand its imaginative response to the reigning conditions of histrionic performance, and perhaps regain at least a partial sense of the way that it engaged its audience.

The West Indian

Cumberland's *The West Indian* plainly exploits the benevolent public's predisposition to kindness. Yet like many sentimental plays, *The West Indian* blends both "laughing" and "weeping" comic techniques.[40] Through lively action, sure characterization, and a subdued but provocative moral ambivalence, *The West Indian* requires a complex response from the spectator, subtly arousing both scorn and sympathy. Moreover, beyond the sentimental cast of its claims, the action of *The West Indian* dramatizes a conflict between natural and socialized forms of expression. The play repeatedly presents social communication as a problem and, like the actor himself, resolves that problem by discovering the proper balance between feeling and expression. Like the affective actor, the characters in *The West Indian* learn to reconcile the formalities necessary to polite society with the expressive demands of their natural passions.

Cumberland's designs on the spectator's sympathetic response in *The West Indian* govern the play's sense of character. In his *Memoirs* (1806), Cumberland describes the place of character in drama, and how characterization can become an affective instrument in the theater:

As a writer for the stage is a writer to the passions, I hold it matter of conscience and duty in the dramatic poet to reserve his brightest colouring for the best characters, to give no false attractions to vice and immorality, but to endeavor, as far as is consistent with that contrast, which is the very essence of his art, to turn the fairer side of human nature to the public, and, as much as in him lies, to contrive so as to put men in good humour with one another.[41]

Cumberland articulates a notion of dramatic character that reflects his own practice; to address the audience's passions, the comic hero should attract sympathetic praise rather than alienating ridicule. In his plays, Cumberland complicates the "best character"—and introduces a telling dramatic novelty—by making various social outsiders, as well as typical English heroes, the models of virtue. Because Cumberland is concerned both with the effects of benevolent character on the dramatic action and with its capacity to stimulate and improve the theatrical audience, he seizes on the renovation of satiric stage stereotypes to create a broader reformation of social attitudes:

> I perceived that I had fallen upon a time, when great eccentricity of character was pretty nearly gone by, but still I fancied there was an opening for some originality, and an opportunity for shewing at least my good will to mankind, if I introduced the characters of persons, who had been usually exhibited on the stage, as the butts for ridicule and abuse, and endeavoured to present them in such lights, as might tend to reconcile the world to them, and them to the world.   (pp. 203-4)

By redeeming the traditional "butts for ridicule" in the theater— the West Indian and the stage Irishman, in this case—Cumberland hopes to effect a more embracing conversion, one that will ultimately reach beyond the theater. Instead of dividing the theatrical world into a jeering audience and its social victims, Cumberland attempts to invent a sympathetic comedy that will "put men in good humour with one another."[42]

Cumberland's success in this regard is enhanced by his sensitivity to the nuances of familiar stage and literary stereotypes. The "West Indian," like the Eastern nabob, was a well-known character to the eighteenth-century reading and theatergoing public, and Cumberland could easily describe his essential qualities: "a generous spirit, and a vivacious giddy dissipation" (p. 204). But this gloss conceals the explosive contradictions contained in the West Indian's received "character," generally seen as a volatile mixture of natural benevolence and socialized depravity. In the common view, the West Indian inherited his attractive qualities—an impulsive generosity and emotional gusto—from the languid warmth of his native climate, and his more disreputable traits—indolence, sudden cruelty, and sexual profligacy—from the morally debilitating effects of his primitive social environment, particularly from the Caribbean practice of slavery.[43] The traditional West Indian "character" is deeply divided; on a pattern of primitive, natural, and benign virtues, the vices of his society have engrafted a host of perverted and degrading forms of expression.

Although Cumberland moderates the vicious strain of the West Indian in Belcour, his sense of this contradiction in the stock type prompts the central dramatic design of *The West Indian*. Cumberland neatly provides us with a Stanislavskian spine for the play, "to reconcile the world to them, and them to the world," that firmly defines the process of social integration as the leading motive in the play's action. The play is simply plotted on a comic "trial" scheme: once the wayward, prodigal, or exiled character has proven his natural amiability (largely through intention rather than action), he is accepted into the play's society, which itself must be altered in order to accommodate him. But Cumberland develops this paradigm, and develops his altered West Indian in an unusually evocative manner. He emphasizes the disparity between natural and artificial forms of expression, their relation to social harmony, and the means of their reconciliation.

Belcour's foreignness is brilliantly spotlighted in the play's

opening scenes, in which he visits the merchant Stockwell unaware that the merchant is his father. Although Stockwell's confession of paternity to the audience gives Belcour an acceptably
English pedigree, he withholds this revelation from Belcour himself, in order to allow his son to demonstrate his good nature to
the English public. Cumberland quickly sketches in the conflict
between social and natural expressiveness in Belcour's confrontation with English culture. Just as Stockwell completes his introduction, a sailor enters *"ushering in several black Servants,"* bearing Belcour's baggage, and announcing the impending arrival of
"two green monkeys, a pair of grey parrots, a Jamaica sow and
pigs, and a Mangrove dog" (1, 347).[44] In his *Memoirs,* Cumberland recalls that he had inserted this business on Garrick's advice,
the actor having urged him "to give eclat to his entrance, and
rouse the curiosity of the audience; that they may say—Aye, here
he comes with all his colours flying" (p. 216). Garrick knew that
"trumpeters" of this sort would immediately realize the West
Indian's alien manners on the stage. Cumberland, though, instantly moderates the spectator's reaction to Belcour by deftly
balancing the approving comments of the friendly English tar
against the foreigner's exotic retinue. The sailor's warm feelings
toward Belcour mitigate his strangeness, and reassure the audience while they reassure Stockwell: " 'tis no bad prognostic of a
man's heart, when his shipmate gives him a good word." Even
before he arrives onstage, we are prepared to distinguish between
the apparent incivility of Belcour's actions, and the goodness of
his heart, to read his native virtues through his outlandish and
uncouth behavior.

Belcour's appearance in the fifth scene recapitulates and intensifies the disparity between the artifice of social communication
and the requirements of natural expression. Stockwell's expectation of his son—"wild, perhaps, as the manner of his country
is, but, I trust, not frantic or unprincipled" (1, 348)—is confirmed on Belcour's entrance, both in his evident politeness and

in his confusion before the maze of English manners. As Belcour remarks, the unfamiliarity of the London social setting has caused him to behave in an unintentionally inflammatory way:

> accustomed to a land of slaves, and out of patience with the whole tribe of custom-house extortioners, boatmen, tide-waiters, and water-bailiffs, that beset me on all sides, worse than a swarm of mosquitoes, I proceeded a little too roughly to brush them away with my rattan; the sturdy rogues took this in dudgeon, and beginning to rebel, the mob chose different sides, and a furious scuffle ensued.   (1, 349)

Cumberland dramatizes a frequent charge against West Indians, that being "accustomed to a land of slaves," they tended to treat the poor but freeborn English subjects with insulting contempt. The gesture that served well in the Indies offends in London, and isolates the good-natured man from his fellows. Although Belcour's sensitivity to the springs of his own natural passions ("my passions are my masters; they take me where they will") is a sign of his fitness for benevolent society, we recognize that he must be able to adjust the expression of those passions to the decorum of London life. That is, while Belcour is closer to nature than the Londoners, his expressive gestures are not naturally meaningful. He must at once learn to overcome his disruptive gestures, and to harmonize his passions with the social norm of the play. Belcour learns to accommodate his natural benevolence to the forms of expression that animate London society.

The terms of Belcour's trial are reversed in the parallel Rusport-Dudley plot. Stockwell wants to recognize his son, to establish the bonds of family and of feeling that will integrate Belcour into English life. Lady Rusport, on the other hand, undertakes a different kind of trial for her relatives the Dudleys, and judges them according to an inverted standard of values:

> Miss Rusport, I desire to hear no more of Captain Dudley and his destitute family: not a shilling of mine shall ever cross the

hands of any of them: because my sister chose to marry a beggar, am I bound to support him and his posterity? . . . I renounce [Charles Dudley] as my nephew; Sir Oliver renounced him as his grandson; wasn't he son of the eldest daughter, and only male descendant of Sir Oliver; and didn't he cut him off with a shilling? Didn't the poor dear good man leave his whole fortune to me, except a small annuity to my maiden sister, who spoiled her constitution with nursing him? And, depend upon it, not a penny of that fortune shall ever be disposed of otherwise than according to the will of the donor.

(1, 350-52)

Whereas Stockwell makes a trial of Belcour's character in order to acknowledge him, Lady Rusport uses the terms of the will to absolve herself of the claims of kin. In repudiating her family, Lady Rusport ignores the language of sympathy that Stockwell and Charlotte employ, and relies instead on the language of the law. As Charlotte reminds her, the Dudleys are worthy of her interest not only because they are destitute relatives, but also because they are a family of unusual "sensibility" (1, 352). Lady Rusport is plainly insensitive to Charles's good nature; much as our response to Belcour is guided by Stockwell's, our opinion of Charles is phrased not by his aunt, but by Major O'Flaherty:

Upon my conscience, as fine a young fellow as I would wish to clap my eyes on: he might have answered my salute, however—well, let it pass: Fortune, perhaps, frowns upon the poor lad; she's a damned slippery lady, and very apt to jilt us poor fellows that wear cockades in our hats. Fare-thee-well, honey, whoever thou art. (1, 353)

Charles, discouraged, is actually rather rude to the major, but O'Flaherty measures the ensign's actions according to the nature that he reads behind them. Lady Rusport alone denies the duty that she owes to the affable human nature that harmonizes her social world.

[111]

The central action of the play develops the disparity between Belcour's motives and his actions, and makes this discrepancy the primary obstacle to his successful inclusion in society. Particularly where Louisa Dudley is concerned, the West Indian's actions seem mystifying. "I met a young gentleman in the streets," she reports, "who has beset me in the strangest manner."

> I cannot say he was absolutely rude to me, but he was very importunate to speak to me, and once or twice attempted to lift up my hat: he followed me to the corner of the street, and there I gave him the slip.   (2, 357)

Belcour will excuse his importunacy by laying the blame on Nature ("the sun, that was vertical at my birth, and would not wink upon my nakedness, but swaddled me in the broadest, hottest glare of his meridian beams"—3, 370), but Nature is not entirely at fault. Although he is unfamiliar with the proprieties of English wooing, he is mainly hindered by Mrs. Fulmer's deception regarding Louisa's true identity. Mrs. Fulmer plays a delightfully malicious trick on the West Indian:

> have you lived so very little time in this country as not to know that between young people of equal ages, the term of sister is often a cover for that of mistress? This young lady is, in that sense of the word, sister to young Dudley, and consequently daughter to my old lodger.   (3, 372-73)

His natural delicacy forbids him to pursue Louisa after making a substantial gift to her father, but Belcour now finds his honorable scruples apparently removed. No harm in flirting with Captain Dudley's son's mistress, after all. Of course, by treating Louisa as a "sister" and not as a woman of repute, Belcour insolently violates the play's manifest proprieties.

Belcour's natural inclinations are betrayed and distorted through Mrs. Fulmer's manipulation of the "arbitrary" verbal signs that express those inclinations. This deception sunders Belcour's feeling from the terms of its expression, and nearly expels him from polite society. Again and again, Belcour affronts Louisa with his misconceived affections:

> You astonish me! Are you in your senses, or do you make a jest of my misfortunes? Do you ground pretences of your generosity, or do you make a practice of this folly with every woman you meet? (3, 375)

Much like the boatmen, tide-waiters, and water-bailiffs, Louisa is astonished and insulted by Belcour's behavior; his affections seem to take advantage of her distressed family situation. In this form, Belcour's love disrupts the sympathies that would otherwise unite the young couple. For his part, expecting a more professional demeanor, Belcour is also discomfited, silenced by Louisa's unaccountable "assurance" (3, 381). Belcour's misapprehension finally ignites this situation when his advances culminate in a lascivious invitation to pleasure:

> you are welcome to partake my fortune, give me in return your person, give me pleasure, give me love; free, disencumbered, anti-matrimonial love. (4, 386)

As subsequent events suggest, it is the form of Belcour's address to Louisa, and not his attraction to her, that rends the social fabric of the play. When, for instance, O'Flaherty informs Stockwell that Charles has challenged Belcour in defense of his sister's honor—"Ay, the sister; 'tis English, is it not?"—the merchant is "thunderstruck" by Belcour's amorous transgression: "you talked to me of a professed wanton; the girl he speaks of has beauty enough indeed to inflame your desires, but she has honour, innocence and simplicity to awe the most licentious passion" (4, 394). Although there is more than a little Restoration rakishness in Belcour's urgent sexuality, even Stockwell does not chastise him on this account. Taught the wrong social language, Belcour's nature has been misled; he has been unable to read the innocence expressed by Louisa's chaste beauty. Like "sister," Charles's charge of "villain" also becomes a word that frustrates sympathy. Once the insult has been given, only Stockwell's clever manipulation of the dueling code averts the tragedy, reveals Belcour's mistake, and vindicates Louisa's honor.

The major's role here, and in the closing action of the play, reminds us that if Belcour is on trial to the stage audience, the Irish soldier probably made more extensive demands on the theater audience's sympathies. O'Flaherty retains many of the typical features of the stage Irishman, viewed in a more charitable light. Frequently expressing his gratitude to St. Patrick, the major is a Catholic in a play in which Catholicism is not entirely a peripheral issue—Fulmer, too, is a "true son of Loyola" (2, 354). Forced into mercenary armies by laws proscribing service in the British military, he has traveled entensively, and married extensively, too: "I've married five wives . . . and, for what I know, they're all alive and merry at this hour" (2, 364).[45] And, of course, he has an infallible nose for Lady Rusport's "cordial restorative elixir" (2, 368). The Irish major remains a broadly comic figure in *The West Indian*, as Garrick's preference for the comedian Moody over Spranger Barry in the role suggests, but he is no longer a buffoon (*Memoirs*, p. 217).

Furthermore, like Belcour, O'Flaherty is a social outsider. As Cumberland suggests in his *Memoirs*, the major is an exile whose deficiencies of manner and character arise from his inability to perform "in the service of that country, which gave him birth, and which of course he was born to defend" (p. 205). Like Belcour, who struggles under the onus of his Caribbean breeding, O'Flaherty has been injured by artificial social restrictions that have, however mildly in his case, thwarted and deformed his individual nature. O'Flaherty defines a middle ground between Belcour and London; Cumberland's principal dramatic achievement is his canny use of the major to bring about Belcour's, and his own, acceptance into society.

The West Indian variously highlights the major's unerring good nature. O'Flaherty has some splendidly sententious points ("I am an Irishman, honey; mine is not the country of dishonour"—4, 392), and gains our approval through both his quick recognition of Charles's virtue and his instant repudiation of that hard-hearted "hyena," Lady Rusport (2, 368). Moreover, at Garrick's suggestion, Cumberland tied O'Flaherty "closer to the plot," making him especially instrumental to the play's happy resolution.[46] By informing Belcour of Louisa's true identity, and by gaining Charles his fortune and Charlotte in the bargain, the major unravels the principal tangles in the play's action, and links the otherwise independent love plots. In the closing moments of *The West Indian*, the major even becomes a kind of comic chorus. Instead of jeering at the Irishman, the audience is led by his giddy glee:

> Joy, joy, joy! sing, dance, leap, laugh for joy! Ha' done making love and fall down on your knees to every saint in the calendar, for they're all on your side, and honest St. Patrick at the head of them. (5, 401)

Major O'Flaherty articulates the play's final resolutions. He announces Charles's entitlement, and his own decision to retire with old Captain Dudley to Ireland. He interprets Louisa's loving glances at Belcour to the surrounding audience—"for you may see plainly enough by the young lady's looks, that she says a great deal" (5, 403)—and attempts to stand between Lady Rusport and her wrath—"Be advised now, and don't put yourself in such a passion; we were all very happy till you came." Fittingly, it is the major who wishes "we were all fairly set down to supper," a call for comic feasting that seems to prompt Stockwell's long-delayed discovery to Belcour. Stockwell's revelation provides the play's final act of inclusion; as Louisa remarks, "how many new relations spring from this night's unforseen events, to endear us to each other" (5, 405). No longer dominated by Lady Rusport, or distorted (from Belcour's point of view) by the Fulmers, the social world of the play discovers a new harmony, one that includes the amiable West Indian and the rugged Irish major. By arousing our sympathetic approval of Belcour, and by voicing it through O'Flaherty, Cumberland involves the theater audience in this process of social readjustment. As the major puts it, "I think we shall be all related by and by."

The West Indian, then, explicitly raises the problem of social communication in a benevolent context, one that reflects the theater's insistent concern with the meaning of expression. In his "manners, passions and opinions," Belcour is not "as yet assimilated" to the social climate of metropolitan London; "he comes amongst you a new character, an inhabitant of a new world" (5, 399). Although Belcour has been raised in a tropical paradise, and generally possesses an acceptably gregarious character, he must discover the way to make his character affective. He has, as Kames would argue, a natural inclination to society, but through his West Indian breeding his expressive gestures have been skewed from the pattern that the play establishes as its social norm. Naturally, much comedy of manners exploits the social friction generated by foreign or eccentric habits, but Cumberland widens *The West Indian*'s frame of reference by placing the social action of the play in a larger dramatic world. Lady Rusport's London not only includes a number of foreigners like Belcour and O'Flaherty and the Fulmers; its habits are seen in relation to "the fatal heats of Senegambia," to the Fulmers' Boulogne, to the Indies and to Ireland. The geographical backdrop both qualifies and reinforces our parochial attachment to proper London behavior, stressing both the necessary, and the necessarily arbitrary, nature of its social customs. This double focus characterizes the play's action as well. From the society's viewpoint, the outsiders undergo a trial of their amiability; to the characters, the action takes the shape of a search for home and security. A number of characters in the play, like Belcour, are somewhat shiftless, seeking their proper and protected niche—Captain Dudley searches for an ap-

pointment, Major O'Flaherty for a way to retire, Charles and
Charlotte for a way to wed, Stockwell for a son. In the providential
vision of *The West Indian*, the characters inevitably find their
places, but in the process they must learn the lesson of Lady
Rusport's failure, and of the actor's success. They must find a
way to make the artifice of social communication express their
natural, and naturally benevolent, feelings.

She Stoops to Conquer

Goldsmith's *She Stoops to Conquer* has always stood in an ambiguous
relation to the comedy of its day. Goldsmith's play is part of a
lively burst of "laughing" comedy in the 1760s and 1770s, and
is completely in keeping with the thriving manners and satiric
comedies of Foote, Colman, and Garrick. Nevertheless, critics
have tended to rely on the authority of Goldsmith's "An Essay
on the Theatre" (*Westminster Magazine*, 1 Jan. 1773) to consider
the play primarily as a rejoinder to the "weeping" comedies of
Cumberland, Kelly, and others. The proportions of Goldsmith's
attack on sentimentalism have been well and amply surveyed,
but in order to set *She Stoops to Conquer* in relation to the ethics
of sentimental performance, I would like to turn briefly to the
terms of the essay.

Although Goldsmith quickly and acerbically depreciates the
sentimental drama in the "Essay," he stops short of discussing
any individual plays in detail, and leaves the exact features of the
drama he castigates partly in shadow. He shies away from all but
the most general definition of the sentimental, and finally settles
for some vigorous lampooning of the genre as a "kind of *mulish*"
blend of tragedy and comedy that is as easy to "hammer out" as
cheap fiction.[47] Actually, Goldsmith's most cogent criticism is
directed not to the formal features of sentimental drama, but to
its debasing effect on the audience's moral discrimination. Since
"In these Plays almost all the Characters are good, and exceedingly

generous" and "have abundance of Sentiment and Feeling," when they are shown to have "Faults or Foibles, the Spectator is taught not only to pardon, but to applaud them, in consideration of the goodness of their hearts." As a result, "Folly, instead of being ridiculed, is commended, and the Comedy aims at touching our Passions without the power of being truly pathetic." As the "Essay" suggests, and as the final moments of *She Stoops to Conquer* confirm, Goldsmith does not baldly reject an appeal to the audience's "Sentiment and Feeling" in laughing comedy. But he does insist that the spectator's sympathetic response advance society's fundamental interests, and that those interests are moral in nature. To be "truly pathetic," the play must arouse a feeling response consistent with moral principle by ridiculing folly as well as approving virtue. In Goldsmith's view, this restorative function is best served by the humane "art of Laughing."

Goldsmith's desire to produce restorative laughter in the theater impels the action of *She Stoops to Conquer*, a play that firmly unites theatrical and social concerns. A naive attitude toward social performance is the vice of the play's society; chastening laughter and inventive role-playing allow it to recover its moral equilibrium. Moreover, like the actor's dramatic roles, social roles in the play function properly only when they are seen to express actual sentiment and feeling.

The play first suggests a histrionic vision of social activity in its theatrical frame. The prologue burlesques *Hamlet* to invite us into the play, and the epilogue releases us by recalling Jaques' lines from *As You Like It*: "Our life is all a play, compos'd to please,/ 'We have our exits and our entrances.' "[48] Garrick's prologue sensitively announces the histrionic thrust of the play's action and immediately defines the kind of social performance that the play will envision and criticize. The comedian Woodward (who had refused to play "low" Tony Lumpkin) enters in Hamlet's inky cloak, or "mourning suit" in this case, grieving the death of the comic muse at the hand of "sentimentals":

But why can't I be moral?—Let me try—
My heart thus pressing—fix'd my face and eye—
With a sententious look, that nothing means,
(Faces are blocks, in sentimental scenes)
Thus I begin—All is not gold that glitters,
Pleasure seems sweet, but proves a glass of bitters.
When ign'rance enters, folly is at hand;
Learning is better far than house and land.
Let not virtue trip, who trips may stumble,
And virtue is not virtue, if she tumble.
　I give it up—morals won't do for me;
To make you laugh I must play tragedy.

Garrick frequently abused sentimentals, harlequin shows, and other irregular dramatic entertainments in his prologues, but here he uses the prologue to introduce the action of the main piece. Like many characters in the play, Woodward views the expression of serious sentiments as a kind of posturing, a "sententious look" and formulaic speech that belie his true character. But though Woodward the comedian is allowed to "give it up," the central characters in *She Stoops to Conquer* are not let off the hook so easily. Through the action of the play, they are brought not to reject sentiment, but to reject its artificial expression. Like the actor, they learn to adjust their feelings to a sentimental role, while learning to make the role-playing necessary to social performance express their actual feelings.

　The opening scenes of the play generate an uneasy tension between genuine feeling and artificial behavior. Goldsmith swiftly counterpoints two attitudes toward society by contrasting the country isolation of the Hardcastle mansion with the habits of town life. "Is there a creature in the whole country, but ourselves, that does not take a trip to town now and then, to rub off the rust a little?" whines Mrs. Hardcastle, longing for the chance to burnish unused accomplishments (1, 106). To Hardcastle, though, her fondness for the town is merely "vanity and affectation." If she is vain, he is morose; like the Jonsonian humour characters that he resembles, Hardcastle dismisses the novelties of social life with a mildly obsessive vigor—"I love every thing that's old: old friends, old times, old manners, old books, old wine" (1, 107). Hardcastle and his wife define the range of social attitudes that operates in the play. Mrs. Hardcastle, attracted as she is to the vanities of the city, subordinates feeling to propriety, and will press for a respectable but loveless marriage between Constance and Tony. Hardcastle, like Rousseau, repudiates the proprieties of the town as affected, hypocritical fopperies that warp and disguise true character.

As her various performances in the play suggest, Kate can express her virtues through social performance without becoming enchanted, as her mother is, by the posturings of performance themselves. Kate's costuming phrases this flexibility in the theater. To Hardcastle, Kate's dress measures the degree of her infection by the duplicities of the town: "the fashions of the times have almost infected her too. By living a year or two in town, she is as fond of gauze, and French frippery, as the best of them" (1, 110). "Drest out as usual," Kate's attire signifies her declining moral sense to Hardcastle, while it suggests to the audience that her father's notion of social performance is unduly limited. Kate is clearly not Mrs. Hardcastle, and uses the formal requirements of her behavior expressively, receiving and paying visits dressed as befits a young woman of her estate, and wearing her "housewife's dress" in the evening to please her eccentric but kindhearted parent.

In one sense, Kate's dress simply lubricates the familiar mismatched-lovers machine of romantic comedy. But in *She Stoops to Conquer* this conventional device assumes a larger role in the play's significance. The sign-value of clothes critically enabled social performance in eighteenth-century London, and clothing functions similarly in the play as well. In his fascinating discussion of clothes in the eighteenth-century metropolis, Richard Sennett argues that clothing facilitated social interaction by providing the wearer with an easily recognizable social role. Clothing served the public by identifying the wearer's class background to his social audience. One "stepped into clothes whose purpose was to make it possible for other people to act as if they knew who you were," permitting them to respond with the appropriate language and bearing, with respect, with familiarity, or with condescension (pp. 67-68). Sennett clarifies the contribution that Kate's dress makes to the humor of *She Stoops to Conquer*. Kate's housedress means something different to the city-bred Marlow than it does to Hardcastle in the remote country. To Marlow, it is the costume of a serving-woman, and requires the appropriate response, though in fact "It's the dress . . . that every lady wears in the country, but when she visits or receives company" (3, 168). Marlow's mistaken reading of this costume eventually mortifies his assault on a barmaid's virtue as well as his unsociable solemnity with women of his own class, and the errors that arise from Kate's costume also qualify Hardcastle's stern contempt for female "frippery." To Hardcastle, Kate's silks are "superfluous" to the natural, straightforward expression of her character, but the action of the play demonstrates the complications that arise when character is not clearly, and conventionally, presented to the social audience.

Kate's clothing introduces a more provocative dimension of the play, its exploration of the necessary relation between social convention and individual feeling. Kate has no reservations about the clothing that she will wear to the first interview with her intended husband, but she does question whether the formal demands of the situation will hamper the expression of feeling: "our meeting will be so formal and so like a thing of business, that I shall find no room for friendship or esteem" (1, 111). Unlike her father, Kate does not disparage appearance in favor of inner virtue. On the contrary, her affections for Marlow are raised by degrees as Hardcastle's description moves from the attributes of his character to the advantages of his person:

> HARDCASTLE. . . . I am told he's a man of an excellent understanding.
>
> MISS HARDCASTLE. Is he?
>
> HARDCASTLE. Very generous.
>
> MISS HARDCASTLE. I believe I shall like him.
>
> HARDCASTLE. Young and brave.
>
> MISS HARDCASTLE. I'm sure I shall like him.
>
> HARDCASTLE. And very handsome.
>
> MISS HARDCASTLE. My dear Papa, say no more (*kissing his hand*) he's mine, I'll have him.
>
> (1, 112)

But Hardcastle's climactic revelation—"And to crown all, Kate, he's one of the most bashful and reserved young fellows in all the world"—undoes for her "all the rest of his accomplishments. A reserved lover, it is said, always makes a suspicious husband." The disparity between Marlow's feeling and expression presents a nearly insurmountable obstacle to Kate's affection, violating as it does the necessary trust between friends, lovers, and spouses. Insulting Kate's intelligence, Hardcastle will later epigrammatize her view—"a smooth face stands for good sense, and a genteel figure for every virtue" (3, 160)—but this tag distorts Kate's sensible hesitation. She does not argue that every pretty face expresses a gentle disposition, but she knows better than Hardcastle does that unexpressed feeling cannot sustain mutual affection.

The first scene of the play relates inner feeling and expressive behavior to the demands of social performance. The second scene transfers these issues to the alehouse, reinforcing the connection between social role and social class. Like the Hardcastles, the "shabby fellows" of the tavern are obsessed with their social status, and conceive their activities as expressions of their gentility, applauding Tony's ballad, for example, "bekeays he never gives nothing that's *low*" (1, 117). As Goldsmith suggests, they are typified by the bear-master's performing bear, who "ever dances but to the very genteelest of tunes. Water Parted, or the minuet in Ariadne." Kate's claim that excessive shyness impedes the workings of society is confirmed here; by preventing the travelers from asking their way more frequently, Marlow's "unaccountable reserve" is responsible for their loss of direction, and for the subsequent confusions of the evening. But although Marlow holds himself aloof from some social situations, he behaves in other settings with insulting familiarity. Unlike Hastings, who maintains a polite and appropriate distance from the habitués of the Three Pigeons, Marlow keeps his reserve for members of his own class. In the tavern, he frequently indulges his contempt for Tony, most contentiously when he contradicts Tony's description of the Hardcastle children:

> TONY. The daughter, a tall trapesing, trolloping, talk-ative maypole—The son, a pretty, well-bred, agreeable youth, that every body is fond of.
>
> MARLOW. Our information differs in this. The daughter is said to be well bred and beautiful; the son, an aukward booby, reared up, and spoiled at his mother's apron-string. (1, 121)

This kind of "reserve" is not calculated to stimulate the kindness of strangers, and as Tony remarks, "all I have to tell you is, that you won't reach Mr. Hardcastle's house this night, I believe."

Marlow is stonily modest with his equals, and offensively familiar with his inferiors, and this misapprehension of the requirements of social behavior motivates his actions throughout the play, particularly where Kate is involved. To Marlow, "a modest woman, drest out in all her finery, is the most tremendous object of the whole creation" (2, 130), an object that asks of him an impossibly suave performance. In his initial interview with Kate in Act 2, for example, Marlow describes himself as a peripheral "observer" rather than as a participant in the life of his social sphere, articulating the painful inadequacy among his equals that drives him finally into a speechless silence (2, 144). Marlow's reserve is wearisome to Kate, his attractive virtues are "so buried in his fears, that it fatigues one more than ignorance" (2, 148). Conversely, in the barmaid scenes, much as in the tavern scene, Marlow's forthright expression of desire threatens to disrupt rather than to facilitate social harmony. Only Kate's good-natured ability to manage her barmaid performance, and to divert her father's outrage at Marlow's evident impudence, prevents his attempted seduction from throwing the Hardcastle household irrevocably into chaos.

A prevailing strain of theatricality heightens the sense of social performance that informs *She Stoops to Conquer*. Much as the mid-century stage forced its audience to place the actor's performance in the wider context of the social performance taking place in the theater, the action of *She Stoops to Conquer* insistently requires its on- and offstage audiences to evaluate events within a variety of social contexts. This technique underlies the principal mistake of the night, when Marlow and Hastings are led to mistake the Hardcastle mansion for an inn. Although Hardcastle chafes against the affectations of his wife and daughter, he undertakes his own social responsibilities with a keen sense of the proprieties of performance. As host, Hardcastle painstakingly teaches his stable boy and plowhand how to act as table servants, and is both annoyed and antagonized when his guests fail to play their proper parts. Goldsmith repeatedly develops the action of the play through mistakes of this kind, which increasingly disrupt and confuse the play's comic society. In Act 3, for instance, Kate and Hardcastle are placed momentarily at odds through their different views of Marlow's performance:

> MISS HARDCASTLE.   Surprizing! He met me with a respect-
> ful bow, a stammering voice, and a
> look fixed on the ground.
> HARDCASTLE.   He met me with a loud voice, a lordly
> air, and a familiarity that made my
> blood freeze again.

In the same vein, Tony rallies his mother when her "stolen" jewels actually turn out to be missing: "I never saw it better acted in my life" (3, 166). Not recognizing Marlow's confusion about his daughter's identity, Hardcastle is stunned by their apparent lovers' struggle: "So, madam! So I find *this* is your *modest* lover. . . . Art thou not asham'd to deceive your father so?" (3, 174). In the subplot, the feigned love that Constance and Tony perform throughout the play is discredited through a similar kind of mistake, when Tony blunders into Constance's improvised turn with Hastings' elopement letter, and unwittingly exposes the plan to Mrs. Hardcastle.

The closing action of the play hinges on the same kind of theatrical duplicity, placing an evident action in a number of conflicting interpretive contexts. As Sir Charles remarks,

> What a situation am I in. If what you say appears, I shall then find a guilty son. If what he says be true, I shall then lose one that, of all others, I most wish'd for a daughter.   (5, 209)

The scene Kate contrives both exposes and cures Marlow's stage fright among women of his own class. When Hardcastle and Sir Charles step from behind the screen, Marlow's confession to the barmaid is revealed to be his declaration of affection to Miss Hardcastle. Marlow is tricked into realizing the feelings of his character by performing them before a discerning audience. Kate's theatrical device repairs the rift between Marlow's feeling and his public expression. Sir Charles and Hardcastle naturally disparage Marlow's "formal interview" and temper their ridicule of his modesty with their sympathy for his affection for Kate. Kate in particular derides Marlow's artificial role-playing, setting it sharply against his inability to perform adequately *in propria persona*:

> In which of your characters, Sir, will you give us leave to address you. As the faultering gentleman, with looks on the ground, that speaks just to be heard, and hates hypocrisy; or the loud confident creature, that keeps it up with Mrs. Mantrap, and old Miss Biddy Buckskin, till three in the morning; ha, ha, ha. (5, 213)

By exerting the "art of Laughter" Kate, Sir Charles, and Hardcastle mortify Marlow ("Zounds, there's no bearing this; it's worse than death") and engage him in a process of social adjustment and social rebirth.

The return of Hastings and Constance further amplifies this treatment of social performance in the play's final moments. Much as Kate has stooped to a lower social role in order to conquer Marlow's reserve, Constance has "been obliged to stoop to dissimulation to avoid oppression" (5, 214). But whereas Marlow's mask of modesty is forcibly removed, Constance doffs her feigned affection for Tony in order to appeal to Hardcastle's "humanity." Both surrender a disagreeable form of role-playing in order to adopt their properly expressive social roles; for this reason, they request and receive the benevolent sympathy of their betters and peers. Even Tony Lumpkin is released from a kind of false bondage, when he discovers that he has come of age and can assume the role that is most accessible to him without fear of restraint.[49] Of course, Goldsmith slyly qualifies the sentimental overtones of his finale in Mrs. Hardcastle's defeated lament, "Pshaw, pshaw, this is all but the whining end of a modern novel." With mild irony, Goldsmith orchestrates his final social refinement. By exerting feeling consistent with the demands of their social roles, the characters appeal to their audience's sympathies, and are accepted into their social world.

Let me make a few final remarks on plays and playing in the sentimental theater. As we have seen, the actor's performance attempts to reconcile the irrational passions with their conventional expressive forms. Many features of the theater contribute to this end—pointing, formalized roles, the actor's use of pictorial gestures and postures—or, like the disposition of the audience into visible class groupings, implicitly extend the actor's task to his attentive theatrical public. Like the society it serves, the sentimental theater articulates passion through a variety of structuring conventions; it is thoroughly a theater of manners.

I have a particular sense of the word *manners* in mind here, something akin to the French term *mœurs*. For a modern audience, *mœurs* suggests much more actively the expression of character in action than *manners* does.[50] *Mœurs* are manners as moral actions, habitual acts, opinions, and principles that realize character in its personal and social implications; to a degree, *mœurs* is reminiscent of the Brechtian *gest*, though without Brecht's economic overtones. And unlike *gest, mœurs* implies a formal regularity to these expressive acts. *Manners* in this sense encompasses the courtesies of social involvement, simple habits, and also the more subtle and complex enactment that expresses bearing, character, and class.

Manners unify both the sentimental theater and its ambient society. The drama of the period persistently examines the relationship between manners and character; the resolution of social improprieties, whether real or imagined, is both the subject and the process of sentimental dramatic action. A play like *She Stoops to Conquer*, by insisting on the importance of performed character—character realized through proper manner—reflects the pervasiveness of performance as an obligatory social activity. When he steps on to the public stage, Chesterfield's man of the world "must, like the chameleon, be able to take every different hue," and his decision to engage society histrionically is a necessary one. Chesterfield's blithe recollection of the chameleon image of the actor measures the degree to which the ontological instability of the Renaissance actor—remember Richard III promising to "add colors to the chameleon,/ Change shapes with Proteus"—has been blunted.[51] This is not to say that all sentimental roles provide a positive image of the affective actor in the way that Kate and Belcour do. Much as roles like Iago or Faustus exploit the Renaissance actor's demonic capability, the sinister dimension of the sentimental actor's figuration of social performance—his maliciously disengaged manipulation of the mask of feeling—informs the characterization of hypocrites like Mrs. Hardcastle and Mrs. Fulmer, of glib Joseph Surface and cunning Glenalvon.

This concern for *mœurs* thoroughly informs both the dramatic repertory and the nascent dramatic criticism of the period. Collier's challenging critique of Restoration comedy, which provides a model for antitheatrical attack throughout the eighteenth century, partly assails just this feature of the drama, in that by rewarding its Horners and Dorimants, the drama subordinates morals to the polite, engaging, but ultimately hypocritical manners of its rakish heroes. In an important sense, comedy of this kind divorces manner from morals, and explodes the *mœurs* ideal. The sentimental mode, on the other hand, more consistently presents its heroes as both virtuous and well-mannered, even though (as in Belcour's case) the audience must frequently reinterpret the hero's actions extensively in order to recognize his virtue and rehabilitate his reputation for wholesome manliness.[52]

One small effect this interest in manners had on the dramatic repertory can be seen in the rise of a significant minor dramatic genre in the period, the drama of theatrical manners. The eighteenth-century public was particularly fond of plays depicting backstage life, the daily society of the theater. Unlike either

Renaissance or modern metaplays like *The Tempest* or *Rosencrantz and Guildenstern Are Dead*, these plays entirely ignore the metaphysical implications of dramatic art in order to address the social aspect of the theater enterprise. Old favorites like Buckingham's *The Rehearsal* (1671)—Bayes was a Garrick triumph—and newer plays like Garrick's *A Peep Behind the Curtain* (1767) and Sheridan's *The Critic* (1779), subject the social process of the theater to the audience's scrutiny in much the way that conventional comedies allow the theater to expose the histrionic posturing of the social audience. Inasmuch as they turn a sardonic eye on the social life of the theater, these plays and the many like them complement the satiric comedies ridiculing the theatrical excesses of social life. They are the *Clandestine Marriage*s and *School for Scandal*s of theatrical manners.

The significance of manners in theatrical, dramatic, and social worlds sustains the ethos of neoclassical acting. I have not said much here about the acting theorists' use of associationist psychology, but there is an important point of comparison between the actor's conventional representation of a pointed moment of passion, and the vision of mind advanced by the natural psychologists. In its structure of discrete emblems of feeling, the theatrical role is perfectly suited to the sensory orientation of faculty psychology. Hume's notorious description of the mind as "a bundle or collection of different perceptions, which succeed each other with an inconceivable rapidity, and are in perpetual flux and movement" implies that human thought is created in

> a kind of theater, where several perceptions successively make
> their appearance; pass, re-pass, glide away, and mingle in an
> infinite variety of postures and situations.[53]

Not only is social interaction modeled on theatrical representation, self-consciousness itself is the experience of points on the stage of the mind. The actor's coordination of feeling and expression is critical to harmonizing a society made up of individuals such as Hume describes. Hume's mind passively receives the impressions of the external world; the order of nature establishes the order of mental experience. When moved to act, man's motives are revealed through a host of natural "postures"—the language of gesture. His mental life is expressed to the outside world through a gestural system that is itself the natural extension of his inner experience. The actor's emblematic enactment of this process may suggest how this mechanical relation between mind and nature enhances the social involvement that is mankind's ultimate end. By unifying a moment of passion with its expressive form, the actor coordinates his own experience with the audience's feeling response through the medium of conventional, yet natural, signs. In a sense, the actor interrupts the flow of impression-expression-impression, in order to create a moment of significance, of meaning shared by performer and audience. His acting is actively moral because he actively pursues a social relationship with his public. In creating society, rather than simply participating in it, the actor becomes, much like Garrick among lesser players, a "man among marionettes."[54]

[3] Self-Betrayal:
The Optics of Modern Acting

If it be metaphorically the destiny of humanity, it is literally the experience of an actor, that one man in his time plays many parts. A player of any standing must at various times have sounded the gamut of human sensibility from the lowest note to the top of its compass.
  —Henry Irving, "The Stage As It Is" (1881)

Now self-betrayal, magnified to suit the optics of the theatre, is the whole art of acting.
  —Bernard Shaw, "The Immortal William" (2 May 1896)[1]

Henry Irving and Bernard Shaw. The names suggest a constellation of values dividing the old theater from the new: Boucicault and Tennyson versus Ibsen and Chekhov; the star versus the ensemble; the deadly theater versus the immediate theater. Shaw, of course, is largely responsible for this crisp metonymy. As the voice of the new theater, he relentlessly besieged Irving, shelling his overstuffed and egocentric Lyceum Shakespeare with mortars of the new drama. Naturally, Shaw had both personal and strategic reasons for embodying the Victorian stage in the figure of its actor-knight. As an acclaimed actor, and as a recognized arbiter of theatrical taste, Irving's defection to the new theater would lend it instant authority and substance. But more important, Shaw recognized that Irving's ironic intellect, his oddly creative acting, and his often bizarre, highly mannered psychological intensity could be effectively exploited in the incipient modern drama—he "instinctively felt that a new drama inhered in this man."[2]

That Shaw could imagine sharing any stage with Irving is itself arresting, and suggests the extent to which our understanding of the rise of modern actor needs review; much as the late decades of the nineteenth century incubated the attitudes and techniques of the modern drama, they also engendered a sweeping revision of the actor's art. In many respects, this innovation was a stylistic one, providing actors and audiences with a performance technique that seemed (as such innovations always do) more "natural" than its fustian predecessors.[3] Beyond that, though, this reconsideration reviewed not only the actor's mimetic technique, but radically rephrased the artistic justification of his art as well. Before turning to an overview of modern acting theory, I would like to assess the terms of that popular revaluation, and suggest how actors and critics variously conceive the actor, not as tawdry stageplayer, hired masquer, or impersonal mime, but as an artist undertaking the difficult project of authentic Romantic art—"self-betrayal."

Irving's lecture "The Stage As It Is" plays a minor part in the general reconsideration of acting that animates the theatrical press of the 1880s and 1890s, and helps us to define the terms of a controversy that exercised the talents of a host of theatrical professionals—Constant Coquelin, Dion Boucicault, William Archer, and Henry James among them.[4] In public lectures, Irving frequently capitalized on his considerable reputation to upgrade and legitimate acting as a profession. "The Stage As It Is"—delivered to the Edinburgh Philosophical Institution—is a typical instance of this effort. Far from apologizing for his craft, Irving confronts the public prejudice against actors, and urges his staid Scots audience to treat actors like other creative artists, that they may receive "in society, as do the members of other professions exactly the treatment which is earned by their personal conduct." Indeed, Irving subtly assaults his audience's values even through the flattering invocation of Shakespeare's "All the world's a stage"; for in rephrasing these familiar lines, Irving directly undermines the audience's biased vision of acting. In *As You Like It*, Jaques understands that one man may play many parts, and describes those parts as a series of roles or offices (infant, schoolboy, lover, soldier, justice, pantaloon, senile old man), each marked by its typical business (mewling and puking, sighing like a furnace), and costume (satchel, beard of formal cut, slippers, spectacles, youthful hose). Shakespeare's actor becomes an image for the mutability of human identity in relation to the inevitable process of age and the renewing cycles of nature. The actor becomes an appropriate metaphor for our experience because his roles, like our own, are ultimately ephemeral. Irving's recollection of Jaques' lines offers a strikingly different image of the actor, and addresses his audience's assumptions about acting by recasting the actor as a Romantic artist. Irving considers his actor subjectively. The actor emblematizes our experience not simply because he must fill a variety of roles, but because each of these roles exacts a complete, and sometimes painful, commitment. The actor's masks are not easily discarded, nor are they merely the means of his confrontation with the world; "all he learns is embodied in his own personality."[5] Like the poet, the actor discovers the material of his art within himself, expressing his role through a histrionic overflow of powerful feelings. He is a representative figure because his roles require him to sound "the gamut of human sensibility."

Irving implicitly conceives of acting as an art demanding the actor's sincere self-engagement, an authentic confrontation with the self that he hopes will dignify acting to the earnest Victorian public. In this respect, he touches on the major theoretical debate of his day, the "masks or faces" controversy. Fueled by Walter Herries Pollock's translation of Diderot's *The Paradox of Acting* (1883)—to which Irving contributed a preface—actors and critics throughout the 1880s and '90s significantly reviewed the actor's task, using Diderot's distinction between engaged and disengaged acting as a springboard to more immediate concerns. But whereas neoclassical critics attempt to relate the actor's train of feeling to a succession of conventional signs, Victorian critics examine the spontaneity of the actor's feeling more exclusively than his formal expression. In fact, Diderot's terms are not entirely appropriate to this debate, for the actor's emotional engagement is not really the issue at stake, as William Archer's ingenious rebuttal *Masks or Faces?* (1888) suggests. Archer conducts a fascinating survey of contemporary actors, and marshals them into anti-Diderot "emotionalist" and pro-Diderot "mechanical" camps according to the degree of their emotional involvement with their roles. He clearly intends to refute Diderot with the frank remarks of "emotionalist" actors like Salvini and Forbes-Robertson but, despite the actors' testimonies, his study remains inconclusive. Why is the actor's "artistically controlled sensibility" necessary to achieve the truthfulness that forever eludes "even the greatest virtuoso of mechanical mimicry?"[6] Archer doesn't say, but the revelation of actual feeling in performance seems to sustain accomplished acting because it is the sign of a deeper engagement with "real experience." His title carries the implied burden of his argument, for his study suggests that the actor becomes an artist not simply through the revelation of his feelings, but through the exposure of his "face" in performance. "Real" feeling becomes a sign to the audience that the actor's expressive *self* informs the performance. The actor uses his mask to discover and reveal his hidden, vital identity on the stage.

Masks or Faces? fails to resolve Diderot's paradox largely because it fails to redefine Diderot's antithesis between feeling and form by defining the actor's expression of personal emotion as a Romantic act of self-confrontation. The actor's feeling remains a deceptively peripheral issue, for both sides of the emotional question implicitly agree that acting is the art of self-revelation. In "Art and the Actor" (1880), for instance, Constant Coquelin persuasively substantiates Diderot's view of the emotionally disengaged actor: "I am convinced that one can only be a great actor on the condition of complete self-mastery and ability to express feelings which are not experienced, which may never be experienced, which from the very nature of things never can be experienced." And much of Coquelin's discussion, describing the actor as a kind of *bricoleur*—"He borrows from his author, he borrows from stage tradition, he borrows from nature, he draws on his own stock of knowledge of men and things"—naturally seems to oppose him to the "emotionalist" camp (pp. 26, 27). But though he rejects the actor's expression of personal feeling, he simultaneously argues that artistic acting requires the performer to realize his identity onstage. "Mechanical" Coquelin rejects emotional display as the defining condition of acting only to insist on a prior sacrifice, that of the actor's personal selfhood. We need only examine the rampant prejudice against the theater, he argues later in the essay, to see how entirely acting is informed by the actor's identity. Moralizing critics denounce acting because "the renunciation by the actor of his own personality, to assume the character of one, ten, or twenty other people, is apparently a renunciation of his own dignity, and a denial of the dignity of mankind" (p. 37). As Coquelin recognizes, these critics deny the actor the status of artist by seeing his performance as self-denial rather than as self-discovery. Coquelin counters that the actor risks his personal dignity not because he obscures himself in performance, but because in every part he must engage his "personal individuality, directive and creative" toward the performance of a living character. The actor's creative commitment sustains acting as high art: "It is with this individual *self* that he makes you by turn shiver, weep, or smile. . . . He does not abdicate the throne: he reigns supreme" (p. 38). As Coquelin implies, the actor's feelings are of secondary importance. Engaged or disengaged, the actor's "dignity is intact; he is no less a man, and he is an artist."

Coquelin anticipates the most cogent assessment of the modern actor's task to emerge from this controversy, Shaw's "Acting, By One Who Does Not Believe In It" (1889). Like Irving and Coquelin, Shaw keenly pinpoints the Victorian distaste for role-playing:

In English, acting means shamming. The critic, then, despises the stage as a sham, and the actor as a wretched impostor, disguised in the toga of Caesar, and spouting the words of Shakespear—a creature with the trappings and the language of a hero, but with the will of a vain mummer—a fellow that fights without courage, dares without danger, is eloquent without ideas, commands without power, suffers without self-denial, loves without passion, and comes between the author and the stalls much as a plaster of colored earths and oil comes between Raphael and the Cook's tourist. (pp. 12-13)

Since "All art is play; and all play is make-believe," acting can have only limited pretensions as a morally improving art form. Moreover, Archer's "methodical, cold-blooded" effort to make the actor's feeling the criterion of artistic acting seems unpersuasive to Shaw, who recognizes that self-betrayal is the common ground uniting actors otherwise dissimilar in attitude, style, and emotional commitment. Shaw goes on to compare two actors who responded to Archer's survey, the "emotionalist" Salvini and "mechanical" Coquelin. In answer to Archer's queries, Salvini testifies that great acting requires his entire engagement, and as Shaw remarks,

No protest could be more passionate than this. The greatest actor of the day proclaims with all his force that he is no actor at all; that there is no such thing as acting; that he is no sham, no puppet, no simulacrum, but in real earnest all that he pretends to be; that Othello, Hamlet, and Samson are not merely aped by him, but live and suffer in his person; that he throws himself into them because in them he realizes himself as he never could realize himself in the prosaic parts that are played off the stage, such as those of the stockbroker, the lawyer, the painter, or the dust contractor. (pp. 14-15)

Performing on the stage, for Salvini, is not acting at all. It is a form of expressive being, a realization of the inner life that is not possible in the roles offered him off the stage. While Salvini becomes himself through his part, Coquelin in every part "will always be Coquelin," intellectually and emotionally distinct from his role:

> he is one of the few points in the human mass at which individuality is concentrated, fixed, gripped in one exceptionally gifted man, who is, consequently, what we call a personality, a man pre-eminently himself, impossible to disguise, the very last man who could under any circumstances be an actor. Yet this is just what makes him the stage-player *par excellence*.
>
> (p. 16)

Coquelin's approach may be "mechanical" and Salvini's "emotional," but in performance both actors command our attention by revealing themselves. Much as Salvini finds expression through Hamlet or Othello, so too Coquelin's "best part will be that which shews all sides of him and realizes him wholly to us and to himself." In such a part, Coquelin like Salvini "becomes for the first time completely real." As Shaw reminds us, "This is not acting" in the English sense; both actors achieve "the final escape from acting, the ineffable release from the conventional mask which must be resumed as the artist passes behind the wing, washes off the paint, and goes down into the false lights and simulated interests and passions of the street." Whether or not the role demands his immediate feeling onstage, the actor whose performance transcends entertainment to become art must rigorously pursue what Shaw calls here "metaphysical self-realization" through acting (p. 18).[7]

Shaw coordinates a continuing drive to define acting as an *authentic* art, one in which the actor, like Lionel Trilling's Romantic artist, strives to become "as self-defining as the art-object he creates."[8] The issue that truly divides partisans and opponents of the theater at the close of the nineteenth century is not the actor's feeling, but his difficult "self-realization" on the stage. As Jonas Barish has remarked, the Victorian version of the antitheatrical prejudice derives from a Romantic emphasis on "inwardness, solitude, and spontaneity," an attitude embodied in Lamb's strictures against Shakespearean performance, and pervasive throughout the century.[9] While urging "self-realization" as a way to revive acting as an art, theatrical innovators in the 1890s confront a deep-seated conviction: that the actor's necessarily public "self-betrayal" inevitably betrays the self, falsifies the personality it reveals.

This attitude is not confined to naive or unsophisticated observers, nor to those openly hostile to the theater. In "The Art of Acting" (1907), the distinguished theater critic A. B. Walkley takes an exemplary view of the actor's aberrent personality. Entranced by their roles, actors are temperamentally engrossed by superficiality, unduly impressed "by the outward and visible signs of things rather than by the things themselves." The actor's willingness to play a dramatic role is only part of a deeper, nearly pathological attraction to appearances; actors have, Walkley suggests, a constitutional antipathy to "introspective analysis, which is the art of first knowing and then scientifically measuring your own inmost self."[10] Shallow, trivial, and immodest, the "histrionic temperament" necessarily deviates from the masculine reserve of true English character:

> Yet deep down in the hearts of most men there persists the feeling that to make a public show of yourself for money, to be always expressing ideas not your own, and emotions which you do not feel, to pretend in short to be what you are not—to clap a hump on your back and call yourself Richard the Third, as Johnson puts it—is to violate the dignity of a citizen and a free man, to resign the "captaincy of your soul."

By performing on the stage, Walkley's actor resigns his humanity, his dignity as a citizen and the personal value of his soul. The actor is so far from pursuing common social life that he unavoidably lives as a "class apart," permanently marked by his antisocial impersonation and the denial of self it entails: "they sacrifice their Ego, their features, complexions, their whole personality, in the cause of art, so that we may regard the marks their profession sets indelibly upon them as the stigmata of a sort of martyrdom."[11]

Self-betrayal, magnified to suit the optics of the theater, may be the whole art of acting as far as Shaw is concerned, but to many critics the actor's public performance betrays him into tawdry exhibitionism. Walkley's apprehensive vision of the actor's personality is neither idiosyncratic nor extreme, but foreshadows a consistently anxious regard for the actor's self-display that runs throughout modern acting and stage theory. Gordon Craig's "uebermarionette" actor, like Max Beerbohm's "mime," extends Walkley's sense that acting dehumanizes the performer, that "however long the world may last, the nature in man will fight for freedom, and will revolt against being made a slave or medium for the expression of another's thoughts." Even a gifted Shavian actor like Harley Granville-Barker could long for a theater "in desperate defiance of Aristotle," where actors could simply *be* without having to perform themselves actively, a theater "from which doing would be eliminated altogether, in which nothing but being would be left. The task set the actors of it would be to interest their audience in what the characters *were*, quite apart from anything they might *do*."[12]

The fear of violating the audience's slight tolerance for such self-betrayal bore considerably on acting in the last decades of the century. As Michael Baker argues in his study of the Victorian actor, the growing appeal of certain actors in the period is in direct proportion to their increasingly underplayed acting style. What Shaw called the "smart nullity" of the drawing-room style was, in this view, an expression of the actor's unwillingness to transgress the bounds of emotional decorum.[13] Unrestrained, energetic performance demanded a breadth of feeling and a vitality of self denied the audience in life outside the theater, and thus seemed both appallingly vulgar and embarrassingly artificial when presented on the stage. Not surprisingly, one reviewer argues that the new school of acting should not show the energy of spontaneous emotional release, but should "indicate the power of self-control."[14] The vivacity of actresses could be both absorbing and unsettling in this regard. The professional obligations of the Victorian actress automatically placed her outside the pale of domestic feminine decorum; because she worked, she was exotic, attractively threatening. But beyond her experience in the working world, the actress's forceful display of emotion provoked critical concern.[15] Vigorous performance seemed to require the actress's personal exposure, the revelation of her most intimate "face" to the prying stares of the public. The "egoistic force" of a Duse could be, in this respect, disconcerting, almost pornographic, even to a seasoned reviewer like Beerbohm:

> My prevailing impression is of a great egoistic force; of a woman overriding, with an air of sombre unconcern, plays, mimes, critics and public. In a man I should admire this tremendous egoism very much indeed. In a woman it only makes me uncomfortable. I dislike it. I resent it.[16]

As Henry James saw, the opprobrium with which this kind of professional rigor was regarded drove many actresses to the opposite extreme. They acted with repellent coquetry, in an explicitly "amateurish" manner designed to protect them from the vulgarity of the actor's professional display by transforming the brilliant ostentation of the stage into the protected intimacy of a private theatrical.[17]

Yet James, too, could be made uneasy when a woman's personal allure became part of her public performance. During Elizabeth

Robins's rehearsal of Hilda in *The Master Builder*, for instance, James got wind of Ibsen's costuming directions for the part. In a midnight letter, James pleaded with Robins to throw "Ibsen's prescriptions to the winds if practically they betray you." First, in order to make an already unconventional play more accessible to its audience, James advised Robins to respect the stage tradition that required the principal actress to appear in several new gowns in the play. But Hilda's shortened hiking skirt disturbed more than just stage convention. To James, the skirt was too blatant, too revealing; it made too overt a statement of Hilda's sexuality, and betrayed Robins too clearly to her audience:

> Don't be fantastic—be *pretty*, be agreeable, in the right key. I can't help being sorry you have only one gown; if so it ought to have a very positive felicity. A 1000 eyes will peck at it for 2 and ½ hours. Throw yourself into the dressmaker's arms. Be better, be darker, be longer!

Commendably, Robins altered only the distracting sailor collar: "The general air of combined utility and negligence, which he deplored, was an effect I aimed at. . . . As to the obnoxious only dress—no whit 'better,' no 'darker,' no 'longer'—the sole change I offered him was the addition of hobnailed boots."[18]

Although some resented the egoistic force of such actors and actresses, others longed for, and tried to create, a theater that would consistently demand self-betrayal as the standard of theatrical art. To many, the underplayed and self-controlled acting seemed only to imitate the facile role-playing of modern life and the emotional sterility it concealed. Thus, while defining the engagement of the actor's identity as the basis of artistic acting, theatrical innovators naturally oppose this creative acting to the superficial conventions treasured by the tradition-bound theater and its society. Shaw intended the "stagey, brassbowelled" acting he required in his plays to provide a release from the constricting roles of social behavior.[19] From day to day, most of us are walk-ons in the play of life, and Shaw argued that "the walking gentle-man in us does not crave for realization"; it is the magnificent hero lurking within who finds no outlet in the world beyond the theater, and whom the stage must satisfy.[20] Nor is this attitude confined to the theatrical avant-garde. Even the actress Fanny Kemble finds the actor's "dramatic" temperament to be at odds with "theatrical" representation: "the dramatic is the *real*, of which the theatrical is the *false*." The lifeless conventions of the stage are only an extension of the suffocating masks imposed by society at large: "the dramatic temperament, always exceptional in England, is becoming daily more so under the various adverse influences of a state of civilisation and society which fosters a genuine dislike to exhibitions of emotion, and a cynical disbelief in the reality of it, both necessarily repressing, first, its expression, and next its existence." The tragedy of the dramatic temperament is the tragedy of Rosmer or Hector Hushabye, to be thwarted by a world that stifles heroic vitality, much as the conventional theater constricts the actor's expressive art. As Fanny Kemble concludes, "our stage is and must be supplied, if supplied at all, by persons less sophisticated and less civilised," theatrical prim-itives able to ignore the dictates of propriety and act expressively on the stage.[21]

The "masks or faces" controversy illuminates a unique range of popular attitudes toward the modern actor's performance. Cer-tain observers require the actor's complete commitment of self in performance to validate acting as a Romantic art; to some, the actor's expression of genuine feeling testifies to this sacrifice. The actor's self-betrayal witnesses the breadth and vitality of his per-sonality, a vivacity more threatened by the masks of society than by the expressive roles of the theater. Even a disengaged actor like Coquelin, who denies the necessity of emotional involvement, concurs that this "metaphysical self-realization" is the essential stuff of acting. But to consider this self-betrayal as art confounds many attitudes cherished by the Victorian audience and by its children, particularly regarding the delicate privacy of the self and the duplicity of role-playing. The modern actor is fundamentally alienated from the traditional theater, betrayed into triviality by the public nature of his performance. He also requires a technique to sustain the naturalistic verisimilitude of Ibsen, Chekhov, Shaw and others. Historically, Ibsen's plays presented new challenges of action and characterization, challenges that demanded new approaches to preparation and performance.[22] Yet in addition to recasting his technique, the modern actor has also had to reconceive the purpose of acting as an art, and find a means to that "public solitude" that allows him to explore himself authentically in performance, to achieve "what we in actor's jargon call the state of 'I am.' "[23] This new actor, as a chorus of voices reminds us, requires a new theater. To create that theater, particularly to coordinate the actor's problematic relationship to himself, his role, and his audience in a systematic theory of histrionic meaning will become the presiding task of the seminal theoretician of the modern stage, Constantin Stanislavsky.

The revision of the actor as Romantic artist, especially as it is articulated in Stanislavsky's writing, stands in a critical relation to the form and substance of modern drama. Particularly by invoking the actor's self-betrayal as an artistic ideal, and by emphasizing the close synchrony of role and self in performance, English actors and critics decisively anticipate Stanislavsky's innovative prescriptions for the modern stage. As we shall see, they envision an actor whose "metaphysical self-realization" will be exploited and refined in the major plays of the modern canon— in the ambiguous projects of Solness and Rosmer, in the labyrinthine performances of Pirandello's characters, in the provisional role-playing of Pinter's, or of Peter Handke's. Of course, the effect of this ideal on the modern theater has been equally profound. We can see Stanislavsky looming behind Group Theater and Actors Studio productions (and their offspring on the American stage, in film, and television), providing a point of departure for students like Vakhtangov and Michael Chekhov, and defining a guiding antithesis for Meyerhold, Brecht, and perhaps Artaud. Even Jerzy Grotowski, who dispenses with many of the performance goals of Stanislavskian naturalism, finds himself constantly returning to problems first phrased by the Russian master. [24]

That is to say, we should not consider Stanislavsky as part of the "background" of modern drama, as something to fill out the slack time in a class on *The Seagull* or *Death of a Salesman*. Stanislavsky's theory responds to the fresh challenge of the new drama of his time and creates the histrionic instrument it requires. Recent criticism has begun to accommodate Stanislavsky's sometimes obscure stage theory to the intellectual traditions of the nineteenth and twentieth centuries, fleshing out Theodore Hoffman's remark that Stanislavsky "shifted the focus on acting, and brought to it the existential mode."[25] Stanislavsky's particular relevance to the modern stage lies in his unwavering attention to the actor. He precipitates and clarifies the contradictory impulses guiding the Romantic actor's performance, and creates a body of theory that justifies the actor's endeavor as an art. The strength and resonance of Stanislavsky's work derives from his systematic program for a new kind of actor, his prevailing sense not only of how the actor should prepare and perform, but also of the meaning of histrionic performance itself. Stanislavsky defines an art, an attitude, a set of values; he creates an ethos for the modern actor.

The cardinal goal of Stanislavskian production is to achieve an embracing consistency of effect onstage, a "realism" sometimes confused with the detailed naturalism of many of the Moscow Art Theater productions. Timothy J. Wiles suggests that Stanislavsky may have recognized earlier than other practitioners that "what is essentially 'real' about theatrical naturalism lies as much in the reality of the performance itself as in the true-to-life quality of the play's details" (p. 14). Yet Stanislavsky never entirely shed his fascination for the engaging immediacy of stage naturalism, and in an important sense his simultaneous commitment to the naturalistic style and to creating a living reality on the stage represent deeply opposed and contradictory impulses. His auto-biography and production diaries reveal an invariable tendency to conceive of dramatic character within a densely material set-ting, an environment that at once externalizes character and seems to shape and control it.[26] As Raymond Williams remarks, the naturalistic emphasis on "the *production* of character or action by a powerful natural or social environment" was still a provocative novelty in the turn-of-the-century theater. Stanislavsky's thor-ough exploration of dramatic *character*—particularly his sense of character as acting out of the traumas of the past—has its roots in the deterministic orientation of the naturalistic style.[27] But when he considers the *actor's* performance, he rejects the natu-ralistic determination of identity by environment and insists that the actor must be liberated from his stage world, free from the conventions of society and of the theater that threaten to make his acting artificial and inauthentic. Much like the Romantic artist, Stanislavsky's actor must overcome the invalidating re-strictions of his milieu to achieve a genuine, self-creating art form—a "life in art."

In many specific instances, though, Stanislavsky fails to rec-ognize clearly the basic incompatibility of the naturalistic style with his emerging sense of the actor. His familiar model of actor-training is a case in point. As Burnet M. Hobgood suggests in his study of the Stanislavsky system, Stanislavsky's goal is to teach the actor to experience both himself and his role simulta-neously during performance.[28] "Psycho-technique" is critical to this task, providing a means for the actor to vivify the role's responses by grounding them in his own feeling, recollected through "emotion memory." This technique is remarkably well-suited to the demands of naturalistic drama, since it provides the actor/role with a concretely-imagined social and psychological history that can be gradually revealed through the action of the play. Moreover, Stanislavsky conceives of the action of any play as part of a temporal continuum, and centers the actor's preparation on a mastery of the play's prior circumstances. He particularly stresses the importance of the "super-objective" to the actor's preparation, the unbroken line of action "that flows from the past, through the present, into the future."[29] Like the naturalistic drama, Stanislavsky's training is deterministic insofar as it defines the present action—the character's identity and the actor's performance—as the inevitable expression of a fixed and influential past. Not that Stanislavsky considered his theory limited to Ibsen or Brieux; his early notes for the first scene of *Othello* detail an exemplary account of Roderigo, a history that motivates, limits, and explains the role:

> What is the *past* which justifies the *present* of this scene: Who is Roderigo? I imagine that he is the son of very wealthy parents, landowners who took the produce of their village to Venice and exchanged it for velvet and other luxuries. These goods were in turn shipped to other countries, including Russia, and sold at great profit. But now Roderigo's parents are dead. How can he manage such a tremendous business? All he is capable of is squandering his father's wealth. It is this wealth which made his father, and consequently himself, acceptable in aristocratic circles. Roderigo, a simple soul and a lover of gay times, constantly supplies the young blades of Venice with money which, obviously, is never returned. Where does this money come from? Well, thus far the well-established business, managed by old and faithful workers, is still running through force of inertia; but certainly it cannot continue like this much longer.[30]

Stanislavsky's depiction of Roderigo evokes a peculiarly Victorian confidence in the intelligible relation between the physical world, character, and action, one that sustains popular genres like the detective novel and the well-made play, and that recalls the kind of Shakespearean character-study that A. C. Bradley elevated into sophisticated criticism.[31]

Nevertheless, preparation is justified by performance, and the deterministic bias of Stanislavsky's actor-training is offset by a deeper, more original impulse. In chapter 48 of *My Life in Art*, Stanislavsky suggests the personal inspiration—or "sense-memory"—behind his experimental work in the theater. After recalling the depressing events of 1905-1906—the death of Chekhov and Morozov, the failure of the Maeterlinck production, the utter erosion of his own confidence as an actor—Stanislavsky describes himself gazing out into the sea from the cliffs of Finland, and strikes a familiar posture of Romantic alienation: "dissatisfaction with myself as an actor, and the complete darkness of the distances that lay before me, gave me no rest, took away my faith in myself, and made me seem wooden and lifeless in my own eyes" (*LA*, p. 458). Desolate, brooding on the loss of his former "joy in creation," he is suddenly animated by an almost Wordsworthian experience, emotionally invigorated by a vividly histrionic "spot of time." Momentarily, he feels the surge of his original creative excitement in the role of Dr. Stockmann in Ibsen's *An Enemy of the People*. This brief epiphany leads him to reevaluate his naturalistic understanding of acting, and to begin the experimentation that produced his mature work.[32]

The purpose of much of Stanislavsky's subsequent theory is to allow the actor to forego this kind of debilitating malaise, to permit the performer to experience the spontaneous "joy in creation" immediately and effectively while acting. For coupled with the actor's "work on his role" is his searching "work on himself," the extended self-analysis that enables him to recognize and express his own emotional drives in performance.[33] By mastering the character's predetermined past and by synchronizing it with his own motivating desires, the actor becomes ready to realize his own identity on the stage. Paradoxically, then, the deterministic aspects of the actor's preparation produce the freedom to act on native impulses. The committed and creative actor achieves an authentic sense of being through acting, the sense of "I am":

> The difficulty of this aspect of emotional perception is that the actor is now coming to his part not through the text, the words of his role, nor by intellectual analysis or other conscious means of knowledge, but through his own sensations, his own real emotions, his personal life experience.
>
> To do this he must set himself at the very center of the household, he must be there in person, not seeing himself as an observer, as I was doing earlier; his imagination must be active, not passive as before. This is a difficult and important psychological moment in the whole period of preparation. It requires exceptional attention. This moment is what we in actor's jargon call the state of 'I am,' it is the point where I begin to feel myself in the thick of things, where I begin to coalesce with all the circumstances suggested by the playwright and by the actor, begin to have the right to be part of them. (*CR*, pp. 25-26)

The actor, as Wiles notes, must "experience and display the character's feelings *as if for the first time* during each performance"; he must search for new ways to experience himself genuinely in each performance as well (p. 22).

The Stanislavskian actor is exceedingly vulnerable, and his relation to the stage is an almost unremittingly ironic one. His commanding imperative is to pursue the authentic freedom of the "I am," but this desire is continually, and often successfully, frustrated by the circumstances of theatrical performance itself. The actor can only "be" as "other"; his authentic "self-betrayal" is both enabled and betrayed by his pursuit of the mask of his role. What such an actor risks in performance is an inadvertent decline into the inartistic and inauthentic, a slide into mere "acting" instead of creative "being." Failing to freshen "a well-prepared but old role," picking up "mechanical habits," or the inability to concentrate through "lazy habits, inattention, poor health, or personal worries" all contribute to the actor's failure to realize his personal vitality onstage. As a result, he becomes an empty "shell" facing the "abyss of the proscenium," in a condition of personal and professional disintegration—of "I am"-not. Instead of pursuing the self-confirming "joy in creation," the actor adopts the conventional attitudes of the theater and suffers the typically Stanislavskian distemper: "he is incapable of speaking, listening, looking, thinking, wishing, feeling, walking, or even moving, in an ordinary human way. He feels a nervous need to gratify the public, to show himself off and to hide his own state" (*AP*, p. 248).

He finds himself in another kind of double bind as well, for the most implacable obstacle to artistic acting on the stage is the public nature of theatrical performance itself. As we have seen, turn-of-the-century stage criticism frequently denies artist status to actors because the actor's necessary self-display seems almost obscenely exhibitionistic. Like his contemporaries in the English theater, Stanislavsky finds the actor's public performance disturbing, and concurs with Walkley, Craig, and others that the stage poses the most "abnormal circumstance of an actor's creative work—it must be done in public" (*AP*, p. 278). Nevertheless, Stanislavsky fully counters the charge of exhibitionism by creating an introspective acting technique, one that regards artistic acting both as the valuable and dignified expression of the actor's identity, and as the powerful representation of his dramatic character. For this reason, the Stanislavskian actor strenuously avoids the impulse toward gratuitous exhibitionism, a danger imposed on his performance by the conventions of the theater and not inherent in acting itself. The actor purposefully violates Walkley's sense of decorum, realizing himself as an artist by exposing himself deeply and spontaneously on the stage:

Yet strangely enough, when we step on to the stage we lose our natural endowment and instead of acting creatively we proceed to perform contortions of pretentious proportions. What drives us to do this? The condition of having to create something in public view. Forced, conventional untruthfulness is implicit in stage presentation, in the foisting on us of the acts and words prescribed by an author, the scenery designed by a painter, the production devised by a director, in our own embarrassment, stage fright, the poor taste and false traditions which cramp our natures. All these impel an actor to exhibitionism, insincere representation. The approach we have chosen—the art of living a part—rebels with all the strength it can muster against those other current "principles" of acting. We assert the contrary principle that the main factor in any form of creativeness is the life of a human spirit, that of the actor and his part, their joint feelings and subconscious creation. (*BC*, pp. 279-80)

The theater urges its conventions on the histrionic artist, and encourages exhibitionistic display. Artistic acting, on the other hand, testifies to the actor's integrity, since it "cannot be 'exhibited.' . . . All you can 'exhibit' on the stage is the artificial, contrived results of a non-existent experience" (*BC*, p. 280). The actor who tries to "run away from himself and renounce his own ego,"[34] or who acts only "for the purpose of entertaining the spectators,"[35] invalidates himself personally and artistically by ignoring the kind of self-engagement that sustains acting as an art form. Jonas Barish is right to suggest that Stanislavsky "wishes to detheatricalize the theater entirely" by denying its legitimate claim to the artificial, the mimetic, the exaggerated (p. 344). But Stanislavsky's project can more fairly be considered as an attempt to accommodate the theater to the prevailing attitudes of Romantic art, mainly through his redefinition of the actor. Although Stanislavsky recognizes that "the actor's artistic force is considerably retarded by the visual auditorium and the public, whose presence may hamper his outward freedom of movement, and powerfully hinder his concentration on his own artistic taste," his notion of the actor's "public solitude" attempts to reconcile the artist's need for creative autonomy with the invalidating publicness of the stage. When the actor's attention

> is taken away from the spectator, he gains a particular power over the audience, grips it, and compels it to take an active share in his artistic existence. This does not mean, of course, that the actor must altogether cease to feel the public; but the public is concerned only in so far as it neither exerts pressure on him nor diverts him unnecessarily from the artistic demands of the moment, which last might happen to him even while knowing how to regulate his attention.[36]

Finally, Stanislavsky's conception of the actor reveals his mistrust of the material dimension of his stage. Stanislavsky tends to suspect the physically apparent, the manifest; in psychological terms, he regards the subconscious rather than the conscious mind as the motivating source of histrionic art. As David Magarshack has ably demonstrated, the core of Stanislavsky's system of actor-training is concerned with improving the performer's ability to externalize "the subconscious through the conscious" (p. 53), so that he may express the hidden, "largely subconscious life" (*AP*, p. 15) of modern dramatic characters. Genuine identity originates in the nearly inaccessible subconscious, where "our mysterious 'I' has its being" (*CR*, p. 81), and only the actor who is "capable of awakening, in a subconscious way we can hardly understand, the intuition which takes hold of the imagination" will realize that identity on the stage, "will no longer 'play' but act, that is to say, create."[37] Rather mystically, Stanislavsky argues that the actor's engagement of his subconscious justifies the entire *mise en scène*, by creating a living relationship between the actor and the material world of the stage. Much like Borkman or Hedda, Stanislavsky's actor is alienated from his physical milieu, and must attempt to bridge the inner and outer worlds of the play. This was the lesson that Chekhov's drama held for the Moscow Art Theater, that there could be a reciprocal vitality between the actor's living performance and the "life of things" onstage:

> Chekhov discovered to us the life of things and sounds, thanks to which all that was lifeless, dead and unjustified in the details of production, all that in spite of our desires created an outward naturalism, turned of itself into living and artistic realism, and the properties that surrounded us on the stage took on an inner relationship with the soul of the actor. (*LA*, p. 350)

The skeptical regard that Stanislavsky turns toward the expressive capabilities of the physical theater extends to his understanding of theatrical language as well. To Stanislavsky, "Ordinary speech—as in life, so on the stage—is prosaic and monotonous," and requires the informing vitality of the subtext to become an adequate vehicle for theatrical communication (*DA*, p. 28). The subtext, not the text, creates and shapes dramatic meaning. The idea of subtextual meaning substantially innovates the rhetorical orientation of the dramatic tradition. Shakespearean language, for instance, asserts an equivalence between intention and expression; a character's language always seems adequate to his purpose, even when his purpose is to deceive.[38] The Stanislavskian subtext, though, implies that language alone is inadequate to theatrical communication, that it negates or distorts the speaker's meaning, concealing it from himself and from his listeners on- and offstage. As Marianna Stroëva suggests, the subtext is always opposed to the meaning of the text it motivates, containing those meanings not capable of being rendered in language.[39]

As a whole, Stanislavsky's writing on the theater declares a complex of ethical imperatives that define the actor and his art. The actor becomes an artist only when he pursues his own authentic identity through histrionic performance. *Pursues* is a key word here, for the actor labors to achieve this elusive art within the baffling confines of a theater that is hostile to his efforts. Working within the conventions of the stage, the actor must engage his personal subconscious in an effort to transform the inexpressiveness of the text, the requirements of the theater, and the matériel of his stage world. His own preparation, while readying him for artistic acting, is an implicit restriction as well, for the actor embodies a deterministic model of character fundamentally at odds with the autonomous performance he attempts to create onstage. The critical engagement of the self alone permits spontaneous stage action, a kind of acting that liberates the actor from the inauthenticating limitations of the theater and of the theater audience, and makes his performance meaningful. As Shaw recognized, the modern audience seeks this "metaphysical self-realization" in the theater. The audience participates in theatrical play in the hope, however provisional or attenuated, that its own sense of being will be reinforced through the actor's effort and example. In his extensive reconsideration of the practice of the stage, Stanislavsky envisions such a theater, and creates the histrionic art that can sustain it. He places a modern actor on the modern stage.

Since Stanislavsky, modern acting theory has profitably elaborated the actor's alienation from the conventional theater and from the naturalistic stage. Much as Fanny Kemble had done, theorists insistently set the actor's self-realizing performance against the empty role-playing of modern life, both in and out of the theater. In his article on acting in the *Encyclopaedia Britannica* (14th ed., 1929), for instance, Max Reinhardt explicitly opposes creative stage acting to its social counterpart: "The art of the stage affords . . . liberation from the conventional drama of life, for it is not dissimulation that is the business of the play but revelation. Only the actor who cannot lie, who is himself undisguised, and who profoundly unlocks his heart deserves the laurel."[40] Stanislavsky defines the paradoxes of modern acting: theatrical versus the real, acting versus being, public versus private, the theater versus the actor. Modern acting theory upsets the stable equilibrium between the provisional reality of the stage and the actuality of the world around it, though, for the major theorists of acting—Brecht, Artaud, Grotowski—reject a theater whose mission is simply to represent. Instead, they urge the theater to create reality, by forcing the actor to create himself. Stanislavsky's student Vsevolod Meyerhold could envision the stage as a purely histrionic arena, a place for acting rather than representation. In "The Stylized Theater" (1907), Meyerhold argues that stylization liberates

> the actor from all scenery, creating a three-dimensional area in which he can employ natural, sculptural plasticity. Thanks to stylization, we can do away with complicated stage machinery, and mount simple productions in which the actor can interpret his role free from all scenery and specifically *theatrical* properties—free from all purely incidental trappings.[41]

The actor's performance becomes real by being released from its theatrical limitations. The necessary accouterments of the theater—scenery, properties, mechanical effects, perhaps even dramatic roles—are now "incidental," peripheral to the theater's relentless attention to the actor himself.

The modern actor inhabits an existential stage, and the most vivid account of acting in the empty space is not Meyerhold's or Peter Brook's but Sartre's. Jonas Barish has remarked that Sartre's understanding of *authentic* action, the refusal to "settle for a hand-me-down part, one fashioned by others," is intrinsically theatrical, and bears extensively on the project of the modern stage (p. 476). Sartre rebels against the deterministic vision of a composed "character" or personality, and sees identity as "a series of undertakings," not as a fixed psychological entity. Unlike the Stanislavskian role, entwined in "the *past* which justifies the *pres-*

ent," Sartrian character actively repudiates the past. To the extent that "the meaning of the past is strictly dependent on my present project,"

> . . . I alone in fact can decide at each moment the *bearing* of the past. I do not decide it by debating it, by deliberating over it, and in each instance evaluating the importance of this or that prior event; but by projecting myself toward my ends, I preserve the past with me, and by action I *decide* its meaning.[42]

Many of the characters of modern drama, struggling to understand the past, are caught between a Stanislavskian and a Sartrian ontology; the past stands in an uncertain relation to their present actions. For the actor, though, this pursuit of authentic identity is even more problematic than it is for his role. For Sartre's rejection of "psychological determinism" questions both the nature of dramatic character and the dynamics of Stanislavskian performance. To the extent that his preparation "attempts to fill the void which encircles us, to re-establish the links between past and present, between present and future," the actor's performance enacts an invalidating and psychologically determined vision of character and identity. He creates his role's actions as the result of a preconceived "character" and sees his own performance as conditioned by his extensive preparation (*Being and Nothingness*, pp. 78-79). If the actor's preparation provides an explanatory "*nature* productive of [his] acts," it makes those acts "transcendent; it assigns to them a foundation in something other than themselves by endowing them with an inertia and externality eminently reassuring because they constitute a permanent game of *excuses*." In this sense, the Stanislavskian actor's presentation of the "*past* which justifies the *present*" of his performance is inauthentic, a form of "bad faith." But to the extent that his performance *decides* the bearing of the past, confronts his preparation and recreates its relation to the performance itself, his enactment becomes an immediate undertaking of identity, his own and his role's.

The Sartrian actor pursues the Stanislavskian "I am," but conceives of the self/role complex rather differently than Stanislavsky does. Much like Brecht, Sartre dispenses with the theater of "character" and calls instead "For a Theater of Situations" (1947). "Psychological theater," he announces, entails the inevitable "decline of tragic forms. A conflict of characters, whatever turns you may give it, is never anything but a composition of forces whose results are predictable." Traditional character is static, formed, decided; Sartre innovates dramatic character by arguing for "the most moving thing the theater can show . . . a character creating himself, the moment of choice, of the free decision which commits him to a moral code and a whole way of life."[43]

But while Sartre requires the drama to demonstrate the character's moment of choice, no such moment of free decision is possible for Sartre's actor; finally, for Sartre, representation and authentic action are irreconcilable. In "The Actor" (1971), a brilliant rethinking of Diderot's *Paradox*, Sartre defines the actor's task: "to make an absent or fictitious object manifest through the totality of his individuality, treating himself as a painter treats his canvas and palette." The actor gathers unreality into himself, and his behavior is largely dictated by this nonexistent simulacrum of being: "to the true actor each new character becomes a temporary *imago*, a parasite living in symbiosis with him even when he is not on stage and at times unrealizing him when he is about his daily business off the stage by dictating attitudes to him." The actor sacrifices his own being in order to create the image of authentic action for his audience. He is the radical archetype of the inauthentic, denying himself for "the existence of an *appearance*" to the extent that he "becomes a medium for nonbeing" (pp. 162-65). To both Stanislavsky and Sartre, the actor's histrionic project is continually threatened by its inevitable involvement with the fictitious, the unreal. But Sartre's actor unrealizes "himself into the reality he has won" rather than discovering himself against the unreality of the stage (p. 170). Whereas the Stanislavskian actor achieves authentic art through self-realization against the theater, Sartre's actor most fully pursues his project of being when he is entirely unrealized, absent. He creates himself authentically only by abnegating himself entirely to the artifice of the stage.

Sartre's skeptical sense of acting denies the actor all but the most contingent dignity or identity. In many respects, though, his theory has yet to be fully explored, for the major theoreticians of the stage have continued to demand some form of presence from the actor. Artaud's *The Theater and its Double* (1938) is a case in point. Artaud's electric vision of theatrical release is best understood as a perception of theatrical potentiality, not as a systematic body of practical advice. Nevertheless, though he rejects the goals of Stanislavskian naturalism, Artaud extensively reinterprets the histrionic project of the Stanislavsky actor. Instead of performing his creative "I am" by bringing the subconscious to the conscious mind, the "cruel" actor attempts to perform a "true act" by engaging a more primary, "archetypal and dangerous reality."[44] Artaud authenticates the actor's performance by redefining his unrealization. Rather than playing a fictitious role, the actor expresses his subconscious identity directly in performance, ignoring the mediating conventions of the traditional theater. Artaud's priorities place authentic identity in a racial or archetypal unconscious, and the actor substitutes this unconscious for conscious motivation, so that his performance can avoid the derivative patterns of rational thought. Artaud capitalizes on Stanislavsky's use of the motivating subconscious, and he also exploits Stanislavsky's commitment to the life beneath the moribund conventions of language and behavior. Arguing that "beneath the poetry of the texts, there is the actual poetry, without form and without text" (p. 78), Artaud specifies a theater and an actor whose combined purpose is to recover that poetry, the "fragile, fluctuating center" of life that social "forms never reach":

> To break through language in order to touch life is to create or recreate the theater; the essential thing is not to believe that this act must remain sacred, i.e., set apart. (p. 13)

As Charles Marowitz discovered in his experimental "Theater of Cruelty" at LAMDA for the Royal Shakespeare Company (1963), Artaud's diffuse theory largely extends the Stanislavsky actor's "work on himself" into new territory. Both kinds of acting "rely on consciousness to release the unconscious, but whereas the Method actor is chained to rational motivation, the Artaudian actor realizes the highest artistic truth is unprovable." Unlike Stanislavskian acting, with its rationalized "beats" of desire, Artaudian acting dispenses with conscious motivation entirely. As Marowitz suggests, Artaud's " 'fragile, fluctuating centre that forms never reach' refers to states beyond the reach of *linguistic* forms, but accessible by other kinds." Like Stanislavsky, Artaud intends to penetrate the social surface of language to release its explosive, irrational subtext, its primitive vitality: "The potential superiority of an Artaudian theatre—compared even to an over-hauled and much-improved realistic theatre—lies in the fact that its language is not yet discovered, therefore not yet tarnished and empty."[45] Artaud redefines the actor's realization as the onstage discovery of this primitive, unsocialized self.

The search for Artaud's undiscovered language has occupied some of the richest efforts of post-war acting theory. Artaud's theater is anti-mimetic, anti-representational; it locates the bedrock of theater in an immediate stage experience that comprehends the audience's reality in the heightened reality of the performance itself. This sense of theater, elaborated most convincingly in Jerzy Grotowski's "poor theater," informs the range of theatrical experimentation in the radical theater of the 1960s and 1970s. Many of these experiments can be thought of as voicing Stanislavsky's concerns in a more rigorous, Artaudian manner. The Ted Hughes-Peter Brook *Orghast* (1971) production in the ruins at Persepolis, for instance, dramatizes Stanislavsky's anxiety regarding theater language. By combining a poetic language invented for the occasion with an equally pristine lexicon of "archetypal" gestures, *Orghast* attempted to overcome the complicity of all languages in conventional social action.[46] Various attempts to inaugurate a ritualistic theater develop Artaud's search for the transcendent reality that ritual typically enacts. Even the participatory efforts of The Living Theater and The Performance Group touch on Stanislavsky's sense of the give and take between actor and spectator. In attempting, in Richard Schechner's words, to "humanize relationships between performers and spectators," participatory theater extends Stanislavsky's insistence that the audience be in creative sympathy with the actor, and that it refrain from imposing preconceived forms on his performance.[47] Of course, these experiments clearly depart from most of the stylistic and political impulses of Stanislavsky's theater, but in their conception of the actor's task, these efforts extend some of the Stanislavsky actor's essential obligations—to pursue being in performance, to reject the conventional stage—to their final ramifications.

Like Stanislavsky, Grotowski develops his theatrical theory out of the practical work of a performing company. In a sense, Grotowski's actor presents a Stanislavskian reply to the Sartrian actor. Grotowski's actor sacrifices himself to the audience's perception of real being, but instead of playing a fictitious, negating "character," he performs the authentic, immediate revelation of himself. Although Grotowski's actor plays a role in performance, he "must learn to use his role as if it were a surgeon's scalpel, to dissect himself":

> It is not a question of portraying himself under certain given circumstances, or of "living" a part; nor does it entail the distant sort of acting common to epic theatre and based on

cold calculation. The important thing is to use the role as a trampolin, an instrument with which to study what is hidden behind our everyday mask—the innermost core of our personality—in order to sacrifice it, expose it. (*PT*, p. 37)

Much like earlier theorists, Grotowski examines the actor/role complex. And as Richard Schechner suggests in *Environmental Theater* (1973), the principal difference between the Grotowskian actor and his Stanislavskian ancestors is one of perspective. To illustrate, Schechner briefly contrasts the traditional "Olivier" actor (though Olivier might well balk at being labeled "Stanislavskian") and the experimental theater's "performer":

> When Olivier plays Othello, he finds in his own life aspects that are relevant to Othello's life. Olivier may use emotional recall so that at a given moment—say when Othello discovers that Desdemona is innocent—the "proper emotion" is displayed. Olivier recalls the precise circumstances of some deep loss in his own life. Recollecting these brings tears to Olivier's eyes. The audience sees Othello weeping.
>
> In environmental theater the situation is reversed. Using the action of the character as his focus, the performer illuminates his own life. The audience sees the performer through the prism of the character. (p. 224)

As Grotowski's most visible American proponent throughout the '70s, Schechner polemically polarizes the two actors here, overstating the divergent emphases of Stanislavskian and Grotowskian performance. Grotowski's theater reveals the actor's identity more overtly; it innovates the relation between actor and role only in the degree that it depresses the primary importance of the role, and heightens our perception of the actor's independent identity as a theatrical value. The actor/role balance is differently weighed in each theater, but both require the actor's genuine self-discovery on the stage. (Schechner himself notes as much in his controversial review of "The Decline and Fall of the [American] Avant-Garde," where he remembers that many of his Performance Group's training exercises and performance routines simply "took Stanislavski's and Strasberg's ideas of 'public solitude' or 'private moment' further—and brought these exercises out of workshop and into public performances.")[48]

Like his Stanislavskian counterpart, Grotowski's actor performs by overcoming external obstacles to self-revelation. To perform the "total act" that validates Grotowski's theater (*PT*, p. 131), the actor avoids any action that substitutes a socially or theatrically conventional behavior for a spontaneous one. Because Grotowski's company creates its own texts—either by fragmenting and distorting an extant play like *Doctor Faustus*, or by shuffling together a mélange of texts and stories, as in their *Apocalypsis cum figuris*—the performance is a direct outgrowth of the actors' interests. In performance, Grotowski urges the actor to ask, " 'What are the obstacles blocking you on your way towards the total act which must engage all your psycho-physical resources, from the most instinctive to the most rational?' . . . What resistances are there? How can they be eliminated? I want to take away, steal from the actor all that disturbs him. That which is creative will remain within him" (*PT*, p. 209). Again Schechner's sense of the "performer" (note that he *performs* himself, rather than *acting* a role), explicates Grotowski's rather vatic pronouncements more plainly: "The performer does not play a role . . . so much as remove resistances and blocks that prevent him from acting through, wholly following, the impulses that come from within him in response to the actions of a role. In performing, the role remains itself, the performer remains himself"; actor and character have equal status (p. 128).

The modern performer is a Romantic innocent struggling to discover himself through the prism of histrionic performance. Not surprisingly, Grotowski also presents his actor in an ambivalent relation to the spectator: "If the actor has the spectator as

his point of orientation . . . he will be offering himself for sale.
. . . A sort of prostitution, bad taste." Yet the actor cannot
retreat into private performance, for the audience's presence trans-
lates the actor's otherwise gratuitous narcissism into a legitimate
act of sacrificial self-realization:

> But I think the essential thing is that the actor must not act
> for the audience, he must act *vis-à-vis* with the spectators, in
> the presence of the spectators he must do an even more au-
> thentic act in place of the spectators, do an act of extreme yet
> disciplined sincerity and authenticity. He must give himself
> and not hold himself back, open up and not close in on himself
> in a narcissistic way.[49]

Grotowski's sacrificial actor consummates an entire tradition.
Like Irving's actor sounding "the gamut of human sensibility,"
the Grotowski actor risks in an extreme form both exhibitionistic
exposure and offensive narcissism onstage. If successful, he performs the "total act" that sustains Grotowski's theater, the "act
of laying oneself bare, of tearing off the mask of daily life, of
exteriorizing oneself" (*PT*, p. 210). This act requires a remarkably
spare theater; the Lab Theater's productions demand a small audience, few props, no scenery, little lighting, and often dispense
with the stage platform in favor of other, less "theatrical" ways
of deploying actors and audiences. Clearly, Grotowski intends
his theater to evade the tarnished staginess of the traditional
theater as far as possible. The "total act" requires the actor's
"extreme confrontation" with himself, a "sincere, disciplined,
precise and total" act of commitment that engages his "whole
being from his instincts and his unconscious right up to his most
lucid state" (*PT*, p. 57). The actor's utter hazard, and potential
gain, of himself through acting is both the means and end of
Grotowski's theater, whose essential subject is the actor himself.

But for many spectators—and theorists—this kind of theater
eschews the traditional values of the stage so entirely that it can

hardly be recognized as theater at all. The conflation of the actor and his role, the invitation to participate, the lack of spectacle, and the defictionalizing of the stage space often seem to invite a reality that the artifice of the theater should imitate, but not create. And as much contemporary drama implies, the act of self-realization itself may seem increasingly irrelevant to us. As Michael Goldman suggests in *The Actor's Freedom*, the indistinct boundary between the experimental actor's self and his dramatic role reflects "the epistemological crisis of our era, in which the self is seen to be lost among its means of knowledge, indeed in which our methods for knowing the world and articulating the self finally cut us off from both world and self."[50] Although Shaw could confidently urge the actor's "metaphysical self-realization" on the stage as an invigorating image of affective vitality, the contemporary actor's performance tends to disperse rather than to confirm the presence of a guiding self. The contemporary theater's radical identification between role and performer both affirms and denies the presence of a coherent self behind the mask.

The breakdown of the self has been anticipated by the dismantling of dramatic character urged by a host of playwrights, Strindberg, Pirandello, Beckett, Handke, among others. The theorist who most cogently relates the decomposition of character to the actor's project stands firmly apart from the Stanislavskian theater—Bertolt Brecht. The changing geography of Brecht's theater theory has been well mapped by a number of critics, and its effect on the modern stage surely needs no rehearsal. Here, we should consider how Brecht's sense of the actor's "alienated" or "estranged" relation to his role redirects the ethic of modern stage performance.

We can take initial bearings on Brecht from his late essay, "Some of the Things that can be Learnt from Stanislavsky" (1952). Free from some of the polemical necessities of his earlier writing, Brecht here suggests Stanislavsky's influence on his own sense of theater, and on the aesthetic of alienation. Brecht is impressed by the concrete detail of Stanislavsky's productions, Stanislavsky's pursuit of precise "social meaning" onstage. In this vein, Brecht commends the actor's "exact knowledge of himself and of the men he sets out to portray," as well as Stanislavsky's commitment to artistic truth, to the ensemble instead of the star, to coherent and unified production, and to relentless experimentation. Surprisingly, perhaps, Stanislavsky's thorough presentation of character in environment anticipates Brecht's fascination with action in its social context. Brecht especially praises Stanislavsky's grasp of "the diversity and complexity of social life," finding that he "knew how to represent it without getting entangled. All his productions make sense."[51]

Brecht builds his theater around a specific vision of the actor. Although the technical devices of Brecht's theater—the screens, placards, half-curtain, open lighting—openly proclaim the epic theater's assault on naturalistic values, Brecht's commanding innovation lies in his refinement of a kind of acting that changes the fundamental relationship between the actor and his audience. The cardinal principle of Brechtian acting is, of course, the actor's evident estrangement from his own emotions and from the role he plays. The actor's frank acceptance of the public nature of the theater, and of the inevitable artificiality of theatrical performance, marks his furthest remove from the Stanislavsky actor, struggling to make his every action as immediate, as real as possible. While Stanislavsky's actor retreats from the illusions of the stage into "public solitude," Brecht's actor cheerfully exploits both the didactic potential of the stage and the conventions that it provides. He draws the spectator's attention to the fact that he *is* acting, playing a role rather than "living a part." As Brecht notes in *A Short Organum for the Theatre* (1948-49), the actor continually "narrates the story of his character . . . always knowing more than it does and treating its 'now' and 'here' not as a pretence made possible by the rules of the game but as something to be distinguished from yesterday and some other place, so as to make visible the knotting-together of the events" (p. 194). The actor relates his character's actions to their consequences, in order to communicate to his audience a critical perspective on the character's deeds. Though the actor avoids the subconsciously motivated spontaneity of Stanislavskian acting, his performance is nonetheless immediate, taking place *now*. In "Alienation Effects in Chinese Acting" (1936), Brecht argues that his audience should identify "itself with the actor as being an observer" (p. 93). That is, the spectator recognizes the actor's performance as an immediate criticism of the part he presents, a direct communication concerning the dramatic role. The actor's endeavor succeeds only to the extent that he can make "real contact with his new audience" through a "passionate concern for human progress" ("From a Letter to an Actor," p. 235).

Like Stanislavsky, Artaud, and Grotowski, then, Brecht denigrates representation that obstructs the immediacy of the theater. His actors pursue an actual relationship with the audience during performance. But whereas Stanislavsky calls for the actor's authentic self-realization to sustain the theatrical project, Brecht locates the actor's reality in his conscious manipulation of theatrical artifice. The most disabling aspect of performance to the Stanislavskian actor is his inevitable alienation from the theater. Brecht provides the actor with a way to exploit this rift, to turn estrangement to positive ends. By actively distancing himself from his role, the actor is released from the sentimental limitations of conventional "character," and from the unexamined stereotypes of the theater. Through estrangement, Brecht's actor decides his relationship to the audience; he is free to criticize, even to contradict, the role he plays. Although Brecht does not question the actor's existential authenticity, he requires his actor to forego Sartrian "unrealization" by distinguishing him so clearly from his role in performance. In this restricted sense, Brecht demands that the performer actualize himself in the theater, make his critical attitude effectively evident on the stage.

But can he? Can Brecht's actor realize *himself* on the stage, or merely another role, the obligatory mask of the Brechtian actor? The actor's critical stance is in many ways simply a function of the role he plays, rather than an expression of personal attitudes. The role decides how the underlying mask of the "Brechtian actor" will be seen. Would it be possible to know Helene Weigel, even theoretically, from a production of *Mother Courage*, or even to be assured of her personal attitude toward Courage herself? Not really. We could, though, assemble a collection of *gests* critical of Anna Fierling, each aroused and demonstrated through a particular deed. Would these attitudes necessarily reveal an individual vision of Courage, the impress of a self behind Courage's mask? In a sense, Brecht's actor is reminiscent of Sartre's, utterly concealed behind his double mask.

Actually, Brecht's sense of the bearing of the actor's identity on performance is better seen in another light, in the theatricalized vision of interactional psychology and sociology. In Erving Goffman's studies, for instance, the figure of the actor repeatedly phrases an understanding of the relationship between self, role, and situation. Goffman's actor is uncommitted to any role, and, like Schweyk perhaps, achieves stability not through self-discovery, but by presenting himself in the part which most adequately suits his current performance. Like Brecht, Goffman understands the self to be significant only in the context of a specific theatrical "frame," a particular context of social performance. Goffman's actor is released both from the Romantic commitment to self-discovery and from the existential impulse to decide his identity at every turn. To Goffman, the actor images the irrelevance of an irreducible sense of self. The social actor subordinates identity to the theatrical requirements of an inexorably stagey world.

In *Frame Analysis* (1974), for example, Goffman explicitly views the sense of self as a function of the roles we play. To be recognized as a role, a role must suggest that it is a role. But as Goffman rightly argues, it is in the nature of roles to imply that there is a face beneath the mask:

> It is hardly possible to talk about the anchoring of doings in the world without seeming to support the notion that a person's acts are in part an expression and outcome of his perduring self, and that this self will be present behind the particular roles he plays at any particular moment. After all, from any and all of our dealings with an individual we acquire a sense of his personality, his character, his quality as a human being. We come to expect that all his acts will exhibit the same style, be stamped in a unique way.[52]

We interpret the people we meet outside the theater in much the way we interpret a Rosmer or a Vanya created by a Stanislavskian actor. From scene to scene, we construct the guiding "through action" that seems to connect each presentation with the last, building a consistent character that inhabits the various roles we witness. Each of a person's presentations seems to afford us a view of something anterior, a glimpse of what seems to be the actor behind the mask, the true self. But to Goffman, "this discrepancy between person and role, this interstice through which a self peers, this human effect, need no more depend upon the world beyond the current situation than does the role itself" (p. 298). Man plays his proper role in a variety of situations, and in every situation the role seems to afford this glimpse of who he "really is." But do we have a compelling reason to assemble these gleanings into a composite "self," since they are, after all, simply aspects, side effects, of the roles that various situations have required? Not to Goffman:

> that is no reason to think that all these gleanings about himself that an individual makes available, all these pointings from his current situation to the way he is in his other occasions, have anything very much in common. Gleanings about an

individual point beyond the situation to what presumably will be found in all other gleanings of him, but one cannot say that they point in the same direction, for it is their very nature to make themselves felt as pointing in the same direction.

(p. 299)

Although he lacks Brecht's controlling moral purpose, Goffman articulates the nature of alienated performance, from both the actor's and the audience's point of view. We don't see the Brechtian actor himself, we are not asked to see him in the way that we are presumably invited to know the actors of *Akropolis* or of *Dionysus in 69*. We see a face that is actuated by the role it performs. The mask of Mother Courage, of Herr Puntila, of Shen Te, enables us to "glean" a face, the one that the actor makes available to us. And much as we can never dissolve Shen Te and Shui Ta into a single Stanislavskian character, so too we can never finally penetrate the Brechtian actor's double mask.

Brecht's alienated acting and the vision of the self it implies have encouraged a substantial revision of the actor's project, one that rivals, and occasionally joins, the Stanislavsky-Artaud-Grotowski lineage I advanced earlier. Let me return to Charles Marowitz's notes for the "Theater of Cruelty" season to suggest one point of confluence. When auditioning, Marowitz asked each actor to bring a prepared text:

> The actor is asked to perform his two-minute set-piece in his own way without suggestions or interference. Once he has done this, he is given a new character and a new situation and asked to play these, still retaining the text of his original speech. (An actor who comes along with "To be or not to be . . ." is asked to play King Lear in the heath scene, or Romeo in the balcony scene, *through* the Hamlet text.) The task is for the actor to throw himself into a completely different set of circumstances (to improvise) and yet to retain control over his original text (to operate formally). Once the actor has managed

to create a smattering of the new character and the new situation, he is given yet another character and a different situation . . . until he has three balls to juggle at once: his original choice, the first variation, and the second variation. The actor is then given cue-words which refer to each of his characters, and he is asked to switch rapidly between the three different situations without breaking the flow of his original text.

(pp. 164-65)

As Marowitz goes on to explain, the object of this rather intimidating exercise is to create a discontinuous style of acting, acting that disestablishes our sense of fixed character. The audition applies a sequence of Goffmanesque performance "frames" to distort the actor's role. The actor presents his original text—the basic "self" of the exercise—in a number of situations. In each case, the text remains the same, but is thrown into circumstances that demand a new presentation, a new mask. Does Hamlet's soliloquy reveal the Hamlet of *Hamlet* when it is spoken by Hamlet-as-Lear-on-the-heath? Obviously not. The mask alters the face it presents, changing the purpose and meaning of Hamlet's lines, and altering our perception of the character who speaks them. What matters to Marowitz here is that the actor be able to decide the Sartrian *bearing* of the situation on his text, how performance changes the self he has construed, not that he realize a fully-formed, "built" character in every performance. The question is not the Bradleyan "How would Hamlet act in Lear's place?" but one we might expect from Jan Kott, or even from Jacques Derrida: "How would his performance in King Lear's situation deconstruct Hamlet, force us to see the role as a congeries of contradictory potentialities?"

The priority of role to self is realized in another shape in a recent acting textbook, Robert Cohen's *Acting Power*.[53] Conceiving drama principally as a structure of situations, Cohen presents dramatic style as a kind of language, a medium for communication between actors, characters, and audience. Like the language of the text, the play's dramatic style consists of a system of signs that create meaning only through the articulation of relationships. Similarly, he views performance style—whether naturalistic, Artaudian, "poor," Brechtian, or a reconstructed "Elizabethan" or "Restoration" mode—as another independent matrix of signs, one that makes no personal claims on the actor, and requires no ethical commitment from him. Finally, since dramatic roles are a manifestation of textual and performance signifiers, they require only the actor's skillful manipulation of signs. Dramatic roles make no more claim on the actor's self than other expressive signs do, no more than language, musical notation, or the rules of driving. Indeed, because the actor's performance is entirely a function of his theatrical environment, his acting has no bearing on his self-awareness at all, nor does it imply any relation between his identity and the provisional reality of his dramatic role. Free from the imperative to act authentically, the actor is fully restored to the theater. He uses the conventions of the theater at will, harmonizing with the role-playing demands of the stage, and of the world at large. Both inside and outside the theater, the actor is the representative signifying man, cleverly exploiting the arbitrary conventions of his endless performance.

As we can see, the contemporary actor coordinates a sometimes inchoate, always contradictory network of values. Grotowski's actor extends the Stanislavskian commitment to the actor's "I am," rejecting the conventional theater and its falsifying role-playing in order to use his role as a scalpel, to discover and realize himself more truly to the audience. The theater permits a real enactment that is impossible elsewhere in society, among what Shaw called "the false lights and simulated interests and passions of the street." The Goffmanesque actor of Cohen's book, on the other hand, provides a more perfect emblem of disengaged social performance than any of us are likely to achieve, trapped as we are within the inevitable illusion of our own selfhood. Does the actor decide himself truly by pursuing self-realization on the stage, or instead by attuning himself entirely to the requirements of role-playing? Many recent plays dramatize this paradox, insistently opposing the wreck of naturalistic character with the not altogether attractive alternative of relentless role-playing. Pinter dramatizes this dialectic repeatedly, as his characters struggle to enforce a version of themselves—a manifestly fictitious "character"—on others unwilling to accept it. *The Homecoming*, for instance, pits Teddy (who wants to play a kind of upbeat *Ghosts*, a return home that shows just how far he has gone), against Ruth, who easily manipulates the present performance by concentrating on her role in it, rather than on the self she has come to be. David Mamet's *A Life in the Theatre* phrases this antithesis more schematically. The play counterpoints the relationship between Robert (an older actor on the skids of his career) and John (a young actor on the verge of his first big break) and the plays they perform for the public. Throughout the play, Mamet alternates scenes from backstage—in which Robert and John play themselves, i.e., star and understudy, mentor and apprentice, aging lord and young turk—with scenes from the plays they perform onstage every evening. Which set of scenes expresses the relationship between the two actors? Obviously, for us, the answer is both sets, the combined performance of their life in the theater. Examples multiply: think of Bond's Brechtian theater of situations, Stoppard's juxtaposition of divergent planes of theatrical reality in *Jumpers* and *Rosencrantz and Guildenstern Are Dead*, Handke's drama of signifiers, *The Ride Across Lake Constance*, the blurring of self and role in Weiss's *Marat/Sade*, the communal self of van Itallie's *The Serpent*. This version of role-playing presupposes no particular performance style. Indeed, it informs the creative tension between self and role in an otherwise conventional recent film, *My Dinner With André*. Grotowski's presence as André's mentor is thoroughly implicated in the film's design, which exploits the absorbing borders between film roles ("Wally" and

"André"), the actors who play them (listed in the credits as "Wallace Shawn" and "André Gregory"), and the real Mr. Shawn and Mr. Gregory who are fictionalized, represented and distorted, by the film. Contemporary theory rearticulates the problem of modern acting as it is first phrased in the 1880s. The actor is at once seen as an authentic performer and as a stagey charlatan. Where our vision has altered is in our acceptance of his harlequinade as an apt metaphor for our own stagey lives.

Rosmersholm

In many respects, the major roles of Ibsen's drama anticipate the dialectic of modern acting. The modern actor pursues his sense of "I am" in performance against the conventions of his social and theatrical environment. And as Raymond Williams has noted, Ibsen's characters typically face a similar problem: "What happens, again and again in Ibsen, is that the hero defines an opposing world, full of lies and compromises and dead positions, only to find, as he struggles against it, that as a man he belongs to this world, and has its destructive inheritance in himself."[54] Jonas Barish amplifies Williams's remark, by suggesting that this ambivalent relationship between Ibsen's characters and their dramatic world reveals Ibsen's attitude toward the theater. In one sense, Ibsen often seems to pit "theatrical" roles—characters like Torvald Helmer or George Tesman who "define themselves in accord with clichés inherited from popular drama"—against the more energetic characters (Nora, Hedda) who seem to seek a genuine freedom (p. 451). But though Ibsen frequently opposes his papier mâché villains to more fully realized heroes, more often he locates this dialectic within the hero himself, or herself. Ibsen's heroes are caught between an impulse to create the self anew, and a longing to submit to the security of a comfortable, conventional social posture, a melodramatic role; they see the stage both as an arena for authentic self-realization, and as a theater requiring astute role-playing.[55]

Ibsen phrases this inner conflict between self and role through a characteristic form of dramatic action. His drama centers on acts of discovery, on the conscious revelation of social ills, of hidden intention, of the meaning of the past and the present. He unmasks both heroes and villains, revealing how both genuine action and pretentious role-playing are implicated in the compromised stage world. Ibsen's drama is the drama of exposure. To be exposed is to experience an isolation that is at once terrifying and exhilarating. In the most positive case, exposure leads to the robust freedom of Stanislavsky's favorite, Dr. Stockmann—"The thing is, you see, that the strongest man in the world is the man who stands alone."[56] But to be exposed is also to know the bone-chilling mountain waste that lures Brand and Borkman and Rubek, to feel the vertigo of Solness's tower, to hear the paralyzing silence of Helmer's empty home, to face the piano and the pistols in Hedda's desolate parlor. More often than not, Ibsen's dramatic action plays Peer Gynt with his characters, peeling away the onion-like layers of their social posturing.

What this exposure reveals, though, is usually disturbingly ambiguous. Do the characters manage to transcend their roles through a final authentic act, or do they simply reveal the inner hollowness that their role-playing conceals? The dynamics of exposure richly inform the action of *Rosmersholm*, a play that thoroughly counterpoints the hidden and the manifest, the internal and the external. We contrast Rosmer's sheltered liberalism with the *realpolitik* of Kroll and Mortensgaard, Mrs. Helseth's closed windows with Rebecca's birch boughs and flowers, the airless parlor with the wild millrace. As Thomas R. Whitaker remarks in his brilliant reading of the play, the naturalistic box set itself becomes an active metaphor in the play's unfolding action. As the play proceeds, each character tries to stand apart from the action, to be an observing spectator of the events that disclose themselves onstage (Rebecca's concealment in Act 2 is an obvious example). But while each character plays the audience, each character is also playing the actor, is revealed to the others within the confines of the stage world.[57] The set of *Rosmersholm* is an emblem of the theatricality of the play's social world; the performances it contains are largely the public posturings of self-conscious role-players.

Nonetheless, like the Stanislavskian actor, the characters of *Rosmersholm* are searching for a way to perform themselves authentically within the limitations of their stage. First, they attempt to unmask one another, to expose the artificiality of each others' actions by showing them to be false, acted-up. More important, the characters in the play also expose themselves, attempt to show their onstage audience that their actions are authentic, free, self-realizing. Fittingly, *Rosmersholm* proceeds through a series of such ambiguous confessions—of Rosmer's apostasy, of Kroll's role in local politics, of Beata's suffering, of Mrs. Helseth's secret, of Brendel's inadequacy, of Rebecca's mortal duel with Beata—culminating in the play's final exposure, the recognition that leads Rosmer and Rebecca to the millrace. In the course of *Rosmersholm*, each character—Brendel, Kroll, Rosmer, Rebecca, Mortensgaard, even Mrs. Helseth—attempts to capitalize on the dramatic effect of a surprising self-disclosure. Time and again the characters report their motives, their secret intentions to one another, usually in order to present their actions as free and genuine, unconstrained by convention, social opinion, or guilt. A minor character like Ulrik Brendel provides a simple paradigm. Ibsen undercuts Brendel's hypocritical idealism throughout the play, and yet Brendel clearly thinks himself to be involved in an entirely sincere program of self-renovation. By undertaking his lecture tour, Brendel hopes to "put on a new man," overcoming his feeling that he sacrifices the "purity" of his private ideals by making them public (1, 309, 310). Of course, Brendel's disdain of the commoners and his blithe beggary at Rosmersholm suggest that such public action is foreign to his nature, and raise the suspicion that his plans will reveal his dependency rather than his freedom. The play dramatizes the discrepancy between Brendel's character and the role he has chosen to play, his inadequacy for authentic performance.

Kroll's confessions are more complex and contradictory. As the spokesman for the conservative public that lurks on the frontiers of *Rosmersholm*, Kroll sees himself as the savior of customary values, much as Brendel, ironically enough, sees himself as a Pauline "new man."[58] The derivativeness of his ethical perspective is partly suggested in the willingness with which he, not Rosmer, invokes the "Rosmers of Rosmersholm" as a moral standard (1, 305). But unlike Brendel, Kroll is a powerfully destructive figure in the play, and his strength stems from an urgent sense of personal isolation. Kroll has been harshly severed from the nourishing social life that had given him definition and purpose. His home is "lost" to him permanently (1, 312), his students are increasingly intractable, and his respectable brother-in-law has become suspiciously remote. To Kroll, the coherent and sustaining institutions of society have been fully eroded. "Things can never be as they were before" for Kroll, and his savage determination to establish his own vision of the future (by reestablishing the past) lends his actions—in contrast to the airy plans of Brendel and Rosmer—a desperate and uncompromising ruthlessness. Kroll is, in effect, an actor battling to regain his stage.

Rosmer and Rebecca also pursue self-fulfillment in the play, and the fine irony with which their relationship is presented poses one of the central problems of *Rosmersholm*. Brendel appears onstage only twice in the play; both times his stagey revelations interrupt Rosmer's similar confessions of moral purpose, and incarnate a parody of them. Like Brendel's, Rosmer's mission— "liberating" the minds and "purifying" the wills of his countrymen (1, 314)—requires an extroversion belied by his intensely private nature. As Kroll recognizes, Rosmer is "not cut out for that sort of work" (2, 329). And Rosmer's plans are much more reminiscent of Brendel's vague project than they are of Kroll's pragmatic program. Unlike Kroll's politics, Rosmer's private apostasy provides him with a new feeling of belonging, a new-found sense of community, a "home" as Kroll notes (1, 312). As Rosmer suggests, "I shall not be entirely alone, after all" (1, 316); he has learned well from Brendel, and in confessing his freedom to Kroll, he confesses to the audience his real need for a home, his dependence on the sustaining will of Beata and Rebecca. Rosmer's performance is shaped by his stage, while Kroll's performance transforms his.

Rebecca West is by far the most subversive character in the play, and while *Rosmersholm* doesn't really recall the theatrical reflexivity of *Six Characters* or *Hamlet*, many of the qualities that make Rebecca an unstable and dangerous character are those she shares with the Victorian actress. As her careful maneuvering with Kroll in the opening scene suggests, Rebecca is capable of disingenuous, manipulative role-playing. But she is more profoundly threatening, as an exile from conventional society, as an educated working woman, in her free thinking and plain speaking, and especially in her easy intimacy with Rosmer. An unmarried working woman, she is truly a "free agent" (2, 337), and Ibsen's characterization stresses the social indeterminacy of the *femme de trente ans*, a powerful loner who can yet be so easily snubbed even by lowly Mrs. Helseth.[59] Looming behind Rebecca is a more earnest and educated Becky Sharp, a social climber who "angled for admission here to Rosmersholm" (4, 368). Denied a role in family or society, Rebecca creates a part that realizes her desire for security and power immediately in concrete action. Like the Shavian actress, Rebecca maintains the center of this personal power in a blend of intimidating intelligence and seductive sexuality. She has Duse's bewitching "egoistic force," the erotic power that inspires a "desperate infatuation" in her stage audience—even in Kroll—an attaction that nullifies moral discrimination and overwhelms native resistance (3, 354).

The characters' compulsion to confess their freedom to act authentically, their desire to stand clear of any "false and ambiguous position" (2, 328), anticipates the ethical imperatives of Stanislavskian performance. In a practical sense, Stanislavsky's system of actor-training, with its emphasis on a concrete and detailed past released through the present circumstances of the actor's performance, exploits Ibsen's typical process of character-building. But although Stanislavskian preparation is compatible with Ibsen's plotting, it is in his vision of the actor and the stage that Stanislavsky most profoundly masters Ibsen's complex perspective on the theater. Much as Stanislavsky opposes the actor's self-realization to the conventions of the stage and to the determining influence of his preparation, so Ibsen pits the gradual unfolding of the play's past against the characters' desire to achieve spontaneous action. As the play slowly exhumes the events, motives, and evasions of the past, individual identity increasingly appears to be contingent, determined by social and psychological evolution. At the same time, though, the characters' desire for freedom intensifies markedly. For this reason, the final events in an Ibsen play are often extremely puzzling. The development of the play's action is apparently explanatory in the manner of naturalistic action generally—it seems to present a sequence of causes for which the action of the play is the single, ineluctable effect. But the endings of Ibsen's plays often directly undermine our secure reliance on an exclusively "historical" interpretation of the play's action, usually by qualifying the characters' relation to the omnipotent past. *Rosmersholm* is a remarkable instance of this tendency, for our sense of the play depends almost entirely on our appraisal of the final suicide as a potentially authenticating act. Do we see Rosmer and Rebecca redefining the past through their suicide, or do we agree with Mrs. Helseth, as much in the play urges us to do, that they are simply caught in the toils of the past, that "the dead woman has taken them" (4, 381) after all?

Authentic action becomes possible for Rosmer and Rebecca only when their implication in the past has been fully revealed to them. By midway through Act 4, the intricate interdependence of motive and need that unites Beata with Rosmer and Rebecca has been fully illuminated. Rosmer's ambivalent "innocence" has been skeptically qualified by his erotic passion for Rebecca, an attraction that colors his political as well as his personal goals. And we finally see Rebecca as the matrimonial adventurer she has become, understanding the balance of economic and sensual drives motivating her "fight to the death" with Beata. For the first time in the play, Rosmer and Rebecca are stripped of their masks. But Rosmersholm paralyzes its actors; the curse of *Rosmersholm*'s stage is that it "kills happiness," and makes "great and selfless love" worthless because it is, like Brendel's genius, incapable of being realized in action (4, 371). Without the romantic "joy" that enables the actor to "lay hold of life" (2, 340), the desire to act exhausts itself in frustration. Even though Rosmer claims that the past "hasn't any hold on you any more ... hasn't any connection with you ... as you are *now*," Rebecca rightly realizes that "innocent" action is no longer a possibility for them.

The closing action of the play seems to suggest a way out of these invalidating circumstances, a way that leads out of the stage box itself. The first path that Ibsen provides is that of sacrifice, as Rosmer begs Rebecca to justify his faith in her and in himself: "give me back my faith again! My faith in *you*, Rebecca! Faith in your love. Proof! I must have proof!" (4, 373). Rosmer begs Rebecca to perform for him, to play a sacrificial role that will, he hopes, confirm his faith in himself, and in her. But Rosmer is again interrupted by Brendel here, and the macabre vision of the "inescapable condition" of Rosmer's future mission surely qualifies Rosmer's request to Rebecca: "That the woman who loves him goes out into the kitchen and gladly chops off her dainty, pink and white little-finger ... *here*, just near the middle joint. Furthermore, that the aforesaid woman in love ... equally gladly ... cuts off her incomparably formed left ear" (4, 376). Brendel's depiction of sacrifice, as Thomas Van Laan remarks in *The Idiom of Drama*, provides an important anticipation of the suicide to come, suggesting that in leaping into the millrace, Rosmer and Rebecca "enact a purging self-sacrifice that wins them salvation" (p. 174). But we are, by this time, alert to the seductive simplifications of Brendel's mind, and recognize the ironic tenor of his speech in the context of its surrounding action. For even as he imagines a purifying sacrifice for the lovers, he also visualizes Rosmer's continued dependence on Rebecca. Does the suicide merely confirm Rosmer's dependence—on both Rebecca and Beata, joined in death at the millrace—or does he also act genuinely, discover the "joy" of freedom, and decide the meaning of his actions by redefining their relation to his past?

The answer is, naturally, both yes and no. As he would do later in *The Master Builder*, Ibsen presents a final scene that at once reenacts the past—suggesting its pervasive influence on the present—and that reinterprets it. Here, Rosmer first asks Rebecca to "go the same way ... Beata went" (4, 378), urging her to act out the apparently inevitable imperatives of the past. Of course, the play does stress an important equivalence between Rebecca and Beata throughout: both confess to Kroll, write letters to Mortensgaard, and inform Kroll of Rosmer's apostasy.[60] And Rebecca momentarily seems to accept this deterministic view of her current situation—"I am in the power of the Rosmersholm view of life ... *now*. Where I have sinned ... it is right that I should atone" (4, 379). She casts herself in the role of Rosmersholm's inheritor, and acts to expiate the Rosmersholm curse.

Were the play to end at this point, we would, I think, assume that Beata had indeed claimed her victims, and would find *Rosmersholm* much more akin to *Ghosts* in attitude than to Ibsen's later drama. But Rosmer's reply—"Is *that* how you see it?"—

initiates his desire to accompany Rebecca to the millrace, and reflects his rejection of her sacrifice, his desire to decide his performance rather than to suffer it.[61] Rosmer finally understands that he cannot "build on this charming creature," nor on the sacrifice that Brendel obliquely encourages her to perform. But Rosmer does seem to build on one aspect of Brendel's vision of salvation, the fact that it must be done "gladly." The word "gladly" tolls through the closing moments of *Rosmersholm*, ringing through the house that kills happiness, where the children never cry and the adults never smile. The word limns the recovery of the "happiness and contentment" (4, 372) that Rebecca has lost, a gladness that sanctifies, makes "innocent" in its way, the "marriage" that unites Rosmer and Rebecca in death.

> REBECCA. Suppose you were only deceiving yourself. ...
> Suppose it were all a delusion ... one of those
> White Horses of Rosmersholm.
> ROSMER. It could well be. We can never escape them, we
> of this house.
> REBECCA. Then stay, Johannes!
> ROSMER. The husband shall go with his wife, as the wife
> with her husband.
> REBECCA. Yes, but first tell me this: is it you who goes
> with me, or I with you.
> ROSMER. That is something we shall never fathom.
>
> (4, 380-81)

Rosmer and Rebecca reject the determinism that would make their final action contingent. Each impressively recognizes that the White Horses cannot be escaped, that they must create their own relationship to the guilt and to the past that the White Horses represent. They confront their guilt, but do not allow guilt to control their actions here. They go to the millrace "together," reinterpreting Beata's death, and its effects, through their immediate action. They place themselves in a decisive, but not dependent relation to the past that they share. They are finally united in a common purpose. They act "gladly."

In the exquisite final moments of *Rosmersholm*, we see Rebecca and Rosmer finally unmasked, acting with full recognition of purpose and consequence. Their suicide at once recapitulates the past by making its motive forces explicit ("The husband shall go with his wife"), and changes it, places Rosmer and Rebecca in a new relation to Beata's death. But the justifying act of the play is finally hidden from our view, screened through the trivializing voice of Mrs. Helseth: "the dead woman has taken them." Mrs. Helseth offers us a vision of the suicide that runs counter to what we have just come to understand. Seeing Rebecca's white shawl, she places their suicide firmly in the context of the play's history, implying that far from overcoming the past, they are simply enacting its last twist, its resolution. Like Stanislavsky later, whose actor becomes fully realized only through his ability to create himself against the limiting pressures of his preparation, Ibsen here presents an act that, however ambiguously, confronts and transcends both the ghosts of the past and the material world of the present. We recognize the limitations of Mrs. Helseth's conventional morality, and the inadequacy of her interpretation. Much as Rosmer's and Rebecca's elliptical language is barely able to convey the complexity of their inner life, so too Rebecca's shawl becomes a more ambiguous sign than Mrs. Helseth recognizes. And perhaps more clearly than Stanislavsky, Ibsen understands the fundamental disjunction between the actor and his stage world, and envisions that split more absolutely. By forcing us to see within Mrs. Helseth's narrow perspective, Ibsen dramatizes the uneasy relation between actor and stage that defines Stanislavskian naturalism. Ibsen's play itself innovates the idea of the actor, and demands the kind of theoretical revamping of the actor's art that Stanislavsky came to pursue. The justifying action of *Rosmersholm* contrasts the conventional response with the spontaneous act, the inauthentic with the genuine, the theatrical with the real. It leads its actors out of their stage box, releases them from the glare of our reductive observation, and draws them into the dark and private freedom where they perform their final act of exposure.

Heartbreak House

Like *Rosmersholm*, Shaw's *Heartbreak House* implies a specific, and surprisingly Stanislavskian, vision of the actor, an actor who transcends the torpid conventions of the theater to achieve "metaphysical self-realization." Moreover, Shaw's continuing concern with acting as an art, largely expressed in the form of occasional reviews and letters, bends the modern interest in the actor's authentic performance to a characteristically Shavian design. Laying siege to the complacency of the London theater, Shaw strategically advocates the outmoded, broadly heroic acting style of the "drunken, stagey, brassbowelled barnstormers" of his youth, touring titans like Barry Sullivan, and European actors in the classical mold of Salvini and Ristori.[62] Shaw touts the modernity of this now-dated style, wittily praising the melodramatic entertainments (like Jerrold's *Black Ey'd Susan, OTN*, 3, pp. 6-7) that were its vehicles, and castigating the underplayed "cup-and-saucer" acting indigenous to the respectable theater. He attacks the pretentious sophistications of such amateurish acting, and is concomitantly energetic in exhorting actors to meet the prodigious physical and rhetorical demands of his own plays.

Shaw's insistence on the actor's self-realization on the stage shapes his varied practical criticism as well as his more theoretical remarks. Barry Sullivan's "monstrous" vitality, for instance, impressed Shaw as so "superhuman" that "there was hardly any part sufficiently heroic for him to be natural in it" (*OTN*, 1, p. 271). The actor's self-realization thrills the public, but it has more than a voyeuristic appeal. The self provides the critical means for the actor's expression of his role and its place in the action of the play. Thus, Sullivan's secret as Hamlet was "simply that he presented himself as what Hamlet was: a being of a different and higher order from Laertes and the rest. He had majesty and power."[63] Unlike Stanislavsky's actor, who attempts to overcome the tawdry staginess of the stage through public solitude, Shaw's actor realizes his personality through a frank acceptance of the theater's theatricality. Shaw typically sides with spectators like Fielding's Partridge, preferring the spontaneous energy of stagey heroics to the subdued repressions of "realistic" acting:

> Generations of shallow critics, mostly amateurs, have laughed at Partridge for admiring the King in Hamlet more than Hamlet himself (with Garrick in the part), because "anyone could see that the King was an actor." But surely Partridge was right. He went to the theatre to see, not a real limited monarch, but a stage king, speaking as Partridges like to hear a king speaking, and able to have people's heads cut off, or to browbeat treason from behind an invisible hedge of majestically asserted divinity. Fielding misunderstood the matter because in a world of Fieldings there would be neither kings nor Partridges. (*OTN*, 2, p. 236)

By asserting his majestic, powerful identity, the actor enforces the experience of vitality on the audience.

Shaw's vision of the actor is deeply responsive to Stanislavsky's despite obvious differences in style and attitude.[64] More explicitly than Stanislavsky, Shaw emphasizes the power of the self—the "egoistic force" that so repelled Beerbohm—as the transforming agent of the actor's authentic performance. Describing Janet Achurch's admittedly uneven Rita in *Little Eyolf*, for example, Shaw reels before the "superfluity of power and the vehemence of intelligence which make her often so reckless as to the beauty of her methods of expression":

As Rita she produced almost every sound that a big human voice can, from a creak like the opening of a rusty canal lock to a melodious tenor note that the most robust Siegfried might have envied. She looked at one moment like a young, well-dressed, very pretty woman: at another she was like a desperate creature just fished dripping out of the river by the Thames Police. Yet another moment, and she was the incarnation of impetuous, ungovernable strength. (*OTN*, 2, p. 261)

Tempestuous, reckless, inconsistent, yes, but Achurch has the intelligence to grasp and the physical prowess to realize a complex, unconventional role. She attains "the force and terror of Sarah Bernhardt's most vehement explosions without Sarah's violence and abandonment," augmenting the overwhelming force of her performance by appearing to have "reserves of power still held in restraint." Achurch's controlled power—at least on her better nights—not Bernhardt's random impulsiveness, is the measure of Shaw's "heroic actress."

Shaw's plays "must be acted, and acted hard. They need a sort of bustle and crepitation of life which requires extraordinary energy and vitality, and gives only glimpses and movements of the poetry beneath."[65] Hard acting expresses the right, "devastatingly strong" moral tone in the world of the play.[66] The actor's unshaking commitment to self-realization, to physical, intellectual, and rhetorical effectiveness, gives him what Cashel Byron calls "executive power," both in the theater and in the larger world that he shares with the theater audience.[67] Verbal skill is often the sign of vital identity in Shaw's drama. Achurch, again, could drive "some dangerous lines—lines of a kind that usually find out the vulgar spots in an audience and give an excuse for a laugh . . . home to the last syllable," displaying the rhetorical power that testifies to her histrionic commitment and success. Similarly, Lillah McCarthy, "saturated with declamatory poetry and rhetoric from her cradle," is a natural choice for Ann Whitefield, her "love of verbal music in its loftiest ranges" witnessing to the physical and intellectual vivacity requisite in the mother of the Superman.[68] Shaw assaults his audience with eloquence, and stage language generally has an authority for him that it lacks for Stanislavsky. The Shavian actor's powerful rhetoric is critical to his task of self-realization on the stage. Writing to Stella Campbell, for instance, Shaw at one point subordinates the study of character to the study of the character's language, essentially reversing the Stanislavskian balance between the opaque text and the motivating subtext:

> When you play Shakespear, dont worry about the character, but go for the music. It was by word music that he expressed what he wanted to express; and if you get the music right, the whole thing will come right. And neither he nor any other musician ever wrote music without *fortissimi* and thundering ones too. It is only your second rate people who write whole movements for muted strings and never let the trombones and the big drum go.[69]

By concentrating on word music rather than on character psychology, Mrs. Pat takes a markedly un-Stanislavskian approach to building her character. But by conceiving the music of the language, she will be able to let her own trombones and big drum go; through the music of speech, both character and actor will realize themselves effectively onstage. Like the Stanislavsky actor, Shaw's actor must be willing to cut himself "loose completely and remorselessly at every remove," risking self-exposure in order to achieve the self-realization that creates art in the theater.[70] Both Shaw and Stanislavsky envision acting as the art of "self-betrayal," but Shaw modifies the Stanislavskian "I am" by making it public, articulate, and explicit. As far as Shaw is concerned, the Stanislavskian actor's project of being must be "magnified to suit the optics of the theatre."

The Shavian actor's potent self-realization reflects the typical project of the Shavian dramatic hero. Physically, intellectually, and rhetorically gifted, Shaw's heroes, like Peer Gynt, pursue an "ideal of unconditional self-realization," a vital impulse to create themselves through effective action.[71] The life of the Shavian actor/hero is known by his impress on the world—Bluntschli's hotel accords him the rank of "a free citizen," and Undershaft's unashamed munitions work similarly makes him "free and great."[72] But the world of the Shavian hero, like the theater of the Shavian actor, is often too closely circumscribed by convention to permit him the full exercise of his powerful capacity. The Shavian dramatic world thwarts its own deliverance largely by baffling the hero's desire for effective acting. As a result, Shaw's drama is tinged by a distinctly "unpleasant" frustration, the feeling that drives Vivie Warren to slam the door on her "conventional" mother and the world she represents, only to become ironically *"absorbed"* in its abstract mathematical representation (vol. 1, pp. 355, 356). The characters who can act do so only within strict limits. Marchbanks's final rejection of romantic illusion in *Candida* ("I no longer desire happiness: life is nobler than that") is nearly his exit line from the play (vol. 1, p. 594). Shaw's politicians—Caesar, King Magnus, Good King Charles—achieve only impermanent and compromised victories against the widespread ignorance, delusion, and prejudice that confront them. Saint Joan's experience is paradigmatic in this regard, for her final embrace of the world, "the light of the sky and the sight of the fields and flowers . . . everything that brings me back to the love of God," lead inevitably to her embrace of the stake as well (vol. 6, p. 183).

Heartbreak House articulates the fundamental rift between thought and action, culture and power, moral scruple and effective capacity that Shaw details in his bitter preface to the play. This is the alienation that the Shavian actor's metaphysical self-realization must attempt to overcome. The play is borne along on a restless current of incessant movement; as one early critic remarked, "the characters seem to be scurrying about with the intense crazy logic of lunatics."[73] Shotover's darting exits and entrances are symptomatic of the fretful movement of the play, a quality that Shaw underscores in his stage directions. In a typical passage early in the play, Shotover *"seizes* the cup and the tea-pot and *empties* both into the leathern bucket," then *"disappears* into the pantry." A *"thumping"* is heard, and Lady Utterword *"bursts* in much *flustered."* Characteristically *"precipitate* in speech and action," Ariadne approaches Ellie Dunn "with *outstretched* arms," speaks *"vehemently"* to Nurse Guinness, and sits "with a *flounce"* on the sofa. When Shotover returns with the tea, he *"snatches* away the drawing-board," leaving Ellie to pour a cup *"greedily,"* while Ariadne speaks to him *"suffused* with emotion" at first, and finally *"hysterically"* (1, 64-66, emphasis mine). The scene is an energetic one, but its energy is undirected and diffuse. And at the same time, this nervous movement is offset, and sometimes overcome, by the heavy drowsiness that pervades Heartbreak House. The play opens with Ellie drifting off to sleep over *Othello*, left alone because Hesione accidentally fell asleep while preparing her accommodations. In the course of the play, we see Mangan hypnotized, Mazzini Dunn in pyjamas, and various characters dropping out for their naps. The condition of the characters is best visualized in the opening tableau of the third act, where most seem to be dozing, but are kept from sleep by a fitful wakefulness, neither comforted by oblivion nor galvanized to full consciousness.

The contrast between sleep and waking, between dreaming incapacity and active alertness, also pervades the dramatic action of the play. Critics have frequently remarked on the characters' posturing in the play, and on how Shaw unerringly unmasks them—exposing Marcus Darnley's heroics, Ellie's feelings for Mangan, Mangan's corporate power, Pirate Billy's thievery, Hesione's hair. In many respects, though, Shaw's heartbreaking disillusionment is an ambiguous experience, leading neither to effective action nor to self-realization. Boss Mangan may remind us of Crofts, Undershaft, and Broadbent, but he lacks their effective power. When Mangan is heartbroken by Hesione in Act 2, and is exposed as the powerless tool of the financial community in Act 3, this unmasking fails to discover a commanding face beneath. His sniveling assertion of personal dignity—"I'm a man aint I?"—only reveals his tepid poverty of self. As Hesione remarks, "What business has a Boss with a heart?" (2, 128). Even his name is double, since the effective "Boss" and the poetic "Alfred" fail to produce an effective moral nature, but simply cancel each other out. And, as "Boss," Mangan's effectiveness is diminished by his failure to emulate the humanitarian qualities of his complement in the play, Mazzini Dunn. The play insistently places "power and culture . . . in separate compartments" in this way, opposing Mangan to Mazzini, Hastings to Hector, Ariadne to Hesione, the drinking to the thinking Dunns (Preface, p. 15). And as the confusion between the pirate Billy Dunn and his double Mazzini suggests, this antagonistic self-division produces self-destruction, not realization: "Shooting yourself, in a manner of speaking," as Billy remarks to his alter ego.

But the most seriously thwarted characters in the play are its three principals, Shotover, Ellie, and Hector. Shotover plays a central role in the play, as Old Testament prophet, as Shavian mouthpiece, as suffering Lear, and as the final contemplative companion of Ellie's marital quest.[74] Shotover's "mind ray" is an appropriate metaphor in the play's action because it simultaneously expresses his explosive desire to change his world, as well as the speciousness of that wish. Unlike Undershaft's munitions, which both destroy nations and create Perivale St Andrews, Shotover's ray is an abstraction, an attempt to produce change without the intermediate step of worldly action. Shotover is not "unashamed" of his creative capacity, but retreats instead into "deeper darkness" of isolated invention (1, 105). And, of course, Shotover's brilliant inventiveness, his "seventh degree of concentration" relies on the artificial stimulus of demon rum.

Moreover, Shotover's marriage to Ellie Dunn, the "white wife" who replaces his demonic witch of Zanzibar, is an extremely unstable emblem of the union of power and wisdom toward effective action with which Shaw habitually closes his comic drama. To a considerable degree, Shotover's marriage is a capitulation, the skipper succumbing to "the happiness that comes as life goes, the happiness of yielding and dreaming instead of resisting and doing" (2, 148). At Ellie's instigation, he even forsakes rum, and the unexpected sobriety it provides him. And finally, Shotover's invention is also usurped, as the Zeppelin's bombs, and not his mind ray, destroy Boss Mangan.

Ellie Dunn seems to imagine the actor's metaphysical self-realization more positively, if only because her trials remind us of the education of other Shavian heroines. She combines Raina Petkoff's penchant for romantic adventure ("Not romance, exactly. It might really happen," she remarks to Hesione—1, 79), with the disillusioned strength of Blanche Sartorius, and the pragmatic foresight of Ann Whitefield. And like Ibsen's Rebecca West, she is outside the pale of "cultured, leisured Europe," a classless "matrimonial adventurer" forced to be "hard—as hard as nails" in the face of romantic heartbreak (2, 122).

But as Ellie discovers, "heartbreak is not like what I thought it must be" (1, 85), and it is the difference between Ellie's mature heartbreak and the forcible disillusionment of the earlier heroines that measures Shaw's reconsideration of acting. Whereas Mangan's heartbreak exposes only an inner void, Ellie's heartbreak seems to promote the sense of shrewd self-interest that makes effective action possible; as Shotover comments, "A man's interest in the world is only the overflow from his interest in himself" (2, 146). To realize the self in the world, the actor must avoid the hypnotic spell of romantic illusion, and Ellie seems at various points in the play to be on the verge of such "self-betrayal," particularly when she recognizes the nature of heartbreak: "It is the end of happiness and the beginning of peace" (2, 140). Unlike Mangan, who fails rather pathetically even to disrobe, Ellie is "stripped of everything, even of hope," and discovers that "the only real strength" is to "want nothing" (2, 148-49). Free from desire, Ellie is nonetheless paralyzed by the tedium of Heartbreak House, and Shaw projects two contradictory images of heartbroken action toward the close of the play. Early in Act 3, we see the ancient mariner asleep on the siren's shoulder; later, we hear the Dionysian reveller exulting in the music of annihilation. But unlike Cusins in *Major Barbara*, who is "possessed" by Dionysus Undershaft's invigorating power, and unlike Barbara herself, who is *"transfigured"* by the power of Undershaft's gospel, Ellie is not transformed into a Shavian saint by the splendid drumming in the sky. She simply waits for the Zeppelins to return.

Ellie's death-wish is Hector's as well, poignantly so, for Hector more clearly images the frustration of vital self-realization. Ellie develops through heartbreak; the play suspends Hector at the point of heartbreak, where blocked vitality turns inward upon itself.

Hector, left alone, contracts his brows, and falls into a daydream. He does not move for some time. Then he folds his arms. Then, throwing his hands behind him, and gripping one with the other, he strides tragically once to and fro. Suddenly he snatches his walking-stick from the teak table, and draws it; for it is a sword-stick. He fights a desperate duel with an imaginary antagonist, and after many vicissitudes runs him through the body up to the hilt. He sheathes his sword and throws it on the sofa, falling into another reverie as he does so. He looks straight into the eyes of an imaginary woman; seizes her by the arms; and says in a deep and thrilling tone "Do you love me!" The Captain comes out of the pantry at this moment; and Hector, caught with his arms stretched out and his fists clenched, has to account for his attitude by going through a series of gymnastic exercises. (1, 99-100)

Hector's melodramatic performance demands the Shavian actor's tragic stride, his swashbuckling swordplay, and his deep and thrilling voice. But unlike the Shavian actor, Hector fails to realize himself through role-playing; his performance produces only imaginary deeds, and finally degenerates into trivial gymnastics when the world intrudes on his reverie. Mangan has contradictory names, but only Hector has contradictory *personae* in the play. As the romantic Marcus Darnley, Hector seduces women with the forged currency of his fictitious exploits, and as Hesione's dress-up doll Hector Hushabye, he recklessly performs "the most horribly dangerous things to convince himself that he isnt a coward" (1, 84). In one role, Hector invents false heroics, in the other he enacts meaningless ones, but in neither role can he change his stagey world.

Hector is, in fact, a travesty of the Shavian "efficient man," of Bluntschli rather than Sergius Saranoff, whom he resembles in some respects.[75] As many critics of the play have noted, Hector also owes something to Jack Tanner, but to a Jack confined to the drifting "hell" of romantic self-delusion that is Heartbreak House, rather than to the "heaven" that is the home of the "masters of reality" in *Man and Superman*.[76] The only path out of Shaw's hell is through Saint Joan's "beautiful earth"; the transformation of the world is always the goal of the Shavian realist, of the superman, of Undershaft's "money and gunpowder." As the Don argues, "to be in hell is to drift; to be in heaven is to steer" (vol. 2, p. 685). Early in *Heartbreak House*, Hector seems to have something of this ability, rejecting Shotover's destructive ethic in the belief that "my spark, small as it is, is divine" (1, 100). But Hector has been used up, enervated by the atmosphere of his home and the dreaming romance enforced by Shotover's daughters, the "vampire women, demon women" (1, 102). As Hector's energy is increasingly obstructed, his disillusionment becomes deeply disturbing. "The night takes no interest in us," he remarks at the opening of Act 3, abrogating his responsibility to the world in despair: "I tell you, one of two things must happen. Either out of that darkness some new creation will come to supplant us as we have supplanted the animals, or the heavens will fall in thunder and destroy us" (3, 158-59). Hector abdicates his humanity by pleading to a mechanistic and mindless providence for the deliverance that he ought to be striving to create. Hector fittingly ascribes this desolation to the other occupants of Heartbreak House: "We have been too long here. We do not live in this house: we haunt it" (3, 171). Like his relatives and guests, Hector is a role, a posture, an impulse, one that fails to inhabit its body fully and effectively.

In the end, of course, something does happen to provide a brief simulacrum of vital action to the shades of *Heartbreak House*. The muted subtextual fugue of *Rosmersholm*'s finale is given full Shavian orchestration: we hear the splendid drumming of the Zeppelin, the apocalyptic bass of Shotover's "The judgement has come" and the shrill soprano wail of Ellie's "Set fire to the house," the sharp cries of the Shotover sisters, and Randall's stuttering flute, all culminating in the *"terrific explosion"* that shakes the earth, shatters the windows, and staggers the actors. It is a moment of exhilarating release, offering deliverance through final, purifying devastation, the long-anticipated reply to Hector's anguished plea to the heavens to "Fall. 'Fall and crush" (2, 157). We await annihilation or transfiguration, but in the silence, the explosions become muffled and distant. Heartbreak House and the fragile, damned souls that haunt it are passed over by the angels of death, to await the "glorious experience" of destruction on subsequent evenings. And as we listen—returning to 1919, when Shaw completed the play—to the strains of Randall's "Keep the Home Fires Burning," we inevitably contrast our own survival with the depredations of the Great War. What is our relation to the ghosts on the stage? Who haunts the ruin of "cultured, leisured Europe," the departed soldiers, or the pale specters who have endured? *Heartbreak House* addresses our own capacity for effective self-realization through the final image it presents of the actors' similar effort, their plea for destruction. Hector, Shotover, and Ellie are the Salvini, Sullivan, and Achurch of the play, actors committed to "metaphysical self-realization" in their stage world. But though a character like Undershaft can transform and revitalize the conventions of his world through the impress of his powerful identity, such a transformation is impossible in *Heartbreak House*. Shaw dramatizes for us the tragic dimension implicit in Shavian comic acting, what happens to the actor unable to transcend the cup-and-saucer nullity of the traditional stage, and of conventional society. Like the damned souls that linger on— on both sides of the footlights—the failed actor emblematizes what Shaw calls "the tragedy of modern life": "that nothing happens, and that the resultant dulness does not kill."[77]

Six Characters in Search of an Author and *Enrico IV*

Shaw and Ibsen visualize the modern actor somewhat obliquely in the characterization of their major roles; Pirandello envisions his characters more directly as actors. In *Six Characters* and in *Enrico IV* Pirandello nearly allegorizes the complex ambivalence of the modern actor's performance. *Six Characters* clearly images the confrontation between the family of Characters, with their Ibsenesque tale of hidden intrigue and betrayal, and the troupe of Actors whose theatricality dooms the Characters' play to failure. *Enrico IV* is more remarkable in this regard. Here, Pirandello exploits the particular duplicity of naturalistic acting to offer a pessimistic critique of the project of the Stanislavsky actor, and of the naturalistic stage itself.[78]

The stridently experimental quality of *Six Characters in Search of an Author* has promoted, as Francis Fergusson remarks, a "tendency to think of the play as a brilliant plot idea, a piece of theatrical trickery" lying on the fringes of the dramatic tradition.[79] In fact, much of the fascination of the play lies in its invocation of conventional attitudes and techniques. The Characters' story, for instance, recalls the involved and influential pasts of Ibsen's drama, "retrospectively" providing the Characters with a fixed history that becomes fully known to the audience only at the climactic moment—the drowning of the little girl and the suicide of her brother. The Father himself conceives their story in this manner. In his view, the Actors' performance will depict only the high points of the Characters' narrative, and will suggest the impress of the past on the present circumstances through subtle recollection ("this is only the background," he informs them, "I'm not telling you to act this part"—1, 69).

To many critics and audiences schooled on Ibsen, the dramatic action of *Six Characters* seems necessarily to require the full reconstitution of the Characters' confused yet compelling tale. But Fergusson's spine for the play—"to take the stage"—is surely much truer to our experience, focusing as it does the play's principal dramatic conflict (p. 187). Pirandello forcibly shifts our attention away from the Characters' story by intentionally frustrating our attempts to follow it; as Eric Bentley found, the Characters' story, even when the play is over, remains full of unexplained gaps and silences.[80] The leading action of the play is constituted not of the Characters' story, but of its telling, of the interaction between the Characters, and between the Characters and Actors. The Characters take the stage, and they take it away from the Actors themselves. Although the Actors' performance is extremely trying, the Actors' company should be adequate to the Characters' play; like the family, the cast has a self-important leading man, an aggressive second lady, and so forth. Actually, *Six Characters* becomes distorted if the Actors are portrayed as inept, for Pirandello locates his critique of the stage not in the ability of the performers, but in the nature of acting itself. In the struggle between the artificial Actors and the living Characters, Pirandello imagines the critical limitations of the stage and of acting as a means of expressing reality.

Pirandello throws the contrast between Actors and Characters into high relief in the "Madame Pace" scene by performing the scene twice for us, once in each version. When the Characters perform, they are unable to avoid the sense that their recreation of the story in the theater is artificial, that their "own words ring false, as with another sound, not [their] own language" (2, 81). Their enactment, although true to life, is markedly unsuited to the optics of the theater. It takes place "sotto voce, pianissimo, *utterly naturally, in a way it would be impossible to do onstage*" (2, 86). The Actors, for their part, inevitably "*play the scene differently,*" more theatrically than the Characters, becoming ludicrous to us and to the Characters even though there is no "*air of a parody*" about them (2, 92). As the Father notes, "I admire, sir, I admire your actors: this gentleman here (*points to the Leading Man*) this lady (*points to the Leading Lady*) but certainly ... *look*, they're not us" (2, 95).

The Actors' inability to realize the paradoxical vitality of the Characters onstage is not surprising, for to Pirandello all works of art attempt to impose an artificial formal order on the changing flow of life. As he argues in "On Humor" (1908), "life is a continual flux which we try to stop, to fix in stable and determined forms, both inside and outside ourselves," forms like the composed personality, like the Characters' story, and like the Actors' stock lines.[81] In this respect, the Actors and the Characters undertake the task of the traditional epic and dramatic poets, attempting to "*compose* a character" from the contradictory experiences of life, in order to represent "him as consistent in every action." The Pirandellian humorist, on the other hand, "does just the opposite: he will *decompose* the character into his elements . . . representing him in his incongruities" (p. 143). The action of *Six Characters* enacts just this decomposition. By opposing the conventional Actors to the Characters' demanding narrative, Pirandello generates a conflict in which both formalized versions of experience are broken down. Both the Actors and the Characters remain unrealized, unperformed at the end of the play.

Despite the Father's final cry—"What pretence! Reality, reality, ladies and gentlemen! Reality!"—neither the Characters nor the Actors are victorious in their battle for the stage. The Characters' desire to impose narrative coherence on the refractory details of their story is a conservative, formalistic impulse entirely commensurate with the Actors' similarly stilted efforts to digest the Characters' eccentricities within the smooth bounds of their stock parts. Both groups depict an inhuman impulse to contain the flux of life within an arbitrary form. The Characters remain fictitious, while the Actors remain shallow and inconsequential; neither is realized through performance, a frustration that the audience surely shares, and that the Manager finally voices: "Pretence! Reality! Go to hell, all of you! . . . Nothing like this has ever happened to me! They've made me lose a whole day!"

Pirandello realizes his sense of the frustrating impotence of the theater and of its actors more searchingly in *Enrico IV*, largely by synchronizing the audience's experience of the play with the sequence of action that the characters themselves undergo. We enter the theater and take our seats, waiting for the costume drama to begin. The curtain rises, revealing a splendid set: *"Salon in the villa, accurately furnished to look like the throne room of Enrico IV in the imperial palace at Goslar"* (1, 296). Aside from two portraits carelessly modern in appearance, the *mise en scène* has been fleshed out in plush detail, down to the costumes of the first group of actors, *"dressed as German knights of the eleventh century."* The curtain surprises the knights into speech.

> LANDOLFO (*to* Bertoldo *as if continuing an explanation*). And this is the throne room!
>
> ARIALDO. At Goslar!
>
> ORDULFO. Or, if you prefer, in the stronghold of the Hartz!
>
> ARIALDO. Or at Wurms.

LANDOLFO. According to the scene we're playing, it jumps
           about with us, now here, now there.
ORDULFO.   To Saxony!
ARIALDO.   To Lombardy!
LANDOLFO. On the Rhine!

. . .

BERTOLDO   (*who has been looking around, amazed and per-
           plexed, inspecting in turn the room, his costume, and
           the costumes of his companions*). Excuse me, but
           ... this room ... these clothes ... Which Henry
           IV? ... I don't get it: Isn't it Henry IV of
           France? (1, 297-98).

Within seconds, our first dislocation takes place. What kind of
history play is this? Our disorientation precisely reflects the stage
action, for we become aware that the "knight" Bertoldo is also
being introduced to the set, familiarized with the surprising
circumstances of his performance. Bertoldo's stage world is un-
expectedly strange. As a conscientious actor, Bertoldo has prepared and internalized the relevant social and historical dimensions of his role, but has unfortunately built the character of a
servant of the sixteenth-century Henry IV of France, not the
eleventh-century German Emperor. He has, that is, brought the
wrong part to the theater. In the opening moments of the play,
we share with Bertoldo the unsettling erosion of his assumptions
about the reality of the theater, a "traumatic" experience that
will be repeated throughout the evening.

As Eric Bentley remarks, the play is constructed around a series
of such "traumatic collisions," which he conveniently summa-
rizes:

The moment when the protagonist fell from his horse comes
first to mind, but of equal weight is the moment twelve years
later, when he woke up to know he was not the Emperor.

Then there is the moment, eight years after that, which is the occasion of the action presented on the stage, the moment when the other actors in the original drama dare to return to it after two decades: such is Act One. The play moves on to two further traumatic moments: the moment when the planned trauma does not take place, but another one does, as the nameless hero sees the living portraits and the crowd rushes in to say he is sane; and, secondly, the moment in which "Henry" murders Belcredi. (p. 37).

The play operates on its audience through a similarly traumatic process, repeatedly wrenching our confidence in its representational integrity. The historical setting works on us in this way. Pirandello deliberately garbles and interrupts the already obscure doings of the Emperor Henry IV—much as he does with the Characters' story—in order to impede our reconstruction of a historical past for the play's present action. The frustration we experience in ordering this past also colors our efforts to comprehend the play's central role, the nameless figure who plays the king. In the person of "Henry," Pirandello concentrates his critique of naturalistic acting by baffling both actor and audience in their various attempts to consolidate a reliable Stanislavskian "*past* which justifies the *present*" of the play.

By distorting the play's temporal reference, Pirandello also opposes this "historical" model with a rival "psychological" explanation, offering both as competing accounts of "Henry's" behavior. Each account is presented by one of "Henry's" families, his eleventh-century servants and his modern visitors. The servants interpret "Henry's" actions according to the circumstances surrounding the historical Emperor. Landolfo reassures Donna Matilde at the opening of the play in just this way, saying "you too, Marchesa, keep calm. He always remembers that it was due to the intercession of both of you that he was admitted, already half frozen from two days in the snow, into the castle of Canossa and into the presence of Gregory VII, who didn't want to receive him" (1, 319-20). The visitors, having brought their doctor to examine "Henry," predictably take a more psychological, but no less determined, view of "Henry's" behavior. Belcredi, for example, argues that "Henry" had always been deeply alienated from and suspicious of his own feelings, and found necessary relief in the exaggerated posturing of histrionic performance: "that sudden recognition that he was acting, playing a part, at once cut him off from his own feelings, which seemed—not false, because they were real, sincere—but like something that he had to give value to ... somehow, through some intellectual act, in order to make up for the real warmth he felt missing in himself. He improvised, exaggerated, let himself go, see, in order to distract himself and avoid seeing himself in that way anymore. So he seemed inconstant, silly, and ... yes, frankly, often ridiculous" (1, 313). A pathological role-player, and "quite a good actor," "Henry" devised the pageant, and as the result of a fall from his horse, became fixed in "his terrible mask, which wasn't a mask anymore, but the face of madness." If the historical account determines "Henry's" actions according to the paradigm of the Emperor Henry IV, Belcredi's psychological analysis conceives "Henry's" actions as the inevitable result of an essentially histrionic personality. As Di Nolli suggests, madness has made him a "magnificent, terrifying actor."

Pirandello subtly coordinates the historically determined aspect of the naturalistic actor's preparation with the deterministic psychological vision it implies. "Henry's" two ensembles and the sense of character they articulate present the two aspects of the naturalistic actor's task, his "work on his role"—the development of concrete prior circumstances—and his "work on himself"—the creation of a motivating subtext of desire, a consistent personality. Also like the actor, "Henry" sees his stage life as enriched by its relation to a prepared past, but not as determined or explained by it. By his own account, he awakens to the present and voluntarily decides to resist the depredations of time by adopting the unaging mask of Henry IV. Although the role itself is "fixed forever" (2, 355), it enables "Henry" to escape a more seriously invalidating condition, his sudden and arbitrary projection from youth to age. He rebukes his servants for their unwillingness to participate immediately in his theatrical project, to use their role-playing to make themselves more freely alive: "You should have done it for yourselves, this deception [*inganno*], not just played it for me and for the others who came to visit from time to time, but like this, naturally, every day, for no one else (*to* Bertoldo, *taking him by the arm*), for yourself, understand? So that in this fiction [*finzione*] of yours you could eat, sleep, even scratch your back if you had an itch (*turning back to the others*) feeling yourselves alive, truly alive in the history of the eleventh century, here at the court of your Emperor Henry IV!" (2, 355).

"Henry's" oddly ambivalent attitude toward the past, however, creates unusual obstacles for the naturalistic actor, whose task is recapitulated in the role itself. Characters in drama frequently act out of divided or contrary motives; "Henry" poses the actor and his audience with a somewhat different problem, for "Henry's" performance is defined against two justifying pasts, his eleventh-century and his twentieth-century circumstances. As an actor himself, "Henry" carefully manipulates the motivating subtexts each of these pasts implies. Speaking to Donna Matilde in Act I—who once played Henry IV's beloved enemy Matilde of Tuscany, but now plays his mother-in-law Adelaide—"Henry" manages to address her in all of her roles:

> I can't be twenty-six forever, my Lady. I ask you for your daughter's sake too, so I may love her as she deserves, now that I am well-disposed toward her, moved toward her by her pity. There: That's it! I am in your hands. (1, 328-29)

The actor's talents are fully engaged here. In character, Henry IV speaks to Donna Adelaide about his love for her daughter, his wife. But through his remarks, "Henry" communicates to the present Donna Matilde the persistence of his affection for her. "Henry" exploits the eleventh-century mask in order to speak directly in the present, and the actor must realize the subtextual intentions of both Henry IV and the awakened "Henry." He must make Donna Matilde's subsequent feeling—"He recognized me, I'm sure" (2, 334)—at once plausible and improbable.

The play's climactic confrontation in Act 3 presents similar interpretive problems to actors and audiences. Faced with his nephew Charles Di Nolli costumed as young Henry IV, "Henry" avails himself of both past and present frames of reference in order to regain control of their common performance.

DI NOLLI (*taken aback by the cry, stunned*). Go on, what is it?

HENRY IV. It won't be only *your* sister who's dead!

DI NOLLI. My sister? I said *yours*, who you forced right up to the end to come here as your mother Agnese!

HENRY IV. And wasn't she *your* mother?

DI NOLLI. My mother? Of course, my mother!

HENRY IV. But for me your mother died "long ago and far away!" You've just now jumped down from there! (*Points to the frame from which he jumped*) And how do you know whether I haven't wept for her, a long, long time, in secret, even dressed like this? (3, 362-63)

"Henry" glides behind his various roles, brilliantly manipulating Di Nolli by obscuring and confusing the subtextual direction of his lines. In his first remark, he fixes Di Nolli in the role of the younger version of himself—as "Henry"-as-Henry IV—by addressing him as the young "Henry" he impersonates (the sister is "Henry's" sister Agnese). "Henry" then addresses his nephew directly, speaking now to the actor and not the role, by referring to Agnese as "your mother." In his final reply, "Henry" capitalizes on Di Nolli's confusion by equating Di Nolli's mother Agnese with Henry IV's mother Agnese, forcing Di Nolli finally back into the historical frame from which he has just stepped. "Henry" imposes the role of Emperor on Di Nolli as he has already forced the roles of guilty brother and grieving son on him. Finally, "Henry" seizes control of the scene by seizing Frida herself, the image of the younger Donna Matilde-as-Matilde-of-Tuscany. By providing him with a leading lady, they have made his play-acting more authentic than he had imagined possible: "this terrible prodigy; the dream they've made come alive in you, more alive than ever! There you were an image; now they've made you a living person—you're mine! you're mine! mine! rightfully mine!" (3, 370).

Pirandello's hero controverts both the psychological and the historical explanations that are brought to bear on his acting. Like the actor, he defines himself in performance by overcoming the roles that threaten to restrict him; he uses them to gain his own ends. But Pirandello refines "Henry's" relation to the past and his critique of naturalistic acting more fully in the final seconds of *Enrico IV*. "Henry's" capacity to shift his masks specifically addresses the contradictions of Stanislavskian acting, particularly the ambivalent relationship between the actor's preparation and the authentic performance that transcends it. In his masterful evasion of interpretation, "Henry" remains relentlessly unexplained by the competing contexts the play offers. Yet the actor's ability to take unconstrained action is severely limited, undercut by the final twist of the play's plot. Although "Henry," waking from madness, has been able to play the role of Henry IV as a means of preserving himself, the play finally shows him to be hemmed in by his masks rather than liberated by them. In the final seconds of the play, "Henry" impulsively relinquishes control of his performance, permitting others to decide his acting for him. He acts—"I'm not mad? Take that!"—but his action allows his character to be construed in a particularly restrictive way. Choosing between madness and sanity, "Henry" chooses between art and life, role and self, the categories he has so ingeniously sidestepped throughout the play. He accepts the role he has so assiduously avoided, not the role of Henry IV or of the conniving madman, modern "Henry," but the mask that had been forced on him by chance—or by trickery—at the pageant twenty years earlier. He becomes the madman playing the German Emperor. At the close, "Henry" fails to decide the bearing of his actions on the roles he is playing. He allows his roles to decide his actions for him, and becomes inextricably trapped in the masquerade.[82] In Pirandello's final view, no performance can realize the self in all of its variety; every performance traps the actor, betrays him into assuming the grimace of his illusory mask.

Beckett's Actor: *Not I, Play, Endgame*

In performance, Beckett's drama makes extensive demands of the actor, and of the spectator as well. Emptied of psychological motivation, of setting, of spectacle, and often apparently of action, Beckett's plays challenge actors and audiences to create theater from the tatters of the traditional stage. And yet, in many respects Beckett's drama seems less to negate theater than to distill it. Although Beckett's plays eschew the allied diversions of the stage—no scene-painters or fencing-masters, please—they do so not to impress us with the poverty of the theater but instead to rivet our attention to the theater's essential means: the actor. Beckett's drama scrupulously clarifies the actor's art, and substantially reconsiders the modern actor's complex enactment.

Beckett is, of course, a remarkably literal playwright in his use of the materials of drama. As many critics have suggested, he repeatedly forces actors and characters to share the painful and apparently arbitrary circumstances of their common stage.[83] The actors in *Play*, for instance, face specific physical requirements.

Bottled in narrow urns, the actors must either kneel or stand in a grave-trap throughout the performance ("The sitting posture results in urns of unacceptable bulk and is not to be considered"), their cramped fatigue exacerbated by the irritating glare of a spotlight intermittently trained on their faces from very close range ("The optimum position for the spot is at the centre of the footlights, the faces being thus lit at close quarters and from below"). The stage rigidly contains the actors, holding their bodies in an uncomfortable posture, bracing their necks against the slightest movement, forcing their eyes *"undeviatingly front"* into the bright light. The actor's faces must remain absolutely *"impassive,"* and with few exceptions their voices speak tonelessly, varying neither pitch nor emphasis. On the rack, the actors must still overcome the considerable demands of the text itself, for without the reinforcement of coherent dialogue, only intense concentration will enable them to deliver their fragmentary monologues completely and accurately. And, naturally enough, the performance holds a final, dismaying peripeteia for its performers; for in the place of the promised end, Beckett asks them to *"Repeat play,"* to re-enact an already tiring performance, risking in weariness a higher probability of failure.[84]

Play deftly reifies the conditions of stage acting. The actors are sealed "in character," speaking in their turns as the spot discovers them, overheard by an audience they seem not to perceive. In an important sense, *Play* invites us to hold M, W1, and W2 in this double perspective, to see them simultaneously as attenuated characters and as constricting yet evocative dramatic roles. Many dramatic parts enforce on an audience the dual awareness of the role's histrionic dynamics and of the character's represented attributes, but Beckett's meager roles fashion this relation with telling resonance. Comparison with a more evidently "theatrical" role is instructive. The role of King Lear, for example, continually astonishes us through the renewed and increasing demands it makes of the actor. As Michael Goldman argues,

Shakespeare magnifies the dimensions of Lear's suffering by making the histrionic obstacles the actor must articulate and overcome palpable to the audience. Having forced Lear to appear to transcend the full reach of his passion several times in the course of the evening, Shakespeare tests the actor finally in Lear's terrible speech over the body of Cordelia, beginning "Howl, howl, howl, howl!" The actor's technical skill for discriminating and intensifying the four beats of the line must not only be commensurate with the powerful emotional resources of the role, he must seem to enlarge suffering that has already seemed to lie on the extreme verge of his histrionic capacity.[85] Shakespeare realizes the extremity of Lear's feeling by forcing us to attend to the extremity of the actor's task; the actor's performance becomes an enriching reflection of the character's performance. Beckett exploits this dual relationship between the character's and the actor's enactment in a typically rigorous manner. First, Beckett's roles require of the actor an extraordinarily negative athleticism, the ability to endure a cramped and fatiguing stasis that reflects the restraints of Beckett's characteristically repetitive and inconsequential language. Moreover, whereas Lear's rhetoric requires the actor to appear to be going beyond the scope of his abilities, Beckett's limping, legless, or even bodiless creatures speak a halting language appropriately depleted of theatrical resource. The verbal elements associated with "creating a role"—patterns of speech, verbal imagery, habits of memory, general articulateness—are no more limited or ambiguous than the physical means permitted to the actor to express his character onstage—gesture, posture, facial expression, vocal tone.

Beckett's straitjacket roles make an unusual claim on the actor's talents. The complex expressive unity of verbal and physical representation that a line like Othello's "Keep up your bright swords, for the dew will rust them" compels is in varying degrees foreign both to Beckett's actors and to his characters as well. Unlike the romantic drama, in which the actor's verbal and physical magnificence are mutually sustaining, Beckett's plays maintain a dialectical tension between the rhetorical capability that the text exacts and the bodily privations of the actor's physical performance. Although the actor's physical movement—think of Didi, Hamm, Winnie, M, Mouth—makes the limitations of the text concrete on the stage, to a certain extent the physical enactment of a Beckett play threatens the life of the play itself, placing the actor under such difficult physical conditions that his ability to complete the performance becomes questionable.

Beckett dramatizes this dialectic between the actor's physical and verbal performance most directly in the short play *Not I*. Once again, he closely confines his performer. The actress playing Mouth is strapped rigidly into a chair high above the stage, her head firmly anchored so that the spot can focus unswervingly on her mouth. Her eyes must be covered to prevent any reflected light from reaching the audience, and she must speak a complex and repetitive monologue at trip-hammer speed. Unlike Murphy, who enjoys this kind of pastime, she cannot release her mind through the restraint of her body, for she must concentrate on delivering Beckett's elliptical text. Even to speak Mouth's text requires particular physical discipline. As Billie Whitelaw discovered, the text is not only difficult to remember accurately, the rapidity with which the words are spoken tends to cramp the jaw muscles, clenching Mouth's mouth blessedly, but inartistically, shut.[86]

In the theater, we never see the actress playing Mouth, and may be unaware of her hardships. Inevitably, though, we wonder about her body and how it is concealed, and this curiosity leads us to a finer point concerning the dialectic between text and body that *Not I* examines. For the action of *Not I* focuses this dichotomy not only in Mouth's performance, but also by juxtaposing Mouth's recitation and Auditor's brief physical response, his/her resigned gesture of "helpless compassion."[87] Beckett intensifies the textuality of Mouth's recitation by disembodying the actress, and by insisting on an unnaturally rapid delivery of her monologue. Similarly, he heightens Auditor's physical function in the drama by restricting him/her to bodily movement. Only through Auditor's increasingly diminished gestures do we understand that he/she is, in fact, *listening* to Mouth. By sundering Mouth and Auditor, Beckett depicts the essential fiction of the actor's embodiment of his role. The actor's physical presence limits his ability to inhabit the text fully; his body, however fragile, is necessary to the realization of the dramatic text as theatrical play. Beckett literalizes the essentials of theater, the contingent and dramatic interdependence between the actor's bodily resources and the role that the text commands.

For all its strangeness, *Not I* provides a striking image of the vital duplicity of acting. As Robert Weimann reminds us, it is "no accident that the verb corresponding to the Greek word for actor—*hypokrites* (*hypokrinomai*)—means 'to interpret,' and less often 'to answer.' The Ionian equivalent of *hypokrites* was *exegetes*, whose characteristic meaning is familiar to us today."[88] This etymology suggests to Weimann that the actor's task is at once to *represent*—to disappear from view while he imitates a false, fictional reality—and to *interpret*—to remain personally accessible as an actor, to provide the public with an "interpretive" prism through which to evaluate the "represented" actions he performs. Acting invariably articulates this dynamic equipoise between the actor's implied absence as "representer," and his immediate presence as "interpreter," the two histrionic modes that Mouth and Auditor emblematize onstage.

As we have seen, modern acting theory provides this dialectic with a characteristic ethical range, one that Beckett amplifies in his dramatic vision of the actor. The Stanislavskian actor depicts a thoroughly motivated character within a detailed naturalistic environment, and clearly undertakes his performance primarily in the "representational" mode. But Stanislavsky prohibits the actor from entirely absenting himself from the stage, urging him to develop his "emotion memory" as a way to combat rote characterization, and to actuate himself immediately on the stage during performance. That is, while he "represents" a stage world clearly distinguished from the audience's by the fourth wall of the proscenium, the actor is simultaneously driven to experience *himself* in performance, to achieve the "interpretive" presence that Stanislavsky calls 'the state of 'I am.' " In Stanislavsky's theory, the actor's "interpretive" function, his ability to sense the "I am" authentically on the stage, sustains his most lifelike, most thoroughly "representational" acting. Brechtian performance reverses the Stanislavskian bias, focusing our attention first on the actor's "interpretive" function—his alienated enactment—and then on the role he "represents" to us. Brecht's actor presents himself to the audience explicitly as an actor; his perceptible presence as a performer is prior to his absence as a character. In more recent theory, the balance is again readjusted. The "interpretive" impulse of Grotowski's actor's revealing "total act" extends the Stanislavskian commitment to self-engagement with the dramatic role. But Grotowski's actor maintains a vital balance between himself and the role he plays, neither subordinating the "interpretive" to the "representational" mode, as Stanislavsky does, nor reversing the poles, as Brecht requires. Grotowski's actor creates an evident interplay between self and role, using the role as a "scalpel" to discover similar aspects of himself to the audience.

Not I insistently phrases this histrionic dialectic between absence and presence, role and self, that modern acting theory elaborates. As "representer," Mouth's actress undertakes to absent herself through the text, a text which here exactly describes her own situation. Mouth, for one, has certain actress-like qualities, not least her need for frequent prompting. More important, though, Mouth's narration dramatizes the actress's "representational" absence, as she obsessively tells the tale of "she," vehemently refusing to relinquish the third person, the fictional mask that expresses her desire to be "not I." But Auditor remains to remind us of the actor's "interpretive" function, that the play requires the actor's presence as an actor, as combination mime and rhetor.

Indeed, one ramification of this dialectic between text and body is to suggest the unique theatricality of Beckett's spare dramaturgy. *Play* accentuates the distinction between physical presence and verbal absence by concealing the actors' bodies in the short, narrow urns. As visual metaphors, the urns help to place the action of *Play* in its purgatorial context, but their size and shape continually direct attention to the problem of the actors' bodies. Because they seem incapable of containing human forms, the urns force us to distinguish between actor and character. We don't ask how the character M fits into his urn, especially since he doesn't complain of discomfort in the way Winnie does, but we invariably wonder how the actor who plays him is stuffed in there. Far from being distracting theatrical trickery, the urns encourage us to amplify the characters' plight through the actors' performance. The characters' desire to be released from their relentless narration ("Dying for dark") is given expressive point by the stark immobility of the actors, unable to escape our view. Try to think of how different our response to *Play* would be if the three heads simply appeared on three television screens, or were floating above a curtain, behind which the actors could be comfortably seated, and easily ignored. Their bodies would be effectively hidden, but we would lose entirely the physical dimension of the actors' painful presence, the difficulty of being there onstage that *Play* is, in this sense, all about.[89]

The actors' bodily stress dramatizes the presence of both actors and characters on the stage, and redirects our attention to the text/body dialectic. Although the text provides the mask that conceals the actor, it also provides him with the material of his art, the shape of his enactment. Similarly, the urns conceal the actor in order to make his physical presence as actor manifest to the audience, to make the perception of the actor's performance part of our experience of the play of *Play*. The urns heighten our awareness of the actor's dual function as "interpreter" and "representer," since we come to experience the dramatic situation (characters in urns reciting on cue the disjointed narrative of a lovers' triangle) through the recognition of the histrionic situation (actors onstage performing arduous roles). The spoken text of the play, emptying the characters' voices of all "vocal" qualities except sound itself, serves a similar end. By denying the actor the full use of his vocal instrument, Beckett makes us aware of the histrionic obstacles the role presents, much in the way that Shakespeare does with Lear. Though the role still conceals the actor, the roles of *Play* so challenge the actor to divest himself of his expressive means that they make us increasingly aware of his expression, of the fact that he can communicate at all under such straitened circumstances. The actor's denial becomes, for us in the audience, the sign of his present achievement, his ability to give life to the character he plays even when stripped to his histrionic essentials.

Finally, the title of *Play* suggests that this complex interplay between text and performer is an essential aspect of all theatrical play, as we can see by comparing the stage play *Play* with a radio play like *Embers*. Whether the actor playing Henry is standing or seated, perched in a sandbox in the studio, or even bound naked in a rocker is immaterial to our experience of *Embers*. In fact, much of the attraction of *Embers* lies in the way that it toys with our ability to decide who is really "there" with Henry, wherever he is. We hear the sound of the sea—the static that Henry's voice must drown out if we are to know that *he* is there as we scan our radio dial up and down the band—and the various noises that Henry's sound-master imagination can command, steps, voices, hooves, waves. But why doesn't Ada make sitting noises too? Where did Addie and the music master come from? Why do the hooves finally fail to clip-clop at Henry's bidding? The refractoriness of the reality the sounds create is critical to our experience of the richness of radio as an imaginative medium.

For radio is, of course, the medium of the disembodied voice, and Beckett suggestively builds the limitations of the medium into the action of *Embers*, a play that tests the creative capability of the radio voice, and of the radio auditor as well. *Play* similarly dramatizes the essential dynamics of stage performance, by reducing the actor's activity to the mere fact of his physical presence, and by limiting his verbal enactment to hushed recitation. But as we have seen, this paring down of the actor's available resources only makes us more aware of his performance as an actor. Beckett's keen attention to the actor suggests the specific theatricality of *Play*, its response to the theater's necessary counterpoise between self and role, presence and absence, through the medium of the actor's body.

Granted, the dialectic between text and body that animates Beckett's drama at least partly reflects his Cartesian fascination with the mind's ambiguous implication in the physical body. But in histrionic terms, Beckett consistently endows the actor's body with a theatrical quality that suggests the actor's "interpretive" immediacy, at the same time that the motions of the mind that the spoken text articulates generally imply the actor's "representational" absence. The vision of performance that *Play* concentrates is evoked more diffusely in Beckett's more spacious plays. Think of Krapp, for instance, whose bodily presence, exaggerated not only by his clownish costume, but also by his eating and drinking, and by the pratfall that he nearly takes on the banana peel, so sharply qualifies the absent voice that dominates the play, the voice from the machine that bids farewell to love. In *Happy Days*, as Winnie is gradually immobilized, Willie becomes more active. While the almost invisible actress is reduced in Act 2 to reciting an increasingly impoverished text (no more allusions to Shakespeare and Milton), the actor becomes a strikingly theatrical presence, making his climactic entrance in *"top hat, morning coat, striped trousers,"* crawling to that stagiest of properties—and the one that most surely arouses our expectation of action—the revolver. *Waiting for Godot* has been so exhaustively beset by mind/body criticism that I hesitate to add to it here; let me briefly suggest that one of the many ways that *Godot* imagines this performance dialectic is by contrasting the pair of clowns whose only recourse is to talk—Didi and Gogo—with the melodramatic star and his entourage, whose talk is subordinate to his journey, his "tragic" imitation of an action.[90] Even Beckett's most minimal play *Breath* maintains this dialectic, while presenting a stage experience that lies on the borders of drama. In *Breath*, the actor is literally not there, for his breath and the two cries are prerecorded. But once again, the slight action of the play counterpoints the physiological breath—inhale, exhale—with the verbal sound, the two cries perhaps suggestive of the beginning and end of language. *Breath* presents the final *reductio* of Beckett's analysis of acting, demonstrating the exiguous dramatic potential that the theater retains when the stage is finally divested of its actors.

Endgame, the play that offers Beckett's single most comprehensive role, similarly phrases a presiding concern for the dynamics of enactment. The metaphor of the theater, and of the "dramatic machine" that occupies the stage, is central to the action of the play, and critics have amply documented *Endgame*'s theatrical reflexivity.[91] Hamm is, of course, part ham tragedian ("Can there be misery . . . loftier than mine?") and part tragic victim, an actor with Richard Crookback in his repertoire who also reminds us of Richard II, of brooding Hamlet, and of dispossessed Lear. In this sense, Hamm portrays the actor's "representational" aspect, by self-consciously placing himself within "this farce" as a dramatic character. But inasmuch as he also plays a stage-wise Prospero to Clov's hobbled Ariel, Hamm also betrays an ability to stand outside the action that is "taking its course," and comment on (literally "interpret") the rhythms of his own performance—"This is deadly," "This is slow work," "This is not much fun," "Will this never finish" and so on. Hamm undertakes his performance both as "representation" and as "interpretation," and explicitly endures the vexing conflation of absence and presence that his playing creates.

Endgame frequently counterpoints verbal and physical enactment. Play is, naturally, an important aspect of the activity we witness in *Endgame*; the weary caesura that punctuates Hamm's opening line—"Me—(*he yawns*)—to play"—anticipates the deflected action of the play to follow. Blind, approaching deafness, unable to stand, unable to sit, legless, hungry, and bleeding, the characters in *Endgame* are all like Hamm's three-legged dog, staggering lopsidedly through their performances. "Every man his specialty" indeed. The actions of the play are similarly truncated, slowly succumbing like Nagg's kiss or Hamm's brief journey to the grinding inertia that pervades the tiny world. Verbal activity is also deformed, unraveling in the manner of Hamm's story:

> I'll soon have finished with this story.
> (*Pause.*)
> Unless I bring in other characters.
> (*Pause.*)
> But where would I find them? (p. 54)

In his final scene, Hamm concisely fuses the actor's representational impulse toward absence and the interpretive presence that the stage requires. He points our attention to the activity he represents to us—ending—with interpretive commentary, "I'm warming up for my last soliloquy." But acting becomes for Beckett a trenchantly pessimistic metaphor of experience. Role-playing frees neither Hamm nor Clov, and the absence they desire is sharply tempered by their capacity to endure. As actors, neither Hamm nor Clov can simply "stop playing" as Clov begs; they must play to the end, finish. And yet though their bodies prevent them from becoming fully absent, they also seem unable to use performance in the Stanislavskian sense, to achieve a vital sense of presence, the magic "I am" of the naturalistic actor. Clov particularly remarks on this aspect of their acting just before he makes his partial exit: "Clov, you must learn to suffer better than that if you want them to weary of punishing you—one day. I say to myself—sometimes, Clov, you must be there better than that if you want them to let you go" (pp. 80-81). The speech is, true to form, enfolded in irony. As part of Hamm's "farewell" scene, Clov's address has a rote quality, emphasized by his *"fixed gaze"* and toneless delivery. And although Clov voices a desire to "be there" more vigorously, this wish raises more questions than it answers. How much more painfully could he be there? We may, finally, have the sense that the speech is Clov's "last soliloquy," an overtly theatrical gesture of completion. Much like Didi's "Astride of a grave and a difficult birth" speech, Clov here voices the gesture of tragic *anagnorisis*, a gesture that may be simply part of the actor's "making an exit." Unable to be utterly absent (he doesn't leave the stage, after all), Clov can "be there" only as an actor making a splendid "point." He might well ask with Didi, "What have I said?" And while Clov stands silently by, dressed in his traveling attire, Hamm discards his props and lowers his tiny curtain. Like the actors in *Play*, both remain motionless, trapped on the stage that neither fulfills nor releases them. In *Endgame*, Beckett bleakly envisions the histrionic dialectic between absence and presence that informs later plays like *Happy Days, Play,* and *Not I.* His actors are caught between an absence they desire and a gallingly histrionic presence, condemned to be there for us as actors in their endless charade.[92]

Old Times

Harold Pinter's *Old Times* evidently invokes an important modern dramatic and histrionic tradition. The structure of *Old Times* decisively recalls William Archer's landmark reading of Ibsen's *The Wild Duck*, where Archer argued that Ibsen innovated the drama most profoundly not in his social criticism, but in his consummate mastery of the "retrospective method":

> the unravelling of the past is a task of infinite subtlety and elaborate art. The execution of this task shows a marvellous and hitherto unexampled grasp of mind. Never before, certainly, had the poet displayed such an amazing power of fascinating and absorbing us by the gradual withdrawal of veil after veil from the past.[93]

Archer rightly senses that Ibsen defines a new dramaturgical relationship between the present and its past, and sees the "unravelling of the past" as the source of our theatrical pleasure. Surely, though, Ibsen's retrospective action appeals to more than the sleuth in us. We are absorbed most immediately by the process of this revelation of the past, by the characters' attempts to evade, discover, and revise themselves under the pressure of an increasingly burdensome knowledge of it. Moreover, because it provides a suitable dramatic structure for the release of the actor's carefully prepared network of subtextual intentions, the retrospective method is deeply conjoined to the Stanislavskian technique. Much as Ibsen opposes the revelation of the past to its effects in the present, so Stanislavsky opposes the deterministic aspect of the actor's retrospective preparation to a contrary impulse, the imperative to act authentically in the present of the stage. For this reason, the actor's forcible rupture from, and simultaneous realization of his prepared past is reflected dramatically less in the clockwork precision of the past's well-made exposition than in the disturbing disconnectedness of the past that looms so portentously behind much of modern drama.

Pinter's drama is a case in point. Pinter's families bear the burden of the past somewhat differently from the way the Alvings, the Lomans, or the Tyrones do. Instead of recovering the past— as Aston in *The Caretaker* and Teddy in *The Homecoming* both fail to do—Pinter's characters tend to use the past as a weapon for controlling the present. Pinter uses the Ibsenesque retrospective structure largely to express this shift in attitude. *Old Times* and *Betrayal* are the clearest examples, since both plays end by imaging a cataclysmic incident from deep in the past; the reversed sequence of scenes in *Betrayal* at once literalizes and syncopates the retrospective paradigm in stage action itself. But instead of providing a fixed point of reference—as, for instance, Mary Tyrone's appearance with her wedding dress does at the close of *Long Day's Journey*—the past in Pinter's drama stands in ambiguous relation to the present action. In *Old Times*, Pinter particularly heightens this uncertainty by setting his diffuse action against the more substantial and familiar plot structures it recalls. The domestic setting, the lovers' triangle, and the undercurrent of sexual misadventure in *Old Times* sketch in the faint outlines of both bedroom farce and of its somber cousin, the problem play (Is Anna a woman with a past?). The play's final tableau boldly sets *Old Times* in the lineage of *Ghosts* by casting a brilliantly inconclusive light on the apparent source of the play's action: the mysterious encounter of Anna, Kate, and Deeley some years earlier in the girls' London flat. As Anna suggests, the play's structure frustrates rather than confirms our assessment of these influential old times: "There are things I remember which may never have happened but as I recall them so they take place."[94]

In an interview with Mel Gussow, Pinter carefully described his characters' stance toward the past in *Old Times*, particularly in the Wayfarers Tavern episode in Act 2:

> The fact that they discuss something that he says took place—even if it did not take place—actually seems to me to recreate the time and the moments vividly in the present, so that it is actually taking place before your very eyes—by the words he is using. By the end of this particular section of the play, they are sharing something in the present.[95]

The past in *Old Times* has the same relation to the characters' present performance that the script of the play has to its actors. Instead of a fixed and influential reality, the past is a malleable metaphor, a fiction that the characters exploit in order to create their roles in the current situation. The various pasts that the characters invent in the play are more like the texts in Charles Marowitz's "Theater of Cruelty" auditions than like Stanislavsky's concrete "prior circumstances." These improvised pasts provide a text for the three characters, one that the current situation refracts and rearticulates. And as an actor himself, Pinter revises the retrospective structure in *Old Times* in order to alter our image of Stanislavskian performance. Pinter's actor, like the characters he portrays, is indeterminate, shifting, hoping to realize a version of himself through the difficult and inconsistent role-playing that the play demands.

Anna, Kate, and Deeley create the past, and they also struggle to control it. Ordering the past is the principal dramatic activity of *Old Times*, and a particular dynamic pattern develops as the characters tell and retell their ambiguous tales—Deeley's "Odd Man Out" scenario, Anna's story of the crying man, the Wayfarers Tavern episode. To perform adequately in the present, one must master the narrated pasts of the play, using them to define both the current circumstances and one's role in them. Anna and Deeley engage each other in this way throughout *Old Times*, manipulating the present through the pasts they gradually come to share. The opening dialogue between Deeley and Kate also suggests this model, as husband and wife maneuver for power, here for an authoritative version of Anna. Deeley's questions about Anna are insistent and categorical, whereas Kate's replies are evasive, non-committal ("Was she your best friend?" he asks; "Oh what does that mean," she replies). But though Kate seems resentful, annoyed at Deeley's probing, she can insist in a way that he cannot on the veracity of her vision of the past. When Deeley implies that Kate's memory may have lapsed ("You haven't seen her for twenty years"), Kate swiftly reminds him, "You've never seen her. There's a difference" (1, 14). In controverting Kate's knowledge of Anna, Deeley violates one of the unspoken conditions of dialogue in *Old Times*. The improvised past may be enlarged or dismissed, but it may not be denied. In so doing, he is here defeated, forced into silence. Without the authority of a "past" text, his role in the dialogue is canceled out, and even his attempt to take a new tack suggests his poor command of the text that he and Kate are writing—he forgets that he had said that Anna was a vegetarian.

Deeley's "Odd Man Out" scenario provides a more suggestive text for Pinter's actors. After Anna arrives, Deeley abruptly takes charge of the conversation, picturing his frustrated exclusion from the Anna-Kate relationship in the "Odd Man Out" narrative. He describes a sexually charged visit to the movies, imaging his fear of the women's intimacy in the vision of the two seductively threatening usherettes, one murmuring obscenities, the other stroking her breasts. He had met Kate at the film, he says, "And then at a slightly later stage our naked bodies met." The "Odd Man Out" story depicts both his anxiety and his possessiveness, his desire not to relinquish Kate to Anna's control. The narrative is both aggressive and defensive. As he pointedly remarks to Anna, "it was Robert Newton who brought us together and it is only Robert Newton who can tear us apart" (1, 29-31).

Anna's reply—"F. J. McCormick was good too"—typifies her response to Deeley throughout the play. She engages Deeley's story, claiming the past that he describes. In fact, she quickly counters his scenario with one of her own, the tale of a man weeping in the London flat she and Kate had once shared. Again, the narrative displaces the immediate situation, offering a transparent image of Deeley defeated, "crumpled in the armchair" (1, 32). But her account has a more complex function, for after describing the man's exit from the flat, she goes on to describe her charming Sundays with Kate, their cozy visits to the galleries, the concerts, the theater, and one Sunday to "some totally unfamiliar district" where they "saw a wonderful film called Odd Man Out" (1, 38). Anna seizes Deeley's "Odd Man Out" image and uses it to express her possession of Kate, both then and now. As both the silence and Deeley's inconsequential reply suggest, Anna neutralizes Deeley by mastering his history, controlling his role in the present circumstances. She creates the present by controlling the bearing of its invented past, staggering Deeley by absorbing his narrative into her own. He is left without a suitable mask, as his increasingly desperate remarks ("My name is Orson Welles") reveal. Without a text, without a role to play in this performance, Deeley truly becomes the odd man out.

In the second act, the bedroom furniture is reversed from its position in the opening scene, and "susceptible to any amount of permutation" (2, 48). Much of the action of this scene follows the pattern of Act 1, as Anna and Deeley gradually embroider the details of the Wayfarers Tavern trope—a flirtation, a party, a woman's underwear—into the recollection of an unsettlingly shadowy affair. Deeley immediately claims Anna as part of his own past, insisting that he remembers her both from the Wayfarers Tavern, and from a party that followed: "It was worthwhile that night. I simply sat sipping my light ale and gazed ... gazed up your skirt" (2, 51). He appropriates Anna's *gaze*, a word that he had questioned in Act 1, and transforms his wife's confidante into the complicit partner of a vaguely voyeuristic liaison. Anna can ignore, modify, or accept Deeley's recollection, and after some resistance, she accepts it. But he continues, attempting as Anna had done earlier to fashion a shared past and then eliminate her from it: "I never saw you again. You disappeared from the area." "No. I didn't," she replies, reserving her ability to revive the narrative to her own advantage (2, 52).

Anna mines Deeley's story extensively later in the scene, after Kate returns from her bath. Reminding Deeley that she frequently borrowed Kate's underwear, Anna picks up the Wayfarers Tavern account, but modulates it to express her intimacy with Kate: "I told her that in fact I had been punished for my sin, for a man at the party had spent the whole evening looking up my skirt" (2, 65). Deeley is once again set in a nameless and insignificant role, and reflects his desperation here in his remarks about Anna's husband "rumbling about alone in his enormous villa." But his fear and exasperation drive him beyond the point of protective fiction: "I mean let's put it on the table, I have my eye on a number of pulses, pulses all round the globe, deprivations and insults, why should I waste valuable space listening to two—" (2, 67). His deprivations and insults are actual, no longer displaced in a recreated past that can be rewritten at will. Anna drives Deeley to confession, to the actor's point of "I am," but self-exposure of this kind is not the liberating act that it is for Stanislavsky. Manipulating the masks of the past, Deeley and Anna are free to revise themselves, to create the roles that their performance requires. To confess, as Deeley does here, is to choose a fixed relation to the past and to the present, to forego the freedom of role-playing. By confessing, he allows the others to fix him in the role of interloper, as Kate quickly demonstrates: "If you don't like it go." Deeley can go to China or Sicily, a threatening prospect—"They'd bloodywell kill me." Nor does Anna hesitate to confirm her victory, reminding Deeley that she came "To celebrate a very old and treasured friendship, something that was forged between us long before you knew of our existence" (2, 68).

But the endgame of *Old Times* belongs to Kate, who suddenly combines Deeley's Wayfarers Tavern story and Anna's story of the weeping man into an oddly ambiguous account of sexual betrayal. Kate tantalizingly recalls and distorts the details of both stories in order to separate herself finally from both Anna and Deeley. As she first explains to Deeley, Anna found him attractive, and was "prepared to extend herself" to him (2, 70). Deeley attempts to retract his story of having met Anna—"If it was her skirt. If it was her," he says to Kate here—but succeeds only in driving Kate and Anna momentarily into closer cooperation, as Anna confidently affirms: "Oh, it was my skirt. It was me. I remember your look ... very well." But like Deeley's confession of frustration, Anna's assertion here also fixes her role in the Wayfarers Tavern narrative. And as Kate turned on Deeley, so she now turns on Anna as well, realizing the subtle antagonism that she has felt for her throughout the play: "I remember you dead" (2, 71).

Kate's final monologue centers on the London flat, and is charged with the sexual undertone that unites the three characters. First, she describes Anna as a kind of invader, who first seized the room and then imitated "my little slow shy smile, my bend of the head, my half closing of the eyes, that we knew so well." Does Anna's impersonation crowd Kate? Did Kate suspect an affair between her roommate and her lover? We can't tell for certain, although Kate's emphasis on Anna's sheets, her dirtiness, and the unnamed man's preference for Anna's bed points in that direction. And much as Anna has eliminated Deeley from the "Odd Man Out" and Wayfarers Tavern narratives, Kate decisively eliminates Anna from their recollected London flat. She buries her: "I felt the time and season appropriate and that by dying alone and dirty you acted with proper decorum." Kate's righteous air carries over into her revision of the weeping-man tale as well. When she brings the unnamed man into the room, she is at first disconcerted by his leaning toward Anna's bed. But Kate finally buries him as well, plastering his "face with dirt." The man resists Kate's assault, suggesting "a wedding instead, and a change of environment," but "Neither mattered." Kate's marriage, and her idyllic recollections of London are both sullied by the elliptical betrayal that Deeley and Anna invent in the play, and she buries her feeling for them as she figuratively buries their fictional avatars in the dim light of that past night.

The final moments of the play work to recall the situation Anna recounted in Act 1, the visual image of the London room that Kate transmutes here. After a long silence, the characters onstage reenact their gestures as Anna described them—Anna switches out the light and lies on the divan; Deeley cries, then peers down at Anna, moves to the door, and returns to Kate, where he lies across her lap. After Deeley moves for the last time, crumpling himself in the armchair, the lights come *"up full sharply. Very bright"* on that desolate and mysterious scene:

> Deeley *in armchair.*
> Anna *lying on divan.*
> Kate *sitting on divan.*

Pinter's retrospective snapshot stands in a disturbing relation to the action of the play, acting as neither summary nor explanation. The past has become disconnected from the present action, although it still sustains and perhaps represents the characters' feelings. Pinter reminds us of various traditional structures in the play in order to measure his revision of them. By allowing his characters to define the place of the past within this retrospective structure, Pinter exploits the contradictions inherent in Stanislavskian acting, and uses them to criticize the naturalistic model of action and character. The play is clearly preoccupied with the past, but the characters act effectively only as long as they can create the past, and use it to define their roles in the current performance. Like the actors who play them, the characters of *Old Times* are involved in a project of realization that is both Sartrian and Stanislavskian. In the search for a constructive role in the play, each member of the *Old Times* triangle must actively, authentically attempt to decide the bearing of the fictive past. For the characters, this past becomes a metaphor for the self, a mask. Similarly, the actors of *Old Times* need not prepare a sequential Stanislavskian biography of the characters, but instead assemble a set of immediate goals and impulses, to be realized through the act of creating a past, or pasts. In this respect, both actors and characters are like Goffman's social actor, searching for the mask that will operate most effectively in the current situation, or "frame," of the play. Through vision and revision, Pinter's characters—like Pinter's actors—create the roles that seem to function the most surely in the threatening combat of their common performance. Whether or not any performance expresses the "real" Deeley, Anna, or Kate is, in *Old Times*, immaterial. What each character seeks is a secure role in the performance at hand, a voice in the silence of their stage.

To take action in modern drama is often to recapitulate the actor's baffling performance. Like the actor, the major roles of modern plays often are driven to act authentically against a range of invalidating constraints, against imposed and sometimes "theatrical" conventions, and against the deterministic influence of the past. The most familiar theatrical and dramatic structures are designed toward this end, to permit both the actor and the character he plays to enact and dramatize the problem of authentic acting. In the course of my discussion, I have had occasion to compare roles and actors, preparation and performance. Here, I would like to make a few observations on the relationship between dramatic setting and the stage itself as environments for acting.

By finding the actor's public performance in the theater to be the most "abnormal circumstance of . . . [his] creative work" (*AP*, p. 278), Stanislavsky phrases the abiding concern of modern acting theory. Like Stanislavsky, the major theorists of the stage all understand the actor's relationship with the provisional reality of the stage to be an ambivalent one, part of his radically equivocal stance toward the theater and the theatrical audience. The physical stage is at once the means to the actor's authentic performance, and, insofar as it is necessarily false, audience-directed, stagey, the most salient obstacle to such a performance. This rift is characteristically dramatized in the sharp disjunction between character and environment, one that paradoxically counters the naturalistic desire to frame character within a controlling stage world. The physical world of Ibsen's plays, for instance, often seems to extend the characters' inner lives to their material surroundings. The mountains and towers, the Ekdals' forested garret, the burning Alving orphanage, Hedda's piano and General Gabler's pistols, all externalize aspects of various dramatic characters to the audience. But though the stage world often places or describes its characters, it signally fails to receive them, rarely providing the means to realize inner life in action. In *Rosmersholm*, the setting enlarges our understanding of the characters only as long as their acts are contained within it; in order to achieve genuinely independent action, Rosmer and Rebecca must step outside the little world of their stage box. Many Ibsen plays resolve in the manner of *Rosmersholm*, presenting the audience with an onstage witness to an act that cannot be realized within the theatrical frame. At the close of *A Doll's House*, Ibsen carefully specifies that when Nora leaves her husband alone in his comfortable stage room, she exits into an adjoining hallway. Only after some seconds, when we have focused our attention firmly on Torvald Helmer, does the stunning report of the house-door echo through the theater. Similarly, we hear the pistol shot that silences Hedda Gabler, but see only Brack and Tesman, whose responses are entirely incommensurate with the deed they describe—"People don't do such things," indeed. In *The Master Builder*, we watch the excited crowd as they stare in fascination at Solness, a stage audience that dramatizes our desire to witness authentic acting; we are as much voyeurs as they are. Ibsen is, of course, perfectly capable of a splendidly theatrical stage death, but to die onstage in Ibsen's drama, one must escape the suffocating stage room and strike actively into the mountain wilderness of *Brand*, of *John Gabriel Borkman*, and of *When We Dead Awaken*. Even there, where Ibsen compresses the pursuit of being and the attraction of death, there remain the ambiguous, distorting voices of Mrs. Helseth's counterparts, Ella and Gunhild, Maja and the Nun. The discovery of the vital self in Ibsen risks an annihilation and a freedom that can be only tenuously achieved—and is almost certainly misunderstood—within the limits of the stage itself.[96]

The modern stage has difficulty receiving its saints, Shavian or otherwise. An extremely provocative study of Shaw could trace in detail the deterioration of the physical world of his plays, and of the offstage social environment such a world implies. The power of the *Unpleasant Plays* lies in their implication of a threatening social and economic mechanism extending beyond the proscenium. The action of the plays reveals the characters' interrelatedness, fraternal in the case of Vivie and Frank, economic in the case of Blanche and Trench, exposing their connections with each other and with a concretely imagined offstage world. The *Pleasant Plays* and the *Plays for Puritans*, set more remotely in time and space, continue to place the stage action within an implicit offstage society, one that transfers the values of Shaw's London audience to Dick Dudgeon's New Hampshire, to Caesar's Alexandria, or to Raina's Bulgaria. But as Shaw's sense of the possibility of effective action becomes more skeptical, radically so after the First World War, his stage worlds and the societies they imply dematerialize. In *Man and Superman*, our conviction of the capability of the Superman's vitality is stronger during the "Don Juan in Hell" interlude than it is when we return to the diminished concerns of pedestrian England. In *Major Barbara* effective action is realized more clearly in the insulated and ironic fantasy of Perivale St Andrews than in Lady Britomart's familiar parlor or in the streets of West Ham. In *Heartbreak House*, Boss Mangan and Billy Dunn discover with Beckett's Hamm that "Outside of here it's death," but inside Heartbreak House it's "hell," the anxious, frustrated discontent of thwarted will. Shaw's later work, even when set historically like *Saint Joan* or *In Good King Charles's Golden Days*, or in the contemporary political sphere of *On the Rocks* and *Geneva*, recalls the expressionistic texture of nightmare and wish-fulfillment. Like Hector's embarrassed gymnastics, "metaphysical self-realization" becomes increasingly improbable, or like the deeds of Private Meek, capricious and peripheral. The material stage world and the characters it contains become insubstantial, like Aubrey enclosed in the fog at the end of *Too True To Be Good*, evaporating before the vital masters of reality who are its saviors.

Drama since Pirandello has increasingly seen its characters as actors isolated and frustrated within an insistently theatrical dramatic world. "Henry" and the Characters and Actors are compelling figures not because they suggest that life requires role-playing, but in the emptiness that their role-playing reveals, the inability of their acting to express any essential vitality. The stage of *Enrico IV* and of *Six Characters* is not a validating one; its actors are forced into restrictive, trivial, and even boring roles. Recent drama more clearly capitalizes on this sense of the actor-as-actor alienated from the materials of the theater. "Absurd" drama generally intensifies the arbitrary restrictions of character by environment characteristic of the naturalistic drama, frequently by literalizing the limiting circumstances of the stage. Beckett's plays are notably rich in this regard, as are some of Ionesco's plays, particularly *Exit the King*. Pinter's more recent plays, especially *Old Times* and *No Man's Land*, present characters as improvisational actors, creating the script as they interact with, and try to control, other members of the ensemble. Unlike Beckett's comedians, Pinter's actors seem to inhabit a more recognizable stage; but in Pinter's plays, the material world is often remote from the characters' interests, or as in *The Caretaker*, provides props which (like the recollections of *Old Times*) change in function and meaning as they become used in different situations. Brechtian alienation works in this manner, too. By allowing the actor to present himself as both actor and character, Brecht forces us to see character through an evaluative lens that at once identifies the character with his dramatic world and distinguishes him from the material stage. Something like Pinter's actors in this regard, the Brecht actor harmonizes with his stage fully only in the posture of *actor*. His personality is irrelevant both to his role in the drama and to his role as the didactic performer. Brecht's alienated performance underlies the diversity of approaches to playwriting that characterizes the contemporary stage. Some playwrights, Edward Bond, for instance, or the David Hare of *Fanshen*, overtly extend Brecht's work in the theater. Other dramatists require an alienated performance from a character who is himself an actor, as Howard Brenton does in *Hitler Dances* and in *The Churchill Play*. Tom Stoppard torments Rosencrantz and Guildenstern with the arbitrariness of the (to us) familiar milieu of *Hamlet*; Genet's *The Balcony* and *The Blacks*, Weiss's *Marat/Sade*, Handke's *Ride Across Lake Constance* variously enforce a similar dislocation between character and stage world by undermining the reality of the actor's relationship to his role and to the artifice of the stage.

In its typical roles, action, setting, modern drama realizes a characteristic vision of the actor. The complex continuity of this idea is occasionally obscured by the misleading variety of performance styles that have come of age since the turn of the century. The goals of Grotowski's spartan *Doctor Faustus*, or of most productions of Brecht, Beckett, Pinter, or Stoppard, are undeniably different from those of the Moscow Art Theater's *Seagull*. Yet, as Shaw recognized, the experience the modern audience seeks in the theater is the reinforcement of its sense of vitality. To Shaw, the audience's experience of this "life in art" depends almost solely on the actor's rigorous "metaphysical self-realization," his pursuit of the Stanislavskian "I am" through histrionic means. Increasingly, the actor's performance becomes authentic in a different, Sartrian sense, by attempting to realize the actor authentically through the role that he has chosen for himself, the role of actor. Neither form of authentic performance is assured; indeed, the drama suggests that the actor is most likely to be frustrated in this quest. Of all the subtle prejudices that have been held against the actor's art (the vulgarity of emotional display, the duplicity of role-playing), surely the most firmly entrenched is the sense that true art cannot be achieved within the confines of the theater. Yet we enjoy the theater for just this reason. We dare the actor to take this risk, to engage himself strenuously in the baffling project of authenticating the acts of the stage.

Postscript

What's Hecuba to him, or he to Hecuba,
That he should weep for her? What would he do
Had he the motive and the cue for passion
That I have? He would drown the stage with tears
And cleave the general ear with horrid speech,
Make mad the guilty and appall the free,
Confound the ignorant, and amaze indeed
The very faculties of eyes and ears.

—*Hamlet*, 2.2.564-71

Hamlet's confrontation with the player is an evocative metaphor for the experience of stage acting. We have seen Hamlet's outburst at the player's monstrous seeming in the context of Shakespeare's theater, and in relation to the special duplicity of the Renaissance actor. There is something both trivial and menacing to Hamlet in the player's assumption of another identity, in the wanning of his complexion and the flow of his tears. Enthralled by a feigned passion, the actor's physical expression is nonetheless alarmingly potent; had he Hamlet's motive and cue, he would be a man of overwhelming, maddening power. On *Hamlet*'s stage, the actor's performance at once exemplifies man's creative vitality and subverts it, turning the plenitude of God's creation into a barren, sterile promontory.

But Hamlet's actor is more than monstrous. His performance also provides Hamlet with a plan of attack, a way to realize his desires in action. Although the player images the specific instability of the Renaissance actor, he highlights other facets of acting as well. His performance aggravates the painful split between banal role-playing and authentic self-expression that troubles Hamlet throughout the play. At the same time that he questions the actor's monstrous feigning, Hamlet also faces something like the modern actor's dilemma. He attempts to discover a role within himself, to vivify his performance as revenger through a personal identification with the role:

> Bloody, bawdy villain!
> Remorseless, treacherous, lecherous, kindless villain!
> O, vengeance!

In the accents of Grotowski's actor, Hamlet momentarily uses his mask as a scalpel, testing his commitment to revenge by attempting to discover the role of avenger within himself. The rhythm of this histrionic process is strikingly modern as well. Hamlet's immediate mockery of his fustian—"Why, what an ass am I!"—has an ironic impulse reminiscent of Hector Hushabye's flip from swashbuckling tragedy to gymnastic futility, or of Hamm's bitter questioning of his own performance. While enacting the monstrous creativity of the Renaissance actor, the player provokes Hamlet's awareness of another complex of attitudes, the potentially compromising, possibly liberating conflict between the histrionic role and the actor's genuine identity.

The actor images both a subversive duplicity and the possibility of authentic action to Hamlet. His performance also draws the sullen prince closer to the center of social activity in the play. By providing him with a model, the player prompts Hamlet to adjust his feelings to the demands of his social milieu, and to the requirements of his own social role. As Hamlet recognizes, the decorum of revenge raises the problem of the actor's feelings, his ability to inform the histrionic posture with fully considered passion:

> This is most brave!
> That I, the son of a dear father murdered,
> Prompted to my revenge by heaven and hell,
> Must, like a whore, unpack my heart with words
> And fall a-cursing like a very drab,
> A stallion!

The loquacity of the revenger's role invalidates it for Hamlet. Like his inky cloak, the role fails to signify his feelings and motives accurately to his audience. Moved by the player's performance, Hamlet turns to the affective theater to frame his mousetrap, to discover the evidence he needs to play his vengeful part with appropriate feeling. And something like his neoclassical inheritors, Hamlet hopes that "The Murder of Gonzago" will both reflect its courtly audience and stimulate an unequivocal—though hardly benevolent—emotional response.

Hamlet triangulates the actor's duplicity within familiar coordinates—in relation to a transcendent moral order, to the order of society, and to the order of the individual self. When the actor takes his mask, he focuses an absorbing concern for the nature of identity and action, for the relationship between the self and its expressive deeds that is the subject of drama in performance. As I have argued, more laboriously than Hamlet, I'm afraid, the actor embodies a particular vision of that relationship, an ethics of performance that he shares with his audience in the theater. But Hamlet's multivocal response to the player suggests that while the actor's doubleness speaks to the values of his theatrical culture, it also challenges them, eludes them. The actor problematizes the question of self and action that he incarnates onstage. Whether we regard the actor as exploring the "potential space" between uncontrolled fantasy and the abject surrender to reality, between the self, the not-self, and the not-not-self; or as a marginal "threshold figure" performing in the "liminal," antistructural, potential spaces of his culture; or even as the emissary of a Derridean critique of the logocentric construction of "the being of the entity as presence," it seems clear that acting resonates with the central paradoxes of human action: self-making, culture-making, sign-making, meaning-making.[1]

The actor relates the self to its actions and subverts that relation; from this dynamic dramatic action flows. As we have seen, the valuation of the actor is fully implicated in the design of drama, coordinating action, character, setting, the entire body and movement of theatrical play. Hamlet tells us that the player holds the mirror up to nature, to the nature of drama, and to the nature of our own actions. His play may reflect us, distort us, beautify us, but it is the actor who holds the mirror, who creates the alluring interplay between the dramatic world and our own. Looking into the actor's mask, we hope—and sometimes fear—to discover our own features.

Notes

In general, a full citation is provided for the first reference in each chapter; later references are to page number and are incorporated in the text. Where book titles have been abbreviated in the text, explanation is provided in the first reference; a list of journal abbreviations follows:

ArizQ   *Arizona Quarterly*
CritQ   *Critical Quarterly*
E&S   *Essays and Studies*
ECS   *Eighteenth-Century Studies*
ELH   *ELH*
ETJ   *Educational Theatre Journal*
GaR   *Georgia Review*
JEGP   *Journal of English and Germanic Philology*
JHI   *Journal of the History of Ideas*
MD   *Modern Drama*
MLQ   *Modern Language Quarterly*
MP   *Modern Philology*
MuK   *Maske und Kothurn*
PAJ   *Performing Arts Journal*
PMLA   *Publications of the Modern Language Association of America*
QJS   *Quarterly Journal of Speech*
RES   *Review of English Studies*
SEL   *Studies in English Literature 1500-1900*
ShawR   *Shaw Review*
SJW   *Shakespeare Jahrbuch*
SP   *Studies in Philology*
SQ   *Shakespeare Quarterly*
ThR   *Theatre Research International*
TJ   *Theatre Journal* (formerly *Educational Theatre Journal*)
TN   *Theatre Notebook*
TQ   *Theatre Quaterly*

UTQ *University of Toronto Quarterly*
YFS *Yale French Studies*
YR *Yale Review*

Introduction

1. Bernard Beckerman, *Dynamics of Drama* (New York: Drama Book Specialists, 1978), p. 18.
2. See Michael Goldman, *The Actor's Freedom* (New York: Viking, 1975); Jonas Barish, *The Antitheatrical Prejudice* (Berkeley: Univ. of California Press, 1981). Several studies bear on my work in individual chapters: Barish's examination of antitheatrical attitudes (chs. 4-6) in the Renaissance underlies much of my argument in chapter 1. Richard Sennett's discussion of the "metropolitan" theater in *The Fall of Public Man* (1974; rpt. New York: Vintage Books, 1978), chs. 3-6; and Joseph W. Donohue, Jr., *Dramatic Character in the English Romantic Age* (Princeton: Princeton Univ. Press, 1970), ch.9, contributed to my sense of performance in chapter 2. Timothy J. Wiles conducts a survey of modern acting theory that has some points of comparison with my own in chapter 3; see *The Theater Event* (Chicago: Univ. of Chicago Press, 1980).
3. Francis Fergusson, *The Idea of a Theater* (Princeton: Princeton Univ. Press, 1949; rpt. 1968), p. 238.

{1} Is it not monstrous

1. All Shakespeare references are to *The Complete Signet Classic Shakespeare*, ed. Sylvan Barnet, et al. (New York: Harcourt Brace Jovanovich, 1972).
2. Charles A. Hallett and Elaine S. Hallett, *The Revenger's Madness* (Lincoln: Univ. of Nebraska Press, 1980), ch. 5.
3. On metatheater in Shakespeare, see Lionel Abel, *Metatheatre* (New York: Hill and Wang, 1963); James L. Calderwood, *Shakespearean Metadrama* (Minneapolis: Univ. of Minnesota Press, 1971); Jackson I. Cope, *The Theater and the Dream* (Baltimore: The Johns Hopkins Univ. Press, 1973); Howard Felperin, *Shakespearean Representation*

(Princeton: Princeton Univ. Press, 1977); Anne Righter, *Shakespeare and the Idea of the Play* (New York: Barnes & Noble, 1962).

4. E. K. Chambers, *The Elizabethan Stage* (Oxford: Oxford Univ. Press, 1923), vol. 4, p. 270. M. C. Bradbrook treats the social status of actors in Renaissance England in *The Rise of the Common Player* (London: Chatto and Windus, 1962).

5. Thomas Middleton, *A Mad World, My Masters*, ed. Standish Henning (Lincoln: Univ. of Nebraska Press, 1965), 5.1.29-33.

6. Michael Goldman, *The Actor's Freedom* (New York: Viking, 1975), p. 58.

7. On acting style in the period, see S. L. Bethell, "Shakespeare's Actors," *RES*, n.s. 1 (1950), 193-205; John Russell Brown, "On the Acting of Shakespeare's Plays," *QJS*, 39 (1953), 477-84; Alan S. Downer, "Prolegomenon to a Study of Elizabethan Acting," *MuK*, 10 (1964), 625-36; Alan S. Downer, "The Tudor Actor: A Taste of His Quality," *TN*, 5 (1951), 76-81; R. A. Foakes, "The Player's Passion. Some Notes on Elizabethan Psychology and Acting," *E&S*, n.s. 7 (1954), 62-77; Alfred Harbage, "Elizabethan Acting," *PMLA*, 54 (1939), 685-708; B. L. Joseph, *Elizabethan Acting* (London: Oxford Univ. Press, 1951); David Klein, "Elizabethan Acting," *PMLA*, 71 (1956), 280-82; Marvin Rosenberg, "Elizabethan Acting: Men or Marionettes?" *PMLA*, 69 (1954), 915-27; Daniel Seltzer, "The actors and staging," in *A New Companion to Shakespeare Studies*, ed. Kenneth Muir and S. Schoenbaum (Cambridge: Cambridge Univ. Press, 1971), pp. 35-54.

8. Thomas Heywood, *An Apology for Actors* (London, 1612), B4ʳ.

9. C. A. Patrides, *The Phoenix and the Ladder*, Univ. of California English Studies, no. 29 (Berkeley: Univ. of California Press, 1964), pp. 36, 61-62.

10. *Playes Confuted in Fiue Actions*, D5ʳ. All references to Gosson's works are to Arthur F. Kinney, ed., *Markets of Bawdrie: The Dramatic Criticism of Stephen Gosson*, Salzburg Studies in English Literature: Elizabethan Studies 4 (Salzburg: Institut für Englische Sprache und Literatur, 1974).

11. William Rossky, "Imagination in the English Renaissance: Psychology and Poetic," *Studies in the Renaissance*, 5 (1958), 69.

12. Sir Philip Sidney, *An Apologie for Poetrie*, in *Elizabethan Critical Essays*, ed. G. Gregory Smith (London: Oxford Univ. Press, 1971), vol. 1, p. 164.

13. George Puttenham, *The Arte of English Poesie*, in *Elizabethan Critical Essays*, vol. 2, p. 4.

14. Jonas Barish, *The Antitheatrical Prejudice* (Berkeley: Univ. of California Press, 1981), pp. 169-72.

15. Giovanni Pico della Mirandola, *Oration on the Dignity of Man*, trans. Elizabeth Livermore Forbes, in *The Renaissance Philosophy of Man*, ed. Ernst Cassirer, et al. (Chicago: Univ. of Chicago Press, 1948), pp. 224-25. Barish discusses Neoplatonic views of acting, *The Antitheatrical Prejudice*, pp. 106-12. See also M. T. Jones-Davies, " 'The Players . . . Will Tell All,' or the Actor's Role in Renaissance Drama," in *Shakespeare, Man of the Theatre*, ed. Kenneth Muir, Jay L. Halio, D. J. Palmer (Newark, Del.: Univ. of Delaware Press, 1983), pp. 76-85.

16. Juan Luis Vives, *A Fable About Man*, trans. Nancy Lenkeith, in *The Renaissance Philosophy of Man*, p. 393.

17. All references to *Volpone*, ed. Alvin B. Kernan (New Haven: Yale Univ. Press, 1962).

18. *The Complete Works of John Webster*, ed. F. L. Lucas (London: Chatto and Windus, 1927), vol. 4, pp. 42-43.

19. See Ernst Robert Curtius, *European Literature in the Latin Middle Ages*, trans. Willard R. Trask (New York: Harper and Row, 1963), pp. 138-44.

20. Jonas Barish uses this phrase in "The Antitheatrical Prejudice," *CritQ*, 8 (1966), 331.

21. William Prynne, *Histrio-Mastix* (London, 1633), X2^r. Prynne's italics have been omitted.

22. Prynne, *Histrio-Mastix*, Z3^v. John Rainolds, in *Th'overthrow of Stage-Playes* ([Middleburg], 1599), makes a more compelling argument: "For, the care of making a shew to doe such feates, and to doe them as lively as the beasts them selues in whom the vices raigne, worketh in the actors a maruellous impression of being like the persons whose qualities they expresse and imitate: chiefly when earnest and much meditation of sundry dayes and weekes, by often

repetition and representation of the partes, shall as it were engraue the things in their minde with a penne of iron, or with a point of a diamond" (D2ʳ). Ben Jonson, in *Timber*, makes a similar point: "I have considered, our whole life is like a *Play*: wherein every man, forgetfull of himselfe, is in travaile with expression of another. Nay, wee so insist in imitating others, as wee cannot (when it is necessary) return to ourselves: like Children, that imitate the vices of *Stammerers* so long, till at last they become such; and make the habit to another nature, as it is never forgotten." See C. H. Herford and Percy and Evelyn Simpson, eds., *Ben Jonson* (Oxford: Oxford Univ. Press, 1925-52), vol. 3, ll. 1093-99.

23. *Bartholomew Fair*, 5.5.98-100. I refer to the Herford and Simpson text, which preserves Rabbi Busy's Puritan rhythms.

24. Chambers, *The Elizabethan Stage*, vol. 3, pp. 423-24.

25. Katharine Eisaman Maus, " 'Playhouse Flesh and Blood': Sexual Ideology and the Restoration Actress," *ELH*, 46 (1979), 603-607.

26. Maynard Mack, "The World of Hamlet," *YR*, 41 (1952), 502-23; rpt. in *Shakespeare: Modern Essays in Criticism*, ed. Leonard F. Dean (Oxford: Oxford Univ. Press, 1967), p. 252.

27. Robert Weimann, *Shakespeare and the Popular Tradition in the Theater: Studies in the Social Dimension of Dramatic Form and Function*, ed. Robert Schwartz (Baltimore: The Johns Hopkins Univ. Press, 1978), p. 232.

28. Alvin B. Kernan, *The Playwright as Magician* (New Haven: Yale Univ. Press, 1979), pp. 96-98.

29. Lawrence Danson, *Tragic Alphabet* (New Haven: Yale Univ. Press, 1974), p. 47.

30. T. S. Eliot, "Hamlet and His Problems," in *The Sacred Wood* (London: Methuen, 1976), p. 101.

31. David Leverenz, "The Woman in Hamlet: An Interpersonal View," in *Representing Shakespeare*, ed. Murray M. Schwartz and Coppélia Kahn (Baltimore: The Johns Hopkins Univ. Press, 1980), p. 120. On theatrical imagery, see Charles R. Forker, "Shakespeare's Theatrical Symbolism and Its Function in *Hamlet*," *SQ*, 14 (1963), 215-29; see also James L. Calderwood, *To Be and Not To Be* (New York: Columbia Univ. Press, 1983).

32. See Alvin B. Kernan's introduction to his edition of *Volpone*, pp. 1-26. Acting also figures prominently in Jonas A. Barish, "The Double Plot in *Volpone*," *MP*, 51 (1953), 83-92; Alexander Leggatt, "The Suicide of Volpone," *UTQ*, 39 (1969-70), 19-32; Leo Salingar, "Comic Form in Ben Jonson: Volpone and the Philosopher's Stone," in *English Drama: Forms and Development, Essays in Honour of Muriel Clara Bradbrook*, ed. Marie Axton and Raymond Williams (Cambridge: Cambridge Univ. Press, 1977), pp. 48-68. Jonson's attitude toward the theater and toward actors is brilliantly surveyed in Jonas Barish's well-known study, "Jonson and the Loathèd Stage," now ch. 5 of *The Antitheatrical Prejudice*.

33. John Dryden, "An Essay of Dramatick Poesie," in *The Works of John Dryden*, vol. 17, ed. Samuel Holt Monk (Berkeley: Univ. of California Press, 1971), p. 49.

34. Herford and Simpson, vol. 2, p. 57.

35. See Kernan, "Introduction" to *Volpone*, pp. 21-24.

36. Thomas M. Greene, "Ben Jonson and the Centered Self," *SEL*, 10 (1970), 339.

37. Trapped by Lady Would-be in Act 3, Volpone moans "She's in again./ Before I feigned diseases, now I have one" (3.4.61-62), ironically intimating his feelings in the opening of Act 5, " 'Fore God, my left leg 'gan to have the cramp."

38. Modern criticism of *Twelfth Night* has been generally preoccupied with three aspects of the play's design. Since C. L. Barber's seminal discussion of the theme of sexual difference in the play, critics have increasingly seen *Twelfth Night* to dramatize the "difference between men and women." In Joel Fineman's view, *Twelfth Night* forces both characters and audience to "win through" the sexual confusion of Illyria to a refreshing affirmation of the natural and attractive difference between the sexes. Since *Twelfth Night* articulates this theme largely through Viola's impersonation of Cesario, the play has fittingly drawn a host of critics to analyze Viola's role-playing. Finally, a third approach assesses what John Hollander calls "the morality of indulgence" in the play, sometimes phrasing *Twelfth Night*'s moral vision, as Barbara Lewalski has done, in terms of Christian epiphany. Within *Twelfth Night*, of course, these perspectives are suspended, and each phrases an aspect of the play's

comprehensive response to the actor's erotic, histrionic, or demonic feigning. See C. L. Barber, *Shakespeare's Festive Comedy* (Princeton: Princeton Univ. Press, 1959), p. 245; Joel Fineman, "Fratricide and Cuckoldry: Shakespeare's Doubles," in *Representing Shakespeare*, p. 82; on role-playing, see Charles Brooks, "Shakespeare's Heroine Actresses," *SJW*, 96 (1960), 134-44; J. Dennis Huston, " 'When I Came to Man's Estate': *Twelfth Night* and Problems of Identity," *MLQ*, 33 (1972), 274-88; F. H. Mares, "Viola and Other Transvestite Heroines in Shakespeare's Comedies," in *Stratford Papers 1965-1967*, ed. B.A.W. Jackson (Canada: McMaster Univ. Library Press, 1969), pp. 96-109; Joseph Summers, "The Masks of *Twelfth Night*," *University Review*, 22 (1955); Thomas Van Laan, *Role-Playing in Shakespeare* (Toronto: Univ. of Toronto Press, 1978), pp. 72-85; see also John Hollander, "*Twelfth Night* and the Morality of Indulgence," in *Modern Shakespearean Criticism*, ed. Alvin B. Kernan (New York: Harcourt Brace and World, 1970), pp. 228-41; and Barbara K. Lewalski, "Thematic Patterns in *Twelfth Night*," *Shakespeare Studies*, 1 (1965), 168-81.

39. J. L. Styan, *Drama, Stage and Audience* (Cambridge: Cambridge Univ. Press, 1975), pp. 166-67.

40. Toby to Cesario of Andrew: "he is a devil in private brawl" (3.4.240-41); Toby to Andrew of Cesario: "he's a very devil; I have not seen such a firago" (3.4.278-79).

41. William Rankins, *A Mirrour of Monsters* (London, 1587), B2^r-B2^v.

42. See Bernard Spivack, *Shakespeare and the Allegory of Evil* (New York: Columbia Univ. Press, 1958), pp. 202-3.

43. Joan Hartwig makes this point in "Feste's 'Whirligig' and Comic Providence in *Twelfth Night*," *ELH*, 40 (1973), 501-13.

44. See Lynda E. Boose's discussion of marriage rituals in "The Father and the Bride in Shakespeare," *PMLA*, 97 (1982), 325-47. I refer here to pp. 325, 328.

45. See Lewalski, "Thematic Patterns in *Twelfth Night*."

46. Ralph Berry's phrase in *The Art of John Webster* (Oxford: Oxford Univ. Press, 1972), p. 29.

47. J. R. Mulryne, "Webster and the Uses of Tragicomedy," in *John Webster*, ed. Brian Morris (London: Ernest Benn, 1970), p. 142.

48. All references to *The Duchess of Malfi* are to the Revels Plays edition,

ed. John Russell Brown (Cambridge, Mass.: Harvard Univ. Press, 1964).

49. See René Girard, "The Plague in Literature and Myth," in *"To double business bound": Essays on Literature, Mimesis, and Anthropology* (Baltimore: The Johns Hopkins Univ. Press, 1978), pp. 136-54.

50. See Hereward T. Price, "The Function of Imagery in Webster," in *John Webster*, ed. G. K. Hunter and S. K. Hunter (Baltimore: Penguin, 1969), pp. 176-202. On degree in *The Duchess of Malfi*, see James L. Calderwood, *"The Duchess of Malfi*: Styles of Ceremony," in *John Webster*, ed. G. K. Hunter and S. K. Hunter, pp. 266-80.

51. Stephen Orgel, *The Illusion of Power* (Berkeley: Univ. of California Press, 1975), p. 24.

52. *The Works of John Webster*, ed. F. L. Lucas, vol. 2, p. 236.

53. See Howard Felperin, *Shakespearean Representation*, pp. 188-91; and Arthur C. Kirsch, *Jacobean Dramatic Perspectives* (Charlottesville: Univ. of Virginia Press, 1972), pp. 106-10.

54. See, for example, Berry, *The Art of John Webster*, p. 142; and C. G. Thayer, "The Ambiguity of Bosola," *SP*, 54 (1957), 168.

55. Kernan, *The Playwright as Magician*, p. 158.

{2} Realize the feelings of his Character

1. Denis Diderot's *Le Paradoxe sur le comédien*; I refer to *The Paradox of Acting*, trans. Walter Herries Pollock (London: Chatto and Windus, 1883), p. 38. See also *The Paradox of Acting and Masks or Faces?* (New York: Hill and Wang, 1957). Garrick's letter is in *The Letters of David Garrick*, ed. David M. Little and George M. Kahrl (Cambridge, Mass.: Harvard Univ. Press, 1963), no. 528. The editors translate the quotation from Horace's *Epistles*, 2.1.211-13: "With airy nothings wrings my heart, inflames, soothes, fills it with vain alarms like a magician."

2. On Garrick's influence on painting see Lance Bertelsen, "David Garrick and English Painting," *ECS*, 11 (Spring 1978), 308-24; for correspondence, see Garrick, *Letters; Mme Riccoboni's letters to David Hume, David Garrick and sir Robert Liston, 1764-1783*, ed. James C. Nicholls, in *Studies on Voltaire and the Eighteenth Century* (Oxford:

The Voltaire Foundation at the Taylor Institution, 1976); James Boaden, *The Private Correspondence of David Garrick*, 2 vols. (London, 1831). For memoirs, see James Boswell, *Life of Johnson* (London: Oxford Univ. Press, 1976); Thomas Davies, *Memoirs of the Life of David Garrick*, 2 vols. (London, 1808); Richard Cumberland, *Memoirs* (London, 1806); John Alexander Kelly, *German Visitors to English Theaters in the Eighteenth Century* (Princeton: Princeton Univ. Press, 1936); Georg Christoph Lichtenberg, *Lichtenberg's Visits to England*, trans. Margaret L. Mare and W. H. Quarrell (Oxford: Oxford Univ. Press, 1938). For Garrick's extensive influence as a bibliophile, see George Winchester Stone, Jr. and George M. Kahrl, *David Garrick: A Critical Biography* (Carbondale: Southern Illinois Univ. Press, 1979), ch. 6. Garrick also appears in J. G. Cooper, *Letters Concerning Taste* (London, 1755); and in Joshua Steele, *Prosodia Rationalis* (London, 1775), which contains a musical transcription of Garrick delivering Hamlet's "To be or not to be"; and in William Hogarth, *The Analysis of Beauty* (London, 1753).

3. Bernard Beckerman, "Theatrical Perception," *ThR*, 4 (1979), 162.
4. Joseph W. Donohue discusses the problem of "Punch's feelings" in *Dramatic Character in the English Romantic Age* (Princeton: Princeton Univ. Press, 1970), ch. 9; I am also indebted to his examination of the plays I discuss in this chapter. There are a number of now classic studies of the eighteenth-century actor; see especially Alan S. Downer, "Nature to Advantage Dressed: Eighteenth-Century Acting," *PMLA*, 58 (1943), 1002-37; Earl R. Wasserman, "The Sympathetic Imagination in Eighteenth-Century Theories of Acting," *JEGP*, 46 (1947), 264-72. Of more recent vintage, see George Taylor, " 'The Just Delineation of the Passions': Theories of Acting in the Age of Garrick," in *Essays on the Eighteenth-Century Stage*, ed. Kenneth Richards and Peter Thomson (London: Methuen, 1972), pp. 51-72. Lise-Lone Marker and Frederick J. Marker persuasively examine Aaron Hill's revolutionary synthesis of feeling and form in acting theory in "Aaron Hill and Eighteeth-Century Acting Theory," *QJS*, 61 (1975), 416-27.
5. The language of gesture has an extensive tradition, stretching back to classical rhetorics, Aquinas' division between irascible and con-

cupiscible sins, Renaissance rhetorical handbooks, and seventeenth-
and eighteenth-century painting manuals. See Alan T. McKenzie,
"The Countenance You Show Me: Reading the Passions in the Eight-
eenth Century," *GaR*, 32 (1978), 758-73; Brewster Rogerson, "The
Art of Painting the Passions," *JHI*, 14 (1953), 68-94; and Herbert
Josephs, *Diderot's Dialogue of Language and Gesture: Le Neveu de Rameau*
(Columbus: Ohio State Univ. Press, 1969).

6. Charles Churchill, *The Rosciad*, in *The Poetical Works of Charles Churchill*,
   ed. Douglas Grant (Oxford: Oxford Univ. Press, 1956), l. 962.

7. Jeremy Collier, *A Short View of the Immorality, and Profaneness of the
   English Stage* (London, 1698), pp. 1, 15.

8. Francis Gentleman, *The Dramatic Censor; or, Theatrical Companion*
   (London, 1770), vol. 1, p. 19.

9. J. G. Cooper, *Letters Concerning Taste*, p. 3.

10. Robert Lloyd, *The Actor* (London, 1760); I cite from (London:
    C. W. Beaumont, 1926), ll. 254-56.

11. Aaron Hill, "The Art of Acting," in *The Works of the late Aaron
    Hill, Esq.* (London, 1753), vol. 3, pp. 390-91. Many of the essays
    in *The Prompter* have been collected by William W. Appleton and
    Kalman A. Burnim, eds., *The Prompter* (New York: Benjamin
    Blom, 1966).

12. Aaron Hill, *An Essay on the Art of Acting*, in *Works*, vol. 4, p. 357.

13. See Josephs, *Diderot's Dialogue of Language and Gesture*, p. 210.

14. Aaron Hill, letter to David Garrick, 3 Aug. 1749, in *Works*, vol.
    2, p. 378.

15. John Hill, *The Actor* (London, 1755), p. 90.

16. I refer to the Modern Library edition of *Tom Jones* (New York:
    Modern Library, 1950), Bk. 16, ch. 5.

17. The meaning of sentiment and sensibility in the period is a vexed
    question; a good introduction is R. S. Crane, "Suggestions Toward
    a Genealogy of the 'Man of Feeling,' " *ELH*, 1 (1934), 205-30.
    For representative statements of the benevolist position, see Francis
    Hutcheson, *An Essay on the Nature and Conduct of the Passions and
    Affections* (3d. ed., London, 1742; rpt. Gainesville, Fla.: Scholars'
    Facsimiles and Reprints, 1969); and the Earl of Shaftesbury's classic
    Characteristics of Men, Manners, Opinions, Times, ed. John M. Rob-

inson (New York: Bobbs-Merrill, 1964). On the rise of benevolism, see Ernest Tuveson, "The Importance of Shaftesbury," *ELH*, 20 (1953), 267-99; and "Shaftesbury on the Not So Simple Plan of Human Nature," *SEL*, 5 (1965), 403-34.

18. Henry Home, Lord Kames, *Elements of Criticism* (New York: Collins and Hannay, 1830), ch. 15. The first edition of this work is 1762; I refer to an edition that incorporates Kames's changes in subsequent editions.

19. Oliver Goldsmith, *The Citizen of the World*, Letter 21, in *Collected Works of Oliver Goldsmith*, ed. Arthur Friedman (Oxford: Oxford Univ. Press, 1966), vol. 2. Lien Chi Altangi describes the house: "The rich in general were placed in the lowest seats, and the poor rose above them in degrees proportioned to their poverty. The order of precedence seemed here inverted; those who were undermost all day now enjoyed a temporary eminence, and became masters of the ceremonies. It was they who called for the music, indulging every noisy freedom, and testifying all the insolence of beggary in exaltation."

20. *The Plays of David Garrick*, vol. 1, ed. Harry William Pedicord and Fredrick Louis Bergman (Carbondale: Southern Illinois Univ. Press, 1980), p. 12.

21. Arthur H. Scouten, *The London Stage 1729-1747: A Critical Introduction* (Carbondale: Southern Illinois Univ. Press, 1968), p. clxxiii. On the behavior of audiences, see Leo Hughes, *The Drama's Patrons* (Austin: Univ. of Texas Press, 1971); and Harry William Pedicord, *The Theatrical Public in the Time of Garrick* (New York: Columbia Univ. Press, 1954).

22. Charles Beecher Hogan, *The London Stage 1776-1800: A Critical Introduction* (Carbondale: Southern Illinois Univ. Press, 1968), p. cxcvi.

23. Earl of Shaftesbury, *Characteristics*, p. 295.

24. In his provocative examination of the changing meaning of public performance between the eighteenth and twentieth centuries, Richard Sennett carefully discusses the nature of social role-playing in the eighteenth-century "metropolis"; his emphasis on Diderot leads him to somewhat different conclusions than I draw here. See *The*

Fall of the Public Man (1974; rpt. New York: Vintage Books, 1978), ch. 6.

25. Philip Dormer Stanhope, Earl of Chesterfield, *Letters to His Son* (New York: The Chesterfield Press, 1917), vol. 1, p. 130.

26. See Boswell's *Life of Johnson, passim.* For example, on p. 1252: "Johnson, indeed had thought more upon the subject of acting than might be generally supposed. Talking of it one day to Mr. Kemble, he said, 'Are you, Sir, one of those enthusiasts who believe yourself transformed into the very character you represent?' Upon Mr. Kemble's answering that he had never felt so strong a persuasion himself; 'To be sure not, Sir, (said Johnson;) the thing is impossible. And if Garrick really believed himself to be that monster, Richard the Third, he deserved to be hanged every time he performed it.' "

27. Jean-Jacques Rousseau, *Politics and the Arts: Letter to M. d'Alembert on the Theatre*, trans. Allan Bloom (Ithaca: Cornell Univ. Press, 1973), pp. 79-80.

28. Lionel Trilling, *Sincerity and Authenticity* (Cambridge, Mass.: Harvard Univ. Press, 1971), p. 64.

29. On Rousseau, see Sennett, *The Fall of Public Man*, pp. 116-19; and Jonas Barish, *The Antitheatrical Prejudice* (Berkeley: Univ. of California Press, 1981), pp. 260-90, *passim.*

30. Denis Diderot, *Letter on the Deaf and Dumb*, in *Diderot's Early Philosophical Works*, trans. Margaret Jourdain (London: Open Court, 1916), p. 174.

31. M. de Cahusac, "Geste," *Encyclopédie* (Paris, 1751-1780).

32. Stone and Kahrl, *David Garrick*, p. 102.

33. Garrick's synthesis of pictorial and "natural" styles is discussed by Donhoue, *Dramatic Character in the English Romantic Age*, pp. 230-32; Stone and Kahrl, *David Garrick*, ch. 2; and Alastair Smart, "Dramatic Gesture and Expression in the Age of Hogarth and Reynolds," *Apollo*, Aug. 1965, 94-95.

34. Charles Le Brun, *A Method to learn to Design the Passions*, trans. John Williams, *Augustan Reprint Society Publication Numbers 200-201*, ed. Alan T. McKenzie (Los Angeles: Univ. of California Press, 1980), pp. 20-21.

35. Thomas Wilkes, *A General View of the Stage* (London, 1759), p. 82.

36. Stone and Kahrl discuss the version of *Douglas* that Garrick read in *David Garrick*, p. 128.

37. David Hume, *Four Dissertations* (London, 1757), pp. v-vi.

38. These plays were among the ten most popular tragedies performed at each of the major houses, Drury Lane and Covent Garden, throughout the Garrick period; see George Winchester Stone, Jr., *The London Stage 1747-1776: A Critical Introduction* (Carbondale: Southern Illinois Univ. Press, 1968), pp. clxii-clxv.

39. All references to *Douglas* are to Home's *Works* (Edinburgh, 1822), vol. 1. I refer in the text to act and page number.

40. See Robert J. Detisch, "The Synthesis of Laughing and Sentimental Comedy in *The West Indian*," *ETJ*, 22 (1970), 291-300. Detisch discusses the play's "laughing" techniques, as well as Major O'Flaherty's leading role in the last act of the play.

41. Richard Cumberland, *Memoirs*, p. 202.

42. On Cumberland's use of stage stereotypes, see Donohue, *Dramatic Character in the English Romantic Age*, pp. 95-113. Donohue also examines Cumberland's use of the "trial" scheme.

43. Wylie Sypher, "The West Indian as a 'Character' in the Eighteenth Century," *SP*, 36 (1939), 503-20.

44. All references in the text are to act and page numbers, and refer to the edition of *The West Indian* in *Eighteenth-Century Plays*, ed. John Hampden (London: J. W. Dent and Sons, 1928). I refer to the 1970 edition, entitled *The Beggar's Opera and Other Eighteenth-Century Plays*.

45. In his *Memoirs*, Cumberland notes two criticisms made of O'Flaherty. Lord Lyttleton thought *"listening . . .* as a resource never to be allowed in any pure drama," and suggested that it detracted from the major's reputation as a gentleman. A more insightful remark was made by "Nugent Lord Clare, not *ex cathedrâ*, but from the saddle on an easy trot. His lordship was contented with the play in general, but he could not relish the five wives of O'Flaherty; they were four too many for an honest man, and the over-abundance of them hurt his lordship's feelings; I thought I could not have a

better criterion for the feelings of other people, and desired Moody to manage the matter as well as he could; he put in the qualifier *en militaire*, and his five wives brought him into no further trouble; all but one were left-handed, and he had German practice for his plea"; see pp. 221-23, 226.

46. James Boaden, ed., *The Private Correspondence of David Garrick*, vol. 1, p. 387.

47. On Goldsmith's "Essay," I am indebted to Robert D. Hume's fine study, "Goldsmith and Sheridan and the Supposed Revolution of 'Laughing' Against 'Sentimental' Comedy," in *Studies in Change and Revolution*, ed. Paul J. Korshin (Menton, Yorkshire: Scolar Press, 1972), pp. 237-76. See also Ricardo Quintana, "Oliver Goldsmith as a Critic of the Drama," *SEL*, 5 (1965), 435-54. References to the "Essay" are to *Collected Works of Oliver Goldsmith*, vol. 3.

48. References to act and page numbers of *She Stoops to Conquer* are to *Collected Works of Oliver Goldsmith*, vol. 5. Garrick's Shakespearean allusions in the prologue are reinforced within the play. Marlow priggishly cites *Hamlet* to Tony in the tavern ("We wanted no ghost to tell us that"), and Kate places her barmaid performance firmly in the comic tradition by recalling "Cherry in the Beaux Stratagem" (3, 168). Kate also defines Tony's theatrical line by recalling one of Falstaff's lines just prior to Tony's entrance in the alehouse scene. See *1 Henry IV*, 5.1.125.

49. An excellent study of Tony Lumpkin's place in the play is Herbert F. Tucker, Jr., "Goldsmith's Comic Monster," *SEL*, 19 (1979), 493-99.

50. See Allan Bloom's note in *Politics and the Arts: Letter to M. d'Alembert on the Theatre*, p. 149, n. 3.

51. See Barish, *The Antitheatrical Prejudice*, pp. 99-110.

52. See Paul E. Parnell's provocative article, "The Sentimental Mask," *PMLA*, 78 (1963), 529-35.

53. David Hume, *A Treatise of Human Nature*, ed. L. A. Selby-Bigge (Oxford: Oxford Univ. Press, 1978), pp. 252-53. On associationist psychology, see M. H. Abrams, *The Mirror and the Lamp* (Oxford: Oxford Univ. Press, 1953), ch. 7; Martin Kallich, "The Association

of Ideas and Critical Theory: Hobbes, Locke, and Addison," *ELH*, 12 (1945), 290-315; Kenneth MacLean, *John Locke and English Literature of the Eighteenth Century* (New York: Russell and Russell, 1962); Walter J. Ong, "Psyche and the Geometers: Aspects of Associationist Critical Theory," *MP*, 49 (1951), 16-27. For a sense of how fully the actor's performance typifies this vision of feeling, thought, and action, compare this anecdote from Edmund Burke's *A Philosophical Inquiry into the Origin of our Ideas of the Sublime and Beautiful*, ed. J. T. Boulton (New York: Columbia Univ. Press, 1958), p. 133: the physiognomist Campanella, when "he had a mind to penetrate into the inclinations of those he had to deal with, composed his face, his gesture, and his whole body, as nearly as he could into the exact similitude of the person he intended to examine; and then carefully observed what turn of mind he seemed to acquire by this change. So that, says my author, he was able to enter into the dispositions and thoughts of people, as effectually as if he had been changed into the very men. I have often observed, that on mimicking the looks and gestures, of angry, or placid, or frighted, or daring men, I have involuntarily found my mind turned to that passion whose appearance I endeavoured to imitate; nay, I am convinced it is hard to avoid it; though one strove to separate the passion from its correspondent features."

54. Lichtenberg, *Lichtenberg's Visits to England*, p. 6.

{3} Self-Betrayal

1. Henry Irving, "The Stage As It Is," rpt. in *The Drama* (Boston: Joseph Knight, 1892), p. 43. Bernard Shaw, "The Immortal William," in *Our Theatres in the Nineties* (London: Constable, 1932), vol. 2, p. 113. This work is abbreviated *OTN*, and further references are incorporated in the text.

2. Bernard Shaw, "Preface," in *Ellen Terry and Bernard Shaw: A Correspondence*, ed. Christopher St. John (New York: Putnam, 1931), p. xx. Shavian acting receives incisive comment from Martin Meisel, *Shaw and the Nineteenth-Century Theater* (Princeton: Princeton Univ. Press, 1963), chs. 2-4; and Harold Fromm, *Bernard Shaw and the*

Theater in the Nineties (Lawrence: Univ. of Kansas Press, 1967), ch. 7.

3. There are several fine studies of acting style in the period; see Alan S. Downer, "Players and Painted Stage—Nineteenth Century Acting," *PMLA*, 61 (1946), 522-76; and Michael Baker, *The Rise of the Victorian Actor* (Totowa, N.J.: Rowman and Littlefield, 1978), ch. 2.

4. The documents in this debate are: Constant Coquelin, "Art and the Actor" (1880); Dion Boucicault, "The Art of Acting" (1882); Dion Boucicault, Constant Coquelin, and Henry Irving, "Actors and Acting" (1887). These works were gathered in series 2 and series 5 of the Dramatic Museum of Columbia University *Papers on Acting*, published in 1915 and 1926; they are conveniently reprinted in Brander Matthews, ed., *Papers on Acting* (New York: Hill and Wang, 1958), and all references are to this edition. See also Henry Irving's "Preface" to *The Paradox of Acting*, trans. Walter Herries Pollock (London: Chatto and Windus, 1883); William Archer, *Masks or Faces?* (London: Longmans, Green, 1888); and Bernard Shaw, "Acting, By One Who Does Not Believe In It," rpt. in *Platform and Pulpit*, ed. Dan H. Laurence (New York: Hill and Wang, 1961), pp. 12-23. References to these works are included in the text. This controversy has been well surveyed by Alfred Emmet, "Head or Heart: The Actor's Dilemma," *TQ*, no. 18, vol. 5 (Jun.-Aug. 1975), 15-21.

5. Henry Irving, "Introduction," to Talma's *Reflections on Acting*, in *Papers on Acting*, p. 42.

6. Archer, *Masks or Faces?*, p. 208. One of Archer's questions, for example, asked actors " 'When Macready played Virginius, after burying his loved daughter, he confessed that his real experience gave a new force to his acting in the most pathetic situations of the play.' Have you any analogous experience to relate? Has a personal sorrow (whether recent or remote) ever influenced your acting in a situation which recalled the painful circumstances to your mind? If so, was the influence, in your opinion, for good or ill? And what was the effect upon the audience?" (pp. 213-14).

7. Shaw's similarity to Stanislavsky has been suggestively explored by

John A. Mills, "Acting Is Being: Bernard Shaw on the Art of the Actor," *ShawR*, 13 (1970), 65-78. Mills presents a view of the actor's "metaphysical self-realization" that I am indebted to here.

8. Lionel Trilling, *Sincerity and Authenticity* (Cambridge, Mass.: Harvard Univ. Press, 1971), p. 100.

9. Jonas Barish, *The Antitheatrical Prejudice* (Berkeley: Univ. of California Press, 1981), p. 326.

10. A. B. Walkley, "The Art of Acting," in *Drama and Life* (London: Methuen, 1907), pp. 101, 100.

11. A. B. Walkley, "The Histrionic Temperament," in *Playhouse Impressions* (London: T. Fisher Unwin, 1892), pp. 235-36.

12. Edward Gordon Craig, "The Actor and the Ueber-Marionette," in *On the Art of the Theatre* (Chicago: Browne's Bookstore, 1911), p. 60; Harley Granville-Barker, "The Heritage of the Actor," *Quarterly Review*, 240 (July 1923), 70.

13. On acting style, see Baker, *The Rise of the Victorian Actor*, chs. 2 and 5; Shaw, *OTN*, 1, p. 274.

14. F. Allen Laidlaw, "The New School of Acting," *Gentleman's Magazine*, n.s. 16 (1876), 473.

15. With regard to the actress as working woman, Shaw was "quite certain that the range of an actress's experience and the development of her sympathies depend on a latitude in her social relations which, though perfectly consistent with a much higher degree of self-respect than is at all common among ordinary respectable ladies, involves a good deal of knowledge which is forbidden to 'pure' women. Any actress who denies this is rightly classed by public opinion as a hypocrite. Further, an actress is essentially a workwoman and not a lady. If she is ashamed of this, she deserves all the mortification her shame may bring on her" (*OTN*, 3, p. 277). Despite Shaw's touting, many actresses remained painfully conscious of their inferiority. Margot Peters's study, *Bernard Shaw and the Actresses* (Garden City: Doubleday, 1980), catalogues a host of circumstances in which the actress's professional status allowed her to be treated with cavalier disregard, even with contempt. On the actress's role in the actor-manager system, see Elizabeth Robins, *Ibsen and the Actress* (London: Hogarth Press, 1928), p. 33.

16. Max Beerbohm, "Duse at the Lyceum," in *Around Theatres* (New York: Simon and Schuster, 1954), p. 82.

17. Henry James, *The Scenic Art*, ed. Alan Wade (New Brunswick: Rutgers Univ. Press, 1948), pp. 110, 120.

18. Letter to Elizabeth Robins from Henry James, 17 February 1893, in Elizabeth Robins, *Theatre and Friendship* (New York: Putnam, 1932), pp. 98, 100. In *Ibsen and the Actress*, Robins recalled seeing Janet Achurch in the English premiere of *A Doll's House*: "The Nora of that day must have been one of the earliest exceptions—she was the first I ever saw—to the rule that an actress invariably comes on in new clothes, unless she is playing a beggar" (p. 10).

19. Letter to Harley Granville-Barker, 19 January 1908, in *Bernard Shaw's Letters to Granville Barker*, ed. C. B. Purdom (New York: Theatre Arts Books, 1957), p. 115.

20. Shaw, "Acting, By One Who Does Not Believe In It," p. 18.

21. Frances Anne Kemble, *Notes Upon Some of Shakespeare's Plays* (London: Richard Bentley, 1882); rpt. as "On the Stage" in *Papers on Acting*, pp. 204-5.

22. For an excellent discussion of how the requirements of acting Ibsen's drama forced the invention of new practices of preparation and production, see Gay Gibson Cima, "Discovering Signs: The Emergence of the Critical Actor in Ibsen," *TJ*, 35 (1983), 5-22.

23. Constantin Stanislavski, *Creating a Role*, trans. Elizabeth Reynolds Hapgood (New York: Theatre Arts Books, 1961), p. 26.

24. Jerzy Grotowski, *Towards a Poor Theatre* (New York: Simon and Schuster, 1968), pp. 117, 206. Subsequent references, abbreviated *PT*, occur in the text.

25. Theodore Hoffman, "Stanislavski Triumphant," in *Stanislavski and America*, ed. Erika Munk (New York: Hill and Wang, 1966), p. 81. In *The Antitheatrical Prejudice*, Jonas Barish succinctly places the antitheatrical strain of Stanislavsky's writing within a network of European cultural attitudes toward the theater, the self, and self-display, tracing the contemporary theater's "rage for authenticity" back to Stanislavsky's wish to "detheatricalize the theater entirely, by reimmersing it in a truer, more authentic naturalness" (pp. 464, 344). More convincingly, Timothy J. Wiles, in *The*

Theater Event (Chicago: Univ. of Chicago Press, 1980), sets Stanislavsky within a larger consideration of affectivity in modern theory and performance. Wiles briefly but effectively describes the complex unity that emerges during Stanislavskian production, the affective event that "integrates the creative aspects of literature, actor, and audience into a totality, one which may change all the parties involved" (p. 3).

26. See, for instance, Konstantin Stanislavski, "Director's Diary, 1905—the MAT Production of Ibsen's *Ghosts*," trans. Elizabeth Reynolds Hapgood, in *Stanislavski and America*, pp. 30-45. Edward Braun conducts a close examination of Stanislavsky's naturalistic practices as a director in *The Director and the Stage: From Naturalism to Grotowski* (New York: Holmes & Meier, 1982), ch. 5.

27. Raymond Williams, "Social environment and theatrical environment: the case of English naturalism," in *English Drama: Forms and Development, Essays in Honour of Muriel Clara Bradbrook*, ed. Marie Axton and Raymond Williams (Cambridge: Cambridge Univ. Press, 1977), p. 205.

28. Burnet M. Hobgood, "Central Conceptions in Stanislavski's System," *ETJ*, 25 (1973), 149-50.

29. Constantin Stanislavski, *An Actor Prepares*, trans. Elizabeth Reynolds Hapgood (New York: Theatre Arts Books, 1936), p. 241, italics omitted. References to this book, to *Building a Character*, trans. Elizabeth Reynolds Hapgood (New York: Theatre Arts Books, 1949); to *Creating a Role*, trans. Elizabeth Reynolds Hapgood (New York: Theatre Arts Books, 1961); and to *My Life in Art*, trans. J. J. Robbins (Boston: Little, Brown, 1924) are abbreviated *AP*, *BC*, *CR*, and *LA*, and appear in the text.

30. Constantin Stanislavski, "From the Production Plan of *Othello*," in *Acting: A Handbook of the Stanislavski Method*, ed. Toby Cole (1947; rev. ed., New York: Crown, 1979), p. 131.

31. See, for example, Helen Faucit's description of Ophelia: "The baby Ophelia was left, as I fancy, to the kindly but thoroughly unsympathetic tending of country-folk, who knew little of 'inland nurture.' Think of her, sweet, fond, sensitive, tender-hearted, the offspring of a delicate dead mother, cared for only by roughly-

mannered and uncultured natures! One can see the lonely child, lonely from choice, with no playmates of her kind, wandering by the streams, plucking flowers, making wreaths and coronals, learning the names of all the wild flowers in glade and dingle, having many favourites, listening with eager ears when amused or lulled to sleep at night by the country songs, whose words (in true country fashion, not too refined) come back again vividly to her memory . . ."; Helen Saville Martin, *On Some of Shakespeare's Female Characters* (London: William Blackwood, 1885), p. 9.

32. David Magarshack, ed., *Stanislavsky on the Art of the Stage* (New York: Hill and Wang, 1961), pp. 14-16.

33. Hobgood offers these translations for the full titles of *An Actor Prepares* and *Building a Character*: "The Actor's Work on Himself in the Creative Process of Experiencing," and "The Actor's Work on Himself in the Creative Process of Embodying," pp. 150, 152.

34. Stanislavsky is quoted by David Magarshack in *Stanislavsky on the Art of the Stage*, p. 54.

35. Constantin Stanislavski, *Stanislavski's Legacy*, ed. and trans. Elizabeth Reynolds Hapgood (New York: Theatre Arts Books, 1968), p. 129.

36. Constantin Stanislavski, "Direction and Acting," in *Acting: A Handbook of the Stanislavski Method*, pp. 24-25. Abbreviated *DA* in text.

37. Konstantin Stanislavsky, "The System and Methods of Creative Art," in *Stanislavsky on the Art of the Stage*, p. 176.

38. Thomas Van Laan, *The Idiom of Drama* (Ithaca: Cornell Univ. Press, 1970), p. 9.

39. Marianna Stroëva, "Tchékov et le Théâtre d'Art (au sujet de la structure des premiers spectacles du Théâtre d'Art de Moscou)," in *La Participation de l'acteur à la réforme théâtrale à fin du 19e et au début du 20e siècle/The Role of the Actor in the Theatrical Reform of the Late 19th and Early 20th Centuries*, ed. Milan Lukeš, 7th International Congress on Theatre Research, Prague, 3-8 Sept. 1973 (Prague: Univerzita Karlova Praha, 1976), p. 177.

40. Max Reinhardt, "THEATRE—The Actor," *Encyclopaedia Britannica*, 14th ed. (London: Encyclopaedia Britannica, 1929).

41. Vsevolod Meyerhold, "The Stylized Theatre," in *Meyerhold on The-*

atre, trans. Edward Braun (New York: Hill and Wang, 1969), p. 62.

42. Sartre discusses identity as a "series of undertakings" in "Existentialism is a Humanism," trans. Philip Mairet, in *Existentialism from Dostoevsky to Sartre*, ed. Walter Kaufman (New York: Meridian Books, 1956), p. 301. The *"bearing* of the past" is analyzed at length in *Being and Nothingness*, trans. Hazel E. Barnes (New York: Pocket Books, 1966), p. 640.

43. Jean-Paul Sartre, *Sartre on Theater*, trans. Frank Jellinek, ed. Michel Contat and Michel Rybalka (New York: Pantheon Books, 1976), pp. 3-4. References to Sartre's theater essays are to this anthology.

44. Antonin Artaud, *The Theater and its Double*, trans. Mary Caroline Richards (New York: Grove Press, 1958), pp. 114, 48.

45. Charles Marowitz, "Notes on the Theatre of Cruelty," in *Theatre at Work*, ed. Charles Marowitz and Simon Trussler (New York: Hill and Wang, 1967), pp. 173, 176.

46. Held in Persepolis in 1971, *Orghast* outlined the Prometheus legend using a language created for the occasion by Ted Hughes. See Geoffrey Reeves, "The Persepolis Follies of 1971," *Performance*, 1.1 (Dec. 1971), 47-70.

47. Richard Schechner, *Environmental Theater* (New York: Hawthorn Books, 1973), p. 60.

48. Richard Schechner, "The Decline and Fall of the (American) Avant-Garde: Why It Happened and What We Can Do About It," *PAJ*, nos. 14-15 (1981); rpt. and revised in *The End of Humanism* (New York: Performing Arts Journal Publications, 1982), p. 51.

49. Jerzy Grotowski, "The Actor's Technique," trans. Helen Krich Chinoy, in *Actors on Acting*, ed. Toby Cole and Helen Krich Chinoy (New York: Crown, 1970), p. 534.

50. Michael Goldman, *The Actor's Freedom* (New York: Viking, 1975), p. 159. See also Elizabeth Burns, *Theatricality* (London: Longman, 1972), pp. 135-36.

51. Bertolt Brecht, "Some of the Things that can be Learnt from Stanislavsky," in *Brecht on Theatre*, ed. and trans. John Willett (New York: Hill and Wang, 1964), pp. 236-38. References to Brecht's theater essays are to this volume.

52. Erving Goffman, *Frame Analysis* (Cambridge, Mass.: Harvard Univ.

Press, 1974), p. 293. See Goffman's earlier volume, *The Presentation of Self in Everyday Life* (Garden City: Anchor Books, 1959).

53. Robert Cohen, *Acting Power* (Palo Alto: Mayfield, 1978).

54. Raymond Williams, *Modern Tragedy* (Stanford: Stanford Univ. Press, 1966), p. 98.

55. As Gay Gibson Cima puts it in her study of the acting of Ibsen's plays in the 1890s, "even in Ibsen's most realistic plays, his creations sometimes act as if they were characters in a melodrama. . . . The actress must reveal where Nora *thinks* she is headed as well as where she actually *is* headed. What Nora, Hedda, and other Ibsen characters envision as they dramatize themselves in the melodramas differs considerably from the outcomes of the realistic plays confining them," p. 19.

56. *An Enemy of the People*, in *The Oxford Ibsen*, vol. 6, ed. and trans. James Walter McFarlane (London: Oxford Univ. Press, 1960), p. 126. References to *Rosmersholm* are to this volume of *The Oxford Ibsen*, and are to act and page number.

57. Thomas R. Whitaker, *Fields of Play in Modern Drama* (Princeton: Princeton Univ. Press, 1977), p. 39. John Northam discusses the setting of *Rosmersholm* in *Ibsen's Dramatic Method* (London: Faber and Faber, 1953).

58. Van Laan, *The Idiom of Drama*, p. 174.

59. John S. Chamberlain discusses Rebecca as a *femme de trente ans* in "Tragic Heroism in *Rosmersholm*," *MD*, 17 (1974), 277-88.

60. The similarities between Rebecca and Beata are convincingly detailed by Marvin Carlson, "Patterns of Structure and Character in *Rosmersholm*," *MD*, 17 (1974), 273-74.

61. The best discussion of Mrs. Helseth's role in the play, and one to which I am indebted here, is Errol Durbach, "Temptation to Err: The Denouement of *Rosmersholm*," *ETJ*, 29 (1977), 477-85.

62. Letter to Granville-Barker, 19 Jan. 1908, in *Bernard Shaw's Letters to Granville Barker*, p. 115. Martin Meisel suggestively discusses Shavian "operatic" acting in *Shaw and the Nineteenth-Century Theater*, chs. 2-4.

63. Bernard Shaw, "Sullivan, Shakespear, and Shaw," rpt. in *Shaw on Theatre*, ed. E. J. West (New York: Hill and Wang, 1958), p. 274.

64. For a somewhat different elaboration of the connections between Shaw and Stanislavsky, see John A. Mills, 65-78.

65. Letter to Stella Campbell, 3 Jul. 1912, in *Bernard Shaw and Mrs. Patrick Campbell: Their Correspondence*, ed. Alan Dent (New York: Knopf, 1952), p. 18.

66. *Bernard Shaw's Letters to Granville Barker*, p. 115.

67. Bernard Shaw, *Cashel Byron's Profession* (Carbondale: Southern Illinois Univ. Press, 1968), p. 86.

68. Bernard Shaw, "An Aside," in *Shaw on Theatre*, pp. 222, 224.

69. Letter to Stella Campbell, 13 Jan. 1921, in *Bernard Shaw and Mrs. Patrick Campbell: Their Correspondence*, p. 248.

70. Letter to Molly Tompkins, 8 Apr. 1923, in *To A Young Actress: The Letters of Bernard Shaw to Molly Tompkins*, ed. Peter Tompkins (London: Constable, 1960), p. 43.

71. Bernard Shaw, *The Quintessence of Ibsenism Now Completed to the Death of Ibsen* (New York: Hill and Wang, 1957), p. 65.

72. All references are to *Collected Plays With Their Prefaces* (New York: Dodd, Mead, 1975), and are to vol. and page numbers: *Arms and the Man*, vol. 1, p. 471; *Major Barbara*, vol. 3, p. 173. References to *Heartbreak House* (vol. 5) are to act and page numbers.

73. Review by J. M. Murray, rpt. in *Shaw: The Critical Heritage*, ed. T. F. Evans (London: Routledge & Kegan Paul, 1976), p. 244.

74. See Stanley Weintraub, "*Heartbreak House*: Shaw's *Lear*," *MD*, 15 (1972-73), 255-65. J. L. Wisenthal discusses the symbolic dimensions of Ellie's progress from romantic Marcus Darnley to spiritual Shotover in *The Marriage of Contraries* (Cambridge, Mass.: Harvard Univ. Press, 1974), p. 146.

75. See Alfred Turco, Jr., *Shaw's Moral Vision* (Ithaca: Cornell Univ. Press, 1976), p. 247. Louis Crompton compares Hector to Sergius Saranoff in *Shaw the Dramatist* (Lincoln: Univ. of Nebraska Press, 1969), p. 159.

76. Wisenthal, *The Marriage of Contraries*, pp. 139-41.

77. Bernard Shaw, "Preface," *Three Plays by Brieux* (New York: Brentano's, 1913), p. xv.

78. References to act and page numbers of *Enrico IV* and *Six Characters in Search of an Author* are to *Opere di Luigi Pirandello*, vol. 4 (Milan: Arnoldo Mondadori Editore, 1971). The translations are my own;

for comparison, see *Henry IV*, trans. Julian Mitchell (London: Eyre Methuen, 1979); and *Six Characters*, trans. Frederick May, rpt. in *Stages of Drama*, ed. Carl H. Klaus, et al. (New York: John Wiley, 1981).

79. Francis Fergusson, *The Idea of a Theater* (Princeton: Princeton Univ. Press, 1949; rpt. 1968), pp. 192-93.

80. Eric Bentley, *"Six Characters in Search of an Author,"* in *Theatre of War* (New York: Viking Press, 1972), pp. 45-46. I refer to Bentley's companion essay *"Enrico IV," Theatre of War*, pp. 32-44, below.

81. Luigi Pirandello, *On Humor*, trans. Antonio Illiano and Daniel P. Testa (Chapel Hill: Univ. of North Carolina Press, 1974), p. 137.

82. Matthew N. Proser, "Shakespeare's *Hamlet* and Pirandello's *Henry IV*," *MD*, 24 (1981), p. 350.

83. Beckett's use of theater as metaphor is discussed by Hugh Kenner, *Samuel Beckett* (Berkeley: Univ. of California Press, 1968); by Ruby Cohn, *Back to Beckett* (Princeton: Princeton Univ. Press, 1973); and by the same author, *Just Play: Beckett's Theater* (Princeton: Princeton Univ. Press, 1980). Acting in Beckett's plays has received comment from Ruby Cohn, "Acting for Beckett," *MD*, 9 (1966), 237; Ruby Cohn, "Plays and Players in the Plays of Samuel Beckett," *YFS*, no. 29 (1963), 43-48; Ted L. Estess, "Dimensions of Play in the Literature of Samuel Beckett," *ArizQ*, 33 (Spring 1977), 5-25; John Fletcher, "Action and Play in Beckett's Theater," *MD*, 9 (1966), 242-50. I am particularly indebted to Enoch Brater's excellent discussion of the performance of *Play* and *Not I* in "The 'Absurd' Actor in the Theatre of Samuel Beckett," *ETJ*, 27 (1975), 197-207.

84. All references to *Play* are to the text published in *Cascando and Other Short Dramatic Pieces* (New York: Grove Press, 1968). Although Beckett's stage direction calls for a straight repeat of the play, the second run-through has been altered in performances under Beckett's direction. See Hugh Kenner, *Samuel Beckett*, p. 220n.

85. Michael Goldman, *"King Lear*: Acting and Feeling," in *On King Lear*, ed. Lawrence Danson (Princeton: Princeton Univ. Press, 1981), pp. 25-46.

86. On the difficulties of performing Mouth, see Ruby Cohn, *Just Play*, p. 109 (on Billie Whitelaw); and Enoch Brater, pp. 199-201 (on Whitelaw and Jessica Tandy).

87. References to *Not I* are to the text published in *Ends and Odds* (New York: Grove Press, 1976).

88. Robert Weimann, *Shakespeare and the Popular Tradition in the Theater: Studies in the Social Dimension of Dramatic Form and Function*, ed. Robert Schwartz (Baltimore: The Johns Hopkins Univ. Press, 1978), p. 2.

89. Beckett refined his sense of the urns' dramatic potential in successive revisions of *Play*. In early drafts, the actors are concealed in large white boxes, then in large white urns. In the fifth, sixth, and seventh drafts of the play, the urns are gradually reduced in size, only assuming their current size and shape in the eighth and final draft. See Richard L. Admussen, "The Manuscripts of Beckett's *Play*," *MD*, 16 (1973), 23.

90. On Pozzo's journey as tragedy, see Bert O. States, *The Shape of Paradox* (Berkeley: Univ. of California Press, 1978), p. 61. References to *Happy Days* (New York: Grove Press, 1961); and to *Waiting for Godot* (New York: Grove Press, 1954).

91. On theatricality in *Endgame*, see especially Hugh Kenner, *Samuel Beckett*, pp. 155-65 (the phrase "dramatic machine" is on p. 162); and Thomas R. Whitaker, *Fields of Play in Modern Drama*. Hamm recalls Richard III and Prospero in specific lines, and his "But deep in what sleep, deep in what sleep already" seems to me to suggest Hamlet's reply, "For in that sleep of death. . . ." Hugh Kenner compares Richard II's "hollow crown" speech with Hamm's situation in the play, p. 160. All references are to *Endgame* (New York: Grove Press, 1958).

92. In a famous early response to *Waiting for Godot*, Alain Robbe-Grillet discusses the problem of "being there" as crucial to the design of *Godot*. His remark that in *Godot* "everything happens as if the two tramps were on stage *without having a role*" perhaps measures the distance between the earlier play and *Endgame*, where Hamm and Clov have only roles to play. See "Samuel Beckett or Presence on the Stage," rpt. in *Casebook on Waiting for Godot*, ed. Ruby Cohn (New York: Grove Press, 1967), pp. 15-21.

93. William Archer, "Introduction," to *The Collected Works of Henrik Ibsen*, vol. 8, trans. William Archer (New York: Scribner's, 1925), pp. xxiv-xxv.

94. Harold Pinter, *Old Times* (Grove Press, 1971), Act 1, p. 32. On the structure of *Old Times*, see Arthur Ganz, "Mixing Memory and Desire: Pinter's Vision in *Landscape, Silence,* and *Old Times*," in *Pinter: A Collection of Critical Essays*, ed. Arthur Ganz (Englewood Cliffs: Prentice-Hall, 1972), pp. 161-78; Robert Skloot, "Putting Out the Light: Staging the Theme of Pinter's *Old Times*," *QJS*, 61 (1975), 265-70; and David Savran, "The Girardian Economy of Desire: *Old Times* Recaptured," *TJ*, 34 (1982), 40-54.

95. Mel Gussow, "A Conversation (Pause) with Harold Pinter," *New York Times Magazine*, 5 Dec. 1971, 43.

96. On actor, character, and setting in Ibsen, see Michael Goldman, "The Ghost of Joy: Reflections on Romanticism and the Forms of Modern Drama," in *Romantic and Modern: Revaluations of Literary Tradition*, ed. George Bornstein (Pittsburgh: Univ. of Pittsburgh Press, 1977), pp. 53-68.

Note to Postscript

1. D. W. Winnicott's discussion of the infant's use of "transitional phenomena" and of the "potential space" in the formulation of fictions that permit the growth of a healthy sense of selfhood is best expressed in *Playing and Reality* (New York: Basic Books, 1971). See also Madeleine Davis and David Wallbridge, *Boundary and Space: An Introduction to the Work of D. W. Winnicott* (New York: Brunner/ Mazel, 1981); and Simon A. Grolnick and Leonard Barkin, eds., *Between Reality and Fantasy* (New York: Jason Aronson, 1978). Victor Turner's theory of "liminality" and "communitas" and their relation to the processual form of "social drama" has, as Turner and others have recognized, important implications for the study of drama and theater; see Victor Turner, *The Ritual Process* (Chicago: Aldine, 1969), esp. chs. 3-4; and *Dramas, Fields, and Metaphors* (Ithaca: Cornell Univ. Press, 1974). On "liminality" in recent performance theory, see Victor Turner, *From Ritual to Theatre* (New York: Performing Arts Journal Publications, 1982); and Richard Schechner, *The End*

of Humanism (New York: Performing Arts Journal Publications, 1982). Finally, the deconstructive impulse of the actor's performance, and Derrida's wider critique of semiotics, have only recently had an effect on theories of performance; see Herbert Blau, *Take Up The Bodies* (Urbana: Univ. of Illinois Press, 1982). I refer to Jacques Derrida, *Of Grammatology*, trans. Gayatri Chakravorty Spivak (Baltimore: The Johns Hopkins Univ. Press, 1976), p. 12. Readers may also be interested in Derrida's remarks on Rousseau's *Letter to d'Alembert*, pp. 302-13. Some of Derrida's remarks concerning Rousseau's sense of theater parallel my own, but have, of course, a rather different provenance.

Index

"Absurd" drama, 226
Achurch, Janet, 183, 184, 193, 250n. 18
acting: absence and presence, 156, 157, 207-208, 211, 213-14; affective, 75, 89, 91, 97, 103, 231; "alienated," 163-68, 208, 226-27; amateurish, 140, 182; and antifeminism, 24; authentic, see authenticity; and being, 149, 156, 159; in conduct books, 13; "cruel," 157; deconstructs "character," 169; and degree, 25, 57, 58; didactic, 14, 30-31, 69, 74, 97, 164, 226; and drama, 5, 9, 68, 71, 127-30, 170-72, 223-32; and duplicity, 3, 4, 9, 26, 34, 43, 48, 87, 92, 125, 143, 207, 228, 230-31; effeminate, 19, 25, 32, 58; "egoistic force," 140, 176, 183; "emotionalist" vs. "mechanical," 134-37; ethics of, 3, 6, 13, 26, 46, 65, 67, 71, 73, 95, 97, 99, 129, 144, 177, 207, 231; and exhibitionism, 149, 162; feeling and expression, 4, 70, 71, 72, 73, 77, 89-90, 95-97, 100, 119, 121, 125, 230, 241n. 4; and "feigning," 14-18, 19, 22-23, 26, 28, 32, 34, 38, 39, 44, 50, 53, 64-66, 67-69, 229; and "framing," 166-68, 169, 223; and gesture, see language of gesture; godlike, 12, 16, 17, 69, 229; of history, 14-16; and identity, 20, 62-63, 67, 87, 96, 134, 135, 141, 147-49, 152, 157, 166,

170, 183, 230, 231; irrational, 69, 157, 158; and "joy in creation," 147, 149, 178, 179; and language, 152, 158, 159, 184-85; "lascivious," 19, 37; and lust, 24, 25, 28, 32, 37; and madness, 24, 26, 28, 30-32, 33, 43, 47, 69, 199, 229; "metaphysical self-realization," 137, 138, 142, 143, 153, 163, 182, 185, 186, 189, 193, 226, 227, 248n. 7; "monstrous," 4, 35, 39, 46, 69, 182, 229, 230; and narcissism, 25, 87, 162; and nonbeing, 156; "ontological subversiveness" of, 18; and "overflow of powerful feelings," 133; and "performing," 161; and plague, 55, 57-60, 66; role-playing, see role-playing; as Romantic art, 5, 132, 150, 166; "sacred and blasphemous," 6; Satanic, 4, 13, 22-23, 24, 45, 46, 47, 48, 49; "self-betrayal," 131, 132, 138, 139, 141, 148, 189, 203; and self-control, 141; and sensibility, 72, 77, 78, 90, 93, 94, 96; sensuous appeal of, 23, 36-38, 41; and sexual indeterminacy, 43, 45, 46, 50, 52, 58; and spontaneity, 40, 84, 96, 133, 138, 140, 149, 153, 177, 183; and subtext, 152; and transvestism, 20, 21, 24-25, 45, 238n. 38; uncanny, 5; uncreates actor, 21, 41, 67, 123; unrealizes actor, 156, 157, 165, 195, 229; violates god's image, 21; and vitality, 163, 182, 183,

Index

Library of Congress Cataloging in Publication Data

Worthen, William B., 1955-
    The idea of the actor.

    Includes index.
    1. Acting.   2. Drama.   I. Title.
PN2061.W67 1984   792'.028   84-42552
ISBN 0-691-06623-X (alk. paper)

45,894

PN   Worthen, William B.,
2061   1955-
.W67
1984   The idea of the
        actor